RECOLLECTIONS OF A **McKINSEY** CONSULTANT

PUSHING THE BOUNDARIES

Herbert Henzler

Published by
LID Publishing Limited
One Adam Street, London WC2N 6LE

31 West 34th Street, 8th Floor, Suite 8004,
New York, NY 10001, U.S.

info@lidpublishing.com
www.lidpublishing.com

A member of:

BPR
Business Publishers Roundtable

www.businesspublishersroundtable.com

© Herbert Henzler, 2016
© LID Publishing Limited, 2016
Reprinted in 2016

Printed in Great Britain by TJ International
ISBN: 978-1-910649-65-7

Cover and page design: Caroline Li

RECOLLECTIONS OF A McKINSEY CONSULTANT

PUSHING THE BOUNDARIES

Herbert Henzler

LONDON   MONTERREY
MADRID   SHANGHAI
MEXICO CITY   BOGOTA
NEW YORK   BUENOS AIRES
BARCELONA   SAN FRANCISCO

Dedicated to...

my Mother and my children

Nicole, Oliver, Eliora, Ilan and Yoran

CONTENTS

PROLOGUE

Throughout my years there were grim moments full of self-doubt. Towards the end of the seventies I consulted for Eumig, then the largest privately held Austrian company and a producer of radios, film cameras (super8) and projectors. I had close contact with one of the two owners, Karl Vockenhuber, so I could detect that the company was going downhill. Together with the owner, I was negotiating with the Austrian Länderbank to see whether there was a chance of salvaging the company. But it was out of my control. The company had made good money for many years with movie cameras and projectors. After their holidays, people would invite friends and neighbors to show their holiday images. That was Eumig's business concept. But then other cameras were offered which were more simple to handle and much cheaper. Eumig's cameras had over 30 different apps in their cameras while Japanese competitors offered "point and shoot" type products at a third of Eumig's sales price. Way too complicated and way too expensive, was the harsh judgment by the market. Vockenhuber just could not cope with this technical disruption.

In 1979 Eumig went bankrupt. I had sleepless nights. My plan had been to open an office in Vienna, but that idea was now gone. The public associated McKinsey with the downfall of Eumig. Karl Vockenhuber, who had been a legend in Austria, called me: "What do they want, do they want to expel me from my own country?". I answered: "Mr. Vockenhuber I cannot imagine that. Let us make a last-ditch effort with the bankers", Vockenhuber invited me into his beautiful home on the outskirts of Vienna near the Vienna forest. Leading me through his villa, he said: "Dr. Henzler I cannot enjoy this any longer. My life achievement is gone". Soon afterwards he died.

That was a life-defining experience; never should anything like this happen to me again. I would do anything to avoid that. But if have to go to the limit, I would do it.

Reflecting on my last years

After I turned 70, I reoriented my professional life. Top management confronted me with the age limit for advisors at Credit Suisse. In addition, my tasks as advisor to the top management were done and implementation was under way. At Credit Suisse, one thought that people in their eighth decade were preparing for a well-deserved retirement. Many examples from the past showed that age limits can have very positive overall effects. Yet, I have problems with it since I still feel very active and retirement can wait. Hence, I have taken on a new challenge and as senior advisor I am helping the independent global Investment Bank Moelis & Company – New York based – with the build up of the German branch. Besides that, I act as a member of the advisory board at New Silk Route – the largest Indian pri-vate-equity fund. Two to three times per year I travel to Mumbai, Pune and New Dehli and get many impressions about the fascinat-ing country which seems to be lagging economically. Since the rupie dropped by 35% over recent years it has been nearly impossible to have satisfactory performance for dollar-based investors. After each trip it seems more difficult to make a coherent judgment about India. The state which has 14 languages imprinted on the rupie is hard to understand and very difficult to govern.

My third area of activities is the professorship at the Ludwig-Maximilian University in Munich where I am teaching master class-es in strategic management. A section of 30 students (preselected) from eight to ten countries provide a challenging environment. It keeps me in touch with the generation "Y" from around the world, and like in the old days, I am eager to see the 360° evaluations about me by the students.

In addition, I am a visiting professor at Moscow School of Manage-ment and enjoy teaching classes on globalization and strategic cases.

Since June 2015 I have been acting as board member in the Russian – German Energy forum, which meets twice a year. Espe-cially in current times, where the Cold War between Russia and the West is showing it's ugly face, this allows me to arrive at a more bal-anced judgment about Russia. What happens in the nine internal time zones is more important than what the West thinks about Russia. Russia wants to be the natural protector for all Russians whereever they live. Deep-seated fears after the historic invasions by the Swedes, the French and the Germans and the still prevailing assessment that Gorbachev and Yeltsin lost the Soviet empire are there. The NATO borders in Poland and the Baltic create a different assessment than in the West.

For over 10 years, I have been counselor to the Bavarian government. During the last years I detected with chagrin that our entrepreneurial level is decaying compared with the sprawling start-up culture in Silicon Valley, New York, Tel Aviv, and even now in Berlin we have a lot of catching up to do. Currently I am spending about a third of my time as angel investor, counselor, board member, speaker and ad hoc task force member for the start-up scene.

But it is not just the economic development which I am supporting. I am also concerned about the social dimensions in our country.

I see that the political advisor still has to go a long way until he/she is taken seriously. Politics is hardly willing to listen to scientific analysis. The concentration on the current generation that wants to go into retirement earlier is highly irritating. When a society ages as rapidly as our own, then we need to find solutions, where people contribute for longer in their active lives, passing on the knowledge to the next generation in order to create a win-win situation. In addition we need to find a way to increase the birth rate. It will be a big challenge for the next generation to find a balance between old and young people since we need both. I hope to contribute my knowledge to some limited degree by coaching youngsters.

After having served both the Catholic church (in the Essen diocese) and the Protestant church (Munich) with McKinsey teams, I got to know the current head of the Protestant church in Germany, Mr. Bedford-Strohm. Having been raised in a Protestant Calvinistic Swabian environment and having been a church-tax paying member of the church, I could not refuse the invitation to come and speak at the Evangelische Academy in Tutzing. This was not easy since the church had in many instances been quite anti-business and a McKinsey partner who stood for efficiency and often for lay-offs in companies was not highly welcome. Over the years I managed to contribute to the open discussion culture and now I am actually helping the Protestant church to prepare the 500th anniversary of the Lutheran Reformation in 2017. In 2015, I attended the Protestant assembly of the church in Stuttgart with over 100,000 participants (at least 40% of them young people under 20 years) and marveled at the utterly "green" positions I encountered and attended lectures on Martin Buber and Christianity.

Dealing with the church poses gigantic organizational issues. Secular trends conflict with continued large-scale attendance. Each year about 100,000 leave the Protestant church and the churchgoers vary between 800,000 on a normal Sunday and 8 million at Christmas. We see a great gap between many young people being confirmed attending the church assembly but leaving the church in adult life. There are over 20,000 pastors but relatively little power over them through the governing body. My enthusiasm for many activities in the mountains (especially skiing) and for soccer, my insatiable interest in other cultures (after my books were translated into Mandarin – I took up learning Chinese), books and music (I started to play piano four years ago) and my family let me lead a fulfilled life each day which gives me the power to lead an active life going forward and to take some responsibility in society.

ACKNOWLEDGEMENTS

L et me thank my clients who formed me and who often have become good friends and helped me in highs and lows of my professional development.

Of the clients there a number of personalities that in many ways have become role models especially Dieter von Sanden, head of communication of Siemens AG, Werner Niefer of Daimler AG and Alfred Herrhausen of Deutsche Bank AG. All these three personalities have contributed significantly to my development and I owe a lot to them. All three are no longer alive. I keep a honorable memory of them.

In addition there were my McKinsey colleagues that over 30 years have been great sources of cooperation and energy. I am especially indebted to Marvin Bower, the ethicist that shaped us as young associates, and to Ron Daniel the long-term MD of McKinsey, who was a real mentor over the various stages of my career.

My office staff under the current leadership of Beate Strobel helped me to perform my role and to bring order to my agenda.

CHAPTER 1

WAR AND THE
CONSEQUENCES
OF WAR

A CHILDHOOD
IN A SWABIAN VILLAGE

The washing trough was comfortable. Each time the sirens started to blare, my mother dressed me and my brother Siegfried in track suits and took us to the basement, where she put us in the washing trough. The neighbor's son Erwin, who was older than us and who went on to become a great soccer player, came over to help at the first blaring of the sirens. Our house had the best basement for miles around, so that ten to twelve neighbors could find shelter in case of bombing alerts. I liked lying in the dark and listening to the grown-ups talking quietly all around us. I only felt an odd tension when they listened silently to what happened outside, which I couldn't grasp at that time because I was only three and a half years old.

When we were able to step out the next morning, we saw roof tiles lying on the street, which must have been knocked off by low flying airplanes. Fortunately, no bombs fell on our village of Neckarhausen. Thus, the tension of the grown-ups subsided fairly quickly and things went back to normal.

The biggest war damage I saw, which was also officially announced, was on a morning in late March of 1945. The municipal bailiff rode his bike through the streets of our village, and every 300 to 400 meters he stopped to announce:

"Attention, attention, the bridge over the river Neckar will be blown up tomorrow morning at 10.20." It was recommended to open the windows in order to avoid any breakage of glass, and children were to stay at home.

Once it happened as we were standing at the windows of our living room and listening to the work of the "Volkssturm" (a national German group), calling upon all men between the ages of 16 and 60 who were able to bear arms, to defend the fatherland's soil as of October 1944.

The noise of the explosion had barely subsided when I ran down to the Neckar. It was a brutal sight: where the bridge had stood for over a hundred years, only debris protruded from the water. The preferred soccer ground of the older kids as well as some of my parents' land on the other bank of the river were out of reach. When I cross the new bridge today, Henry Kissinger, the former US Secretary of State, comes to mind. He once said: "It takes three years to build a bridge, but only three minutes to blow it up."

My war memories are limited to single sequences. I was born in November of 1941 and much too young to really understand what was happening in Germany at that time. I remember a man running into our washhouse screaming: "The enemy is after me!" He threw away his rifle, ripped off his uniform jacket and worked the pump rod. He held his head and upper body under the gushing water. My mother said: "Take a piece of bread." The young man took it grate-fully and then went out through the barn. My mother later explained that he was a soldier who did not want to continue fighting because he considered that the war was senseless, and that he was right.

My mother hailed from Wendlingen, and we spent the first three years of my life there with her parents. In mid-1944, after British bombers dropped bombs on industrial firms in Wendlingen and also destroyed several residential buildings, my mother decided that we should relocate to the house my father had built (at the age of 23) in Neckarhausen about 10 kilometers away.

Thus, I had pictures of fire and destruction in my mind. How-ever, I can't recall having been really afraid, notwithstanding many nights in the bomb shelter. The only explanation I can think of is my mother. I don't know how she managed, but it must have taken a lot out of her.

She had already lost two brothers in the war, one of them miss-ing in action in Latvia, the other was killed in Russia. She attended the memorial services where the Horst Wessel Song, the party hymn of the national socialist party, ("Die Fahnehoch! Die Reihendicht-geschlossen"), was sung, with everyone taking the Hitler greeting po-sition and where she had pushed down her mother's arm. She had started a family with a husband she barely knew. They had been mar-ried in a war ceremony, a quick affair. My father, Albert Henzler, was born in 1913 and was stationed in Chalons-sur-Saône during the French campaign. My mother didn't know whether my father would come back unharmed, or at all. Like many women who shared a similar fate, she had two children, my brother Siegfried and myself. I asked her later how it was possible to have children during the war. My mother responded: "If God puts children on the earth, he will look after them."

She was indeed a very strong woman and continues to be strong at over 99 years of age. She was the focal point of our family, deeply anchored in her Christian faith, providing the solid footing, which was a determinant in the lives of my brother and myself.

Notwithstanding her numerous worries, I remember my mother – with her blonde hair worn pinned up and her rotund figure – as positive and kind, always thinking about others. When the war was over and the first harvests were collected, she and my father loaded the sheaves from the fields on a cart. During that process, some broken spikes always remained lying around on the fields. These were collected by so-called spike-collectors, who walked right behind the carts and wrapped whatever they found in large blankets. Frequently, the spike-collectors were war refugees, and I remember that there were more of them than spikes. Once, they approached the cart very closely to see whether there might be more spikes falling down, and my father said with a demonstrative gesture: "Just go further back and take whatever is left." My mother said: "Just leave it, they already have so little." I remember this scene to this day, as an example of her Christian faith in practice.

Without hesitation, my mother accepted family members in her farmhouse, for example Ruth, the daughter of her fallen brother Gottfried, or her mother-in-law, for whom she cared until her death, as well as two families of war refugees. The latter had been admitted to our house in 1945 by order of the municipality. My father was not happy about having to house four additional people, since he considered them "strangers". And when they told stories about how nice their old homeland had been, he suggested: "They should go back from where they came", overlooking that this was not possible. My mother understood immediately that this was the refugees' way of coping with the loss of their homes. She tried to ease the situation by repeatedly inviting the two couples to our family meals at our kitchen table. "Where there is room for four, there is room for eight," she used to say.

Later, when both Siegfried and I had left home, she was the only person in the village who rented out the top floor of the farmhouse to a Turkish family. After some time, the family moved to a larger apartment a bit further away. But because both parents were working, their daughter, whose name was Schale, stayed with my mother during the week. I considered this somewhat unusual at the time. Initially, Schale didn't do too well in school – her parents' knowledge of German wasn't enough to help with her schoolwork. My mother sat down with her to go through her homework and took care that Schale advanced in school. She stayed with us until she completed basic school. To this day, she calls my mother "Aunt" – Schale is married with three children and lives in Istanbul.

I tried to integrate my mother's Christian charity into my work as a manager at McKinsey, and whenever possible tried to manage the offices with "heart". And frequently, I was able to temper justice with mercy. Once, trouble was brewing because a principal had massively breached McKinsey rules. Whereas I would normally have had to terminate the employee immediately, in this instance I knew that he was having personal issues, was going through a divorce and was separated from his children. Thus, I spoke individually to the three consultants in his team who had made me aware of the breach of rules. "What in your view is the right thing to do? Should I fire Hans (not his real name) or should I show him the yellow card?" After speaking to all three, I thought that they all believed that a second chance was warranted. I then told Hans: "You are being shown the yellow card, and it is a dark yellow. Another one of these and you will be fired." He thanked me with a high degree of loyalty and years later said: "If you had fired me, that would have been the end for me."

At the end of my active time at McKinsey, I was managing 1,400 employees, and there were many areas where things were neither black nor white, but gray. Rental cars required for a Monday morning trip were picked up on a Friday afternoon for a weekend jaunt with the girlfriend, office phones were used for private calls. When the controller advised me of these facts, I replied: "You know, it's not my job to call the employees now and to point out these facts. You can show them the yellow and the dark yellow card. You only have to come to me if it is a red card." Given the high number of consultants, a considerable amount of work would have been required to point out items of misconduct in a gray area. In that case, I would have never been able to manage and lead.

One of my favorite sayings was: "If you work for McKinsey – whether as a partner or a secretary – people look at you differently. Don't sign Christmas or greeting cards simply with "Compliments of". Different things are expected from you. I expect you to display an attitude, which corresponds to what we expect from our clients. If you make a presentation to someone, think about who that person is. And also give some thought to how you dress." I preached these sentiments over and over again.

But back to the post-war period and to my father. He differed from the many other Henzlers in the Nürtingen region in that he was called "Airman Henzler", as he served in the air force. As a boy, I thought whoever served in the air force had to be a pilot. When my father returned from the war, I discovered to my great disappointment that he was only a member of ground staff.

A difficult period started when he returned. I still remember exactly how I felt when he showed up at our house. It was a warm day in June 1945. Siegfried and I were sitting in the kitchen with my mother. She had prepared a local dish called "Gaisburger Marsch", which consisted of Spätzle, a local noodle specialty, and sliced potatoes in a broth. He entered the room through the back kitchen door, slim, almost gaunt, dark-haired, wearing a threadbare uniform, which was full of lice. We could see in his face that he was ill and later a doctor diagnosed him with pleurisy.

He stayed in bed for the next few weeks, cared for by my mother. Slowly, he started to look after our fields and grasslands again, and took care of paying back the mortgages on our house – still in Reichsmarks, the currency at that time. He told me that he had been reluctant to go to war and that he considered the war senseless.

For me, the return of my father was a drastic event. All of a sudden, a man was in the house, a man that I considered a stranger, and who made demands on my mother. I was very much focused on her, and I was allowed to crawl into her bed whenever a storm was on the horizon or the Neckar flooded. But that was out of the question once my father arrived: the matrimonial bed was occupied!

While I was unable to intellectually grasp it, I somehow felt that this man, whom I was supposed to call father, had been marked by the war. When he came back from work in the fields, with his cap covering his dark hair, he sat down at the front end of the kitchen table. He never talked much and simply proceeded to eat whatever my mother put in front of him. His meal finished, he got up immediately and went outside. He very rarely put us children on his lap and never played with us. He was unable to show his affection after the grueling war.

My father had not been wounded, but his health was ruined. He continued to suffer from bouts of pleurisy and pneumonia – he fell ill time and again. And I suspect that his soul had also suffered during the years when he was obliged to serve Hitler as a soldier. He didn't follow the path of many of his contemporaries who became members of the NSDAP, the National Socialist Party. This had nothing to do with opposition, he was an apolitical person through and through – but he was also very sensitive. During the war, his only goal was not to attract attention. Perhaps for that reason he never really gained ground again. Perhaps he didn't want to. As an adult, I sometimes had that impression.

And yet, I frequently heard in the village that he had "sat first" in school, that is he had been at the top of his class. He lost his own father, who died of tuberculosis in 1915, at the age of 36, when he was two. When my grandmother Sophie married another farmer from the village, the man brought five children to the marriage. My father Albert and his sister Maria had to sit at the side table. My father must have gone through horrible experiences – at times, he moved in with relatives in the village because he could not bear living with his older stepbrothers and stepsisters. He was not allowed to take up an apprenticeship, as being a farmer was considered sufficient. Thus, at the age of 14, he started work as a laborer in a mill, and subsequently worked as a semiskilled worker with the "Hellers" – Heller Industries in Nürtingen, who produced machine tools. He had built his own house at the age of 23 and – exceedingly rare in those days – convinced neighbors and relatives to act as guarantors. And he had found a wife in Wendlingen – my mother.

In the postwar years, my father tried to provide for his family by managing the small farm he had inherited and by completing an apprenticeship as a bricklayer. But the work on construction sites proved detrimental to his health, so he started to work as a mechanic for Metabo, a nearby company producing hammer drills and other tools. When I remember my father, I see a constantly tired, even dead tired man and even then, I sensed that success would look different. Later on, I frequently said to myself: not attracting attention will not be my motto. Toiling away unsuccessfully, what kind of life could that be?

Siegfried had similar views. My little brother was born two years and one day after me. Both of us hated farming. We preferred to annoy the war refugee couple living above us or playing football at the river, instead of working in the pen or the barn. We liked it just as little when we were sent to borrow a mower, a chaff cutter or even just a big hay cart from relatives. Frequently, they were sitting in the kitchen eating a meal when one of us was sent there, reciting: "My father sent me and asks whether ....". Embarrassing. Even more embarrassing when the farmer asked: "Why?" Or if we were asked to repeat our question . Maybe that's why we decided then that we were never going to borrow anything as adults. In any event, we never did.

At night, we lay in our beds in the cold room next to the kitchen. Because we knew each other's classmates in school, we played games involving the first and family names of classmates, where they were sitting in class, who we liked and who we didn't. And under our warm blankets, we agreed that we were definitely going to live our lives differently from our parents.

CHAPTER 2

ALL THIS DRUDGERY FOR 30 CENTS PER HOUR

There had been rumors all along that our currency would "go bust". In June of 1948, my mother and father were summoned to the city hall – and each of my parents received 40 Deutsche Marks. I still remember how both of them touched the new currency and couldn't bring themselves to circulate it. But the new currency could not be saved, because we had to buy all the items which were not available in farming: sugar, ersatz coffee, margarine (Sanella) and semolina. My father had wisely stored some apple cider with an innkeeper in Nürtingen, which he managed to sell in exchange for real Deutsche Mark coins. And we made good money whenever we delivered apples to the local Raiffeisen cooperative. Nevertheless, I remember how the Swabian farmers (ethnic Germans from a southwestern region of Germany) cursed the equalization duty they were obliged to pay for the refugees from the east.

Our farmhouse stood a stone's throw away from the river Neckar, at the end of Harz Street. The garden with its fruit trees and beds reached the river, until the construction of a ring road in the 1950s cut us off from the riverbank. The focal point of the house – and of life in general – was the kitchen. Here we spent the evenings; this was where we took our meals and where it was warm. In addition, we had a cozy living room for the odd Sunday visit and the Christmas holidays. There was also the apartment in the attic which housed at first refugees, then my grandmother Sophie and finally Schale and her family. The barn and hay and straw rafters – which had to be carried up there during the summer with incredible efforts – were located in the right part of the house.

The cowshed was at ground level. We had four cows, four goats, two pigs, a bunch of chickens and a dozen geese. They provided meat, milk, eggs, down feathers and we made additional money with any excess. Our vegetable garden provided radishes, salad, cucumbers, peas, beans and many other items, and we harvested cherries, apples and pears from the fruit trees. And then there were the fields, spread over the district on both sides of the Neckar, which amounted to no more than two hectares altogether. My father grew wheat, potatoes and turnips mainly for our own use, but also as fodder for our livestock and to sell to the local Raiffeisen cooperative.

We were self-supporting and thus never suffered. Farmers rarely had money but always enough to eat. The Schlachtfeste (a festival where a pig is slaughtered) were fun events, the self-baked bread was delicious, and I can still remember the dough for our local dumpling specialty being rolled on our beds. In my childhood, milk did not come out of a carton, nor beans from a can, nor eggs from a factory. We had a direct relationship with the food put on the table, because everything came from our cowshed, our garden or our fields.

But there was a high price to be paid. My parents and my grandmother Sophie Bauknecht were constantly on their feet. And us children? The United Nations' convention on the rights of children didn't exist at that time, and I doubt that Swabian peasants would have cared, even today. There was always something useful for a child to do.

Sometimes the neighbors' boys helped as well. One of them was Erwin Waldner, who frequently helped Siegfried and I to get to the basement when the air raid warnings sounded. Even then, Erwin was a model for us younger children, and later became an idol as a striker for the Stuttgart football club (VfB Stuttgart), playing thirteen times for Germany. In 2008, I arranged for the sports facilities in Neckarhausen to be named after this great son of our village.

In early September 1948, shortly after the currency reform, I was told: "School begins." That morning, my mother put the school uniform in front of me. This consisted of a cloth corset, which held a set of straps for the incredibly long woolen socks – although it was still fairly warm outside. In addition, I wore dark blue Bleyle trousers and a pullover. I didn't like wearing the corset and straps, but my mother's orders could not be appealed. Once in school, I saw that the other boys wore similar clothes and were likewise upset about the wood-wool socks, which constantly itched. We did not receive any gifts, which usually came in the format of a large cornet of cardboard filled with sweets and various other small items, and the proceedings were fairly simple. There was a service in the church across the street to celebrate the day.

We were only the third class starting school after the war, a total of 51 children of the Neckarhausen "Stalingrad Year". We were named in such a way because Germany entered the war against Russia in 1941 and in no other year of Hitler's rule were more children born. The propaganda slogan "The Führer needs children" clearly had borne fruit. As a child from a farming village, I was part of the well-to-do people, at least compared with the roughly 20% of refugee children, who had been housed in "New Russia", a district of Neckarhausen. A further 20% of children who had lost their fathers in the war also lived in difficult conditions. But we all felt equal.

The elementary school, located in NürtingerStrasse, was an old, narrow building with creaking floorboards where a tight regime was in place. Our teacher, Mr. Keuerleber ("five minutes ahead of time is on time") required that we sat at our desks at five minutes to eight, waiting for class to begin. At eight, he started with a "finger roll call", meaning that he checked all 102 children's hands, and if he found anything black under a nail, he administered a censure starting with: "Did you attend a funeral?" In most cases, he ended by requiring the offender to wash the blackboard or sharpen the pencils over the weekend.

We constantly memorized things. It was easy for me and I liked it. I can still remember certain verses. When my Kindergarten friend Siegfried Henzler – he had the same name as my brother – recited Heinrich Seidel's "The Little Insatiable" in front of the entire village without a single mistake, he achieved cult status because of the length of this poem.

Mr. Keuerleber also gave me my first nickname. Divinity class, taught by the local priest Mr. Ludwig, centered on Jesus and his disciples. The priest asked for another expression for disciples. I said: "They were his buddies". From then on, my teacher called me "Buddy", which stayed with me for a long time.

At lunchtime, we were given free school meals by American soldiers. We liked peanut butter, chocolate and cocoa, but not corn. "Now we have to eat what cows eat" was the Neckarhausen comment on this American food.

Attending school didn't mean not to continue helping my parents. At least, I wasn't the general handyman any more, but rather occupied an elevated position. I remember well how proud I was when I was promoted to wagoner at the age of ten: my job was to fix the cows' harness, to fix them to the wagon and then to conduct the wagon through the village out to the fields. It was a great feeling to march next to the draft animals, whip in hand and to command them, even if in general they knew what they had to do anyway. Nevertheless, it was a formative experience to assume responsibility. One day, a cow dealt me such a strong blow with its horns that I suffered stomach injuries. After that, I refused to conduct the wagon.

Our four cows not only pulled wagon and plough, but also produced milk. Nowadays, a dairy cow will produce 30 liters of milk per day, but for our cows roughly two liters were considered normal. In the morning and evening, the fresh milk was carried to the local milk station in the center of the village, where the cans were emptied into a tank.

This was considered a plum job. My brother and I competed for it because all the other farm boys went there, too, to deliver their milk. The milk house was the central meeting place for the village boys. We sat on empty milk cans and exchanged information. We gossiped, discussed school or held a council of war in case of difficulties

The amount of milk was automatically registered when the cans were emptied into the tanks. Our milk receipts rarely showed more than four and a half liters of milk per delivery. Deliveries were settled at month end.

Two of our cows were mainly used to work in the fields. At the age of ten, I started to become interested in understanding what the milk business generated in terms of income. I had heard from my parents that we got 28 Pfennigs per liter. How could it be possible that the grocery store Häberle on Brückenstrasse charged 55 Pfennigs ?

We milked the cows, we fed them and we mucked out. We could never sleep in, and when we visited our relatives in Wendlingen on Sundays, we could not afford to miss the six a clock train back because not milking the cows would end in disaster. These couple of liters of milk determined the rhythm of our whole existence, and we received just about half of what the grocery store charged? Who were those receiving the other half and what did they do for that? This was the first time in my life that I acted as a management consultant as I suggested to my parents that their small business should market its milk directly to the refugees in the village in order to capture the retail price themselves. Unfortunately, this concept was doomed because hygiene rules did not permit direct sales from the farms.

Nevertheless, I didn't relinquish the concept. A few months later, I started anew and analyzed the economic situation of our part-time farming business. I wrote down the number of hours worked by my father, mother and grandmother. On the other side, I noted whatever we received in income for selling apples, wheat, eggs, cherries or apple cider, when the monthly milk receipts came in or when my grandmother Sophie went to the farmer's market in Nürtingen to sell potatoes and beans. She used her ancient scales and received very little money, partly due to the fact that she gave away the rest of her goods to refugees.

After a longer period of capturing data – I was going for a larger project – I sat down to calculate the relationship between input and output on a piece of paper. I presented the result, which could be called my first study, to my father: "You make 30 Pfennigs per hour! All this drudgery for 30 Pfennigs per hour! This doesn't make sense."

My findings did not fall on fertile ground. On the contrary, a big fight ensued. "Whatever I have, I got it from my fathers and I have to keep it!" my father hurled at me. Goethe wrote in "Faust" that what you inherit from your fathers, you inherit to own. But my father probably wasn't making a reference to this quote; his comments came from deep inside. And I instantly understood what his sudden outbreak meant: you can't just give away what you inherit, you have to cultivate the fields and meadows that were worked by your ancestors.

My father considered his smart aleck son's calculations of Henzler small business economic viability disrespectful, when all I wanted to say was simply: "It doesn't make business sense."

I only realized much later that other meaningful things exist in life, for example a huge amount of satisfaction can be drawn from eating self-produced bread, where the production process encompasses all the steps from ploughing the fields to sowing the grain, until harvest time and the nightly threshing.

As a boy, I only realized one thing, the relentless drudgery in farming was about the last thing I wanted to do with my life. There was nothing which made this existence even remotely attractive. On the contrary, when I went to school in Nürtingen, I was subject to arrogance displayed by the townsfolk towards us village boys. When I said in my strong local dialect that we had a piece of land in the Heidenhau, which was part of the local fields, they laughed at me and called me and the other village boys "Häberle" (a person considered laughing stock in those days). They also called me "stupid peasant", and that was one of the more harmless cuss words used to make me feel inadequate. Constant work, bad pay and no respect – not my cup of tea.

As I grew older and started to develop an interest in girls, I, as a village boy, ran into some difficulties. While some of my female classmates were quite open and approachable, this wasn't the case for certain more status-conscious daughters of the directors of the Heller company. I was asked once by the mother of one of these families whether I was Mr. Henzler of the Henzler print shop in the Market Square. As I answered in the negative and explained that I hailed from Neckarhausen and only went to school in Nürtingen, that we had a farm and that my father worked for Metabo, my chances of going out with the daughter of the house went down to zero. And this of course went around quickly in small Nürtingen.

CHAPTER 3

TUBERCULOSIS CRISIS

MY MAGIC MOUNTAIN IN SCHWÄBISCH GMÜND

letter arrived which was to have great influence over my future. It came in the summer of 1949 and requested me to appear at the Nürtingen local health authority for an X–ray examination. This request was designed to detect early tuberculosis, and unfortunately it proved justified in my case. When examining my X-rays, the public health officer detected the dreaded spots on my lung tissue. He discussed the case with my mother, and then the standard tuberculosis treatment was set in motion. That meant isolation and, as soon as possible, a stay in the sanatorium.

I wasn't particularly upset since everyone said that I was going to enjoy a couple of weeks of recuperation. No-one mentioned a potentially life-threatening illness. I was told that I was going on some sort of recuperation, which could certainly not do any harm. My mother also stuck to this line. Had she cried, had she said: "My poor child, you have tuberculosis, and you never know whether this illness can be cured," I would have reacted differently. But she pretended everything was all right. Thus, I never even thought of being afraid. Only the fact that my brother Siegfried was billeted out to stay with my grandmother in Wendlingen didn't quite fit the picture.

Schwäbisch Gmünd is located about 50 kilometers north-west of Wendlingen, in the east Württemberg Rems Valley. The Red Cross designed to protect from air raids was still affixed to the roof of the "Sonnenhof". The building had been used as a field hospital during World War Two and was now used as a sanatorium for about 100 children who were supposed to be cured of their tuberculosis in quarantine. However, in those days, no drugs were available, so medical efforts focused on the so-called rest cure.

Day by day, the same monotonous routine applied. Wake-up call, morning ablutions and breakfast in the dining hall. After that, we went to the rest hall where we rested on cots until lunch. We had lunch in the dining hall, after which we went back to the rest hall, back on the cots. A long rest followed. We were allowed to get up for dinner in the dining hall. Then bed rest. No entertainment, no class for schoolchildren and exercise was prohibited. Most of the time we had to lie still, which was incredibly boring. Nowadays, children in such a sanatorium would at least have their iPods. I only had a sheet from the church youth organization, which my mother mailed from time to time, and she came to visit me at the Sonnenhof every six weeks.

I was released after seven months and could go home and finally attend school again. But soon after, a check-up with doctors showed that the tuberculosis had not fully disappeared. I was hospitalized again, this time in in Klein-Ingersheim, three hours away by train. Initially, I was supposed to stay several weeks, which ultimately turned into three months. I realized in both sanatoriums that the newly arrived children suffered considerably. Most were afraid and homesick. Tears kept flowing, and the boys and girls only calmed down a bit after a few days. I fared better right from the start. A nurse asked: "You are new, why don't you cry?" I didn't have any explanation then, but today I believe my behavior was a result of my parents' influence. My mother had managed to convince me that there was no reason to be afraid in this unfamiliar environment, and that things were not that bad. My father also contributed, albeit involuntarily and in an unpleasant manner. He had taken me to the sanatoriums by train. Instead of buying me a ticket, he hid me behind a newspaper when the ticket controller passed by. His behavior not only annoyed but also hurt me. I was rather glad when he checked me in to the sanatorium.

I missed almost a year of school through the stays in Schwäbisch Gmünd and Klein-Ingersheim. What to do with a boy who missed that much class? They discussed whether to downgrade me by one year. But my teacher, Mr. Keuerleber, gave me a break: "Let's see whether he's up to it!" I was allowed to rejoin my old class and managed to catch up greatly after four or five weeks, so that a final decision was made: "The boy will make it!" In that respect, I overcame the effects of the illness with bravura, and felt good about it. However, I struggled to cope with another aspect, when the entire class – in formation and hand-in-hand – went to the sports field, down the street and across the Neckar. There, the teacher told me "Sit underneath the chestnut tree."

While the others ran, jumped, or played with a ball, I had to remain in the shade and watch them. I did not only want to recite poems but also be good at sports and to impress the others. But I was constantly told: "You can't be in the sun, you can't sweat and you can't exert yourself!" I felt excluded, but at the same time I realized that tuberculosis was probably more serious than I had thought. Only a few years ago I re-read Thomas Mann's novel "The Magic Mountain." I even visited the original location in Davos with Axel Heitmann, then CEO of the chemical company Lanxess. At lunch, we discussed similarities and differences between what the literary figure Hans Castorp and I had gone through on the "Berghof". Hans Castorp was the son of a Hamburg merchant and had an exhilarating time, for example, discussing philosophical questions with the writer Lodovico Settembrini and flirting with the Russian Madame Chauchat. Both were out of the question for me. As stated before, I found it a hotbed of boredom. Nevertheless, even if it may sound paradoxical, the illness was a lucky event for me. Because of it, I did not end up on the well-trodden path, the usual way at that time for the son of a small Swabian farmer.

It started with the language. When I came back from the sanatorium and told my classmates about it, they asked "What happened to the way you talk?" In my home area, it was possible to determine from which valley or village people came from by listening to their dialect. And now I came along, eight years of age, speaking high German. Today I know that being in the sanatoriums with their different language settings helped me overcome an issue which may have prevented me from embarking on a national or international career.

Without the illness, I would have inevitably become what was common in Neckarhausen, a skilled worker in the local industry. But I was considered sick and as someone who might potentially fall ill again, and was thus unfit for physical labor. For that reason, it was decided that I should attend middle school. Everyone agreed that I should work in an office, where there was no need to exert oneself physically. I was technically useless. I could deal with Märklin's metal construction set but tinkering and cutting wood shapes wasn't for me. Putting together pressing tools for the Heller Company wasn't right for me.

My parents were frequently warned in the village, "Maria, you are raising a little lord, who will not remember to greet you later on." This showed considerable contempt for change. I heard it again and again until I turned 16. I realized quickly that higher education resulted in better opportunities. For example, English was taught in middle school as of the fifth grade. The language was very easy for me. Once I saw two American soldiers at a local celebration in Neckarhausen. I went to see them and addressed them: "How do you do?" We talked as best as I could. Gradually a cluster of local villagers formed around us and all of a sudden I became a small celebrity. "Look, he can speak English," the locals said. And my mother was also informed that her boy had talked for half an hour with the GIs. What a great feeling: no one other than me in Neckarhausen could talk to the Americans. In addition, I got chewing gum and chocolate. Studying bore fruit.

I liked English but divinity class was difficult because I didn't like Mr. Findeisen, our teacher. Mr. Findeisen provided us with ample opportunities to corner him. While we boys had reached an age where we knew that there were two sexes, he tried to ignore or deny each and every reference to sexuality both in the Bible or in literature. We made fun of asking him precise questions. We had discovered a scene in Schiller's drama "Die Räuber" where Moritz Spiegelberg, the opponent of the crime boss, Karl Moor, described the raid on a convent: "And my guys left them a souvenir which they will have to carry for nine months." We asked Findeisen what that meant. He hemmed and hawed but couldn't bring himself to say the nuns had been raped.

Sport was amongst the best activities in school. I had finally been allowed to fully participate, which I did with enthusiasm and success. I became captain of our school's football team, did track and field and also became a middle-distance runner. I did my first 1,000 meter run at the age of twelve at a school celebration. I still remember the result: Three minutes, fifteen seconds. That was respectable, but first and foremost I realized I was good at endurance.

As a young boy, I had heard reports on the radio from the Olympic Games in Oslo in 1952 and from the ski heroes such as Beni Obermuller and Willi Klein who competed for Germany. I saw photos in the newspapers of the wonderful mountains where skiing took place. I was fascinated and I skied the steep slopes in my fantasy.

In Neckarhausen, skiing was limited to a few farming boys who strapped staves from old apple cider casks to their feet and tried to ski down snowy sloping meadows. Real skiing equipment could be seen a few years later at the sports store Knecht in Nurtingen. I decided to buy real skis, Erbacher Standard, for 39.50 marks.

I worked two or three times a week in a tree nursery and at an hourly rate of 30 pfennig I made 1.50 marks for a five-hour shift. I had enough money in December 1955; but unfortunately I had not taken into account the bindings and the fitting so that I had to earn an additional 12.50 marks, which I managed to do before Christmas.

I acquired the equipment behind my father's back. He would have been strictly against it because skiing was an expensive sport. Spending money on skis was a waste for him. My mother wanted to avoid a fight and implored me not to display my new skis under the Christmas tree, as I had originally planned, but rather hide them in the attic. I discussed the advantages of my own ski equipment with my father over the next few weeks, and the argument that I could help him much faster and bring him his food in the winter carried weight. In any case, he agreed in the end. I took the skis from the attic and went up the Neckar where he just worked in the forest. Poplars had been felled and he was allowed to dig out the roots. When he saw me arriving he said: "Here comes Nurmi on skis!" The Finn Paavo Nurmi was popular before the war since he was the best long-distance runner in the world.

This comparison was slightly over-the-top but I taught myself and made good progress. I went on my first winter vacation at the age of 16 to a youth hostel in Kornau, close to Oberstdorf in the Allgäu. There I attended my first skiing class taught in a fairly rustic Alpine style by no other than Anderl Heckmair, who was the first person to climb Eiger north face in July 1938.

Skiing never lost its hold on me. I worked on my technique for days on end in the Black Forest, more precisely in the Zastler area and later became a certified ski instructor of the German Skiing Association so that I could teach. I did this with some success over my student years and more importantly with my own five children. There is no winter without me pursuing my childhood dream of mobility amid the fascinating mountains and snowy slopes.

There were other important things in addition to school and sports. March 18, 1956 was a decisive day in my life. We had decorated both the interior and exterior of our church, received our confirmation suits and dresses and now had to prove to the entire congregation in the crammed church that we had mastered our divinity lessons. Reverend Jehle asked questions, which we had been assigned a week prior to the event. Peter Sihler and I, who attended middle school, had been assigned two questions each, and all others received one question. The questions covered the contents of a psalm, or the meaning of a commandment, and he also asked questions about the course of the ecclesiastical year and the function of the Holy Ghost.

The person being confirmed had to answer the question correctly. It was more difficult than an exam because the entire village was watching. If someone got stuck, the mishap not only followed him for years, but also his parents and siblings.

I don't remember what I was asked. But I do remember my classmate Günther Koluch being asked to recite the ninth commandment ("You shall not covet your neighbor's house…"), and he couldn't remember the words. So he started to improvise. He spoke about what one should not do – steal a bike, lie to one's teacher, and so forth until Reverend Jehle took pity on him and stopped his recital, thanking him for his contribution.

The culmination of confirmation was the celebration at home, which followed the service. In our area, it was customary that neighbors and relatives gave two marks to the confirmed person, in exchange for yeast cake, a local specialty, and ring cake. My confirmation yielded 210 marks. Unlike most of my friends, I didn't acquire a new bike, but rather bought a used one: It cost 25 marks, and I saved the rest. I made good use of my reserves when the Church Youth Organization organized trips. For example, we went to camps or youth hostels on the Swabian Alb. We spent wonderful days singing, practicing sports, playing games and sitting round the campfire.

I would only have preferred a different camp counselor, since Helmut Krämer got on our nerves. For example, he constantly asked the absurd question: "Who rules, King Football or the Lord?" He repeatedly admonished that: "The Lord sees everything, even what happens in the sleeping bag." In addition, he cut a less than dashing figure when he descended from his Horex motorbike with side-car in his knickerbockers and laced boots.

We met regularly at the Neckarhausen parish hall for two hours on Monday evenings. We played games, books were read, we sang and prayed at the beginning and end of the meetings.

I was deeply impressed by the experience of our Church Youth Organization and the confirmation period. I did not become a regular church-goer. But I found working with the Bible stimulating. In addition, the companionship with other adolescents at sports and games, or when discussing fundamental questions of life shaped my thinking.

The fundaments of Christian faith were laid in my family. As stated before, they became guidelines of my thought and action. The disciple Paul wrote that: "No one lives alone and no one dies alone." (Epistle to the Romans 14.7 – 9). I was equally impressed by Psalm 23: "The Lord is my Shepherd, I shall not lack." Another very important item for me is a poem by the Lutheran theologian Dietrich Bonhoeffer, who was killed in April 1945 in the Flossenburg concentration camp because of his resistance to National Socialism. He wrote in a letter to his fiancée:

"Wonderfully sheltered by good powers, we confidently await what comes.

The Lord is with us in the evening and morning and certainly on any new day."

These lines have kept me grounded both in quiet hours and in turbulent times.

In matters of money in business and with colleagues, I often thought about the biblical saying: "What good is it if man wins the world but suffers damage to his soul?" (Matthew 16:26).

From early on, I have been skeptical about the Church, and the idea of the only true Church or the chosen people were not my cup of tea. But I remained faithful, and leaving the Church was completely out of the question.

Learning was not only for school but also for life, and school was not just for learning. We also provided entertainment. If, for example, a passer-by got soaked, it was generally thought that I was the culprit or at least had a prominent role in the prank. I attach great importance to the fact that in nine out of ten cases, the assumption was correct.

The most spectacular mission I led took place right after our final exams and concerned the teacher Mr. Heger. He drove a Lloyd 300, which we had named a Refugee Porsche, because he hailed from the Sudetenland, an area where many refugees came from. I organized eight or nine guys and together we hauled Heger's Refugee Porsche up five concrete steps to the main entrance door of our school and then through the door right in front of the staff room. We considered this a fantastic job but were sailing rather close to the wind, specifically when the poor teacher told me later that his car had suffered a broken axle when we did this.

And what about my brother's life? While I attended Middle School, Siegfried was originally supposed to complete an apprenticeship at the Heller Tool Company, after graduating from Basic School in Neckarhausen. He started an apprenticeship as a toolmaker, but fell ill with a treacherous intestinal illness after only six months. On the doctor's advice, he dropped out of the apprenticeship and attended Higher Commerce School – against my father's massive resistance but gently supported by my mother. He then went on to Business High School in Esslingen and received a High School diploma. My mother now had two little Lords, as they used to say in our village. Siegfried studied geography and English in Tubingen and subsequently taught in Stuttgart and Ludwigsburg. He went on to become a Certified High School Teacher in Balingen, in Württemberg. He is an excellent pedagogue, a teacher with heart and soul.

I probably drew the energy needed later in life from having been ill with tuberculosis. This weakens significantly, but some who get through the illness develop unimaginable strengths. That was my case. I am no psychologist. I don't know whether the fact of having barely survived generates the will to prove oneself after the crisis, or the urge to live life more intensely. As for myself, I started to lead a life full of activity.

CHAPTER 4

ARRIVING AT DEUTSCHE SHELL IN A YELLOW TIE AND POWDER-BLUE JACKET

I staked all my hopes on an advertisement in the Stuttgarter Zeitung. Deutsche Shell was looking for apprentice sales clerks in the mineral oil business for their Stuttgart branch. My next dream was to get out of Neckarhausen, out of Nürtingen, and to the capital. I could have started an apprenticeship as a clerk at the Heller Tool Company, but didn't want to settle for that.

My grades were good – I received at least a "Good" in all subjects with the exception of French, and Shell was impressed. The head of human resources, Ernst Rommel, offered me an apprenticeship after my job interview. I was happy not to have to work for the Heller Company and proud of making 120 marks per month, twice the amount my classmates who had stayed back in Nürtingen made. I may have had a longer commute to the office, which took about an hour by bike and train. But I didn't mind getting up at 6 am because I could now say to everyone in Nürtingen and Neckarhausen, at the age of sixteen: "Look! I know Stuttgart!"

On the first day of my apprenticeship, I showed up full of anticipation at the imposing Hindenburg building opposite the Stuttgart central train station. I had dressed up, wearing a yellow tie and a powder-blue jacket, my only one. I had been told to report to human resources, where I received my training schedule and was sent to the first station, the registrar's service. This was headed by Mr. Weber, nicknamed the "Tall Weber". He was the boss of a rather smallish clerk also by the name of Weber, who was called the "Small Weber". He taught me the subtleties of filing and the unknown dangers lurking in the background. For example, the papers could fly away if we left for lunch without closing the windows or pinning them down. In addition, it was possible to destroy checks when opening letters.

Specifically, I owe "Small Weber" an insight which played an important role during all of my professional life: once again, a co-worker entered the registrar's service without greeting or showing any other sign of minimum civility. He clearly had an attitude, but Small Weber told me afterwards: "Don't you believe that I'll take great care in filing his papers!" In other words: if he treats me badly, he can get lost and look for his papers next time he needs them til kingdom come. At this moment, I understood that this wasn't a case of the small people's revenge, but rather normal human behavior. We reap what we sow. Of course, Small Weber wasn't an important person, and I was even less important, but that didn't mean that we shouldn't be treated respectfully.

Gradually, I got to know the accounting department. I stood guard over the pumps in the port of Stuttgart when freighters were unloaded. I worked for a few weeks pumping gas ("Full, please?"), planned the routes for delivering oil to the sales offices and registered oil drums in a special accounting department – one which would have been slated for termination by McKinsey after a very short consideration period.

"We all have to start at the bottom of the ladder" was an established expression at Shell. And those were apprentice years when I learned a lot. Very respectable clerks made a huge effort to transmit their savoir faire, and Shell offered English classes; talks were given dealing with chemical topics in order to enable business people to gain a better understanding of the company's products. In addition, we went to vocational school one day per week and learned about the theoretical aspects of our profession.

During my apprenticeship, I also attended a translators' school in Stuttgart two evenings a week, from 18.00 to 20.00, which enabled me to pass the Cambridge Lower Certificate at Heidelberg University's Translation Institute, after approximately one year. Later, when working for Shell's Freiburg branch, I attended the Berlitz school and took a class which entitled me to call myself "Foreign Correspondent in English" once I passed the exam. I also improved my rather limited knowledge of French.

The America House in Stuttgart, which was opened in 1950, housed a library where I frequently borrowed English books. The America House's director was in the process of setting up a conversation club, of which I became an original member. Because Baden-Württemberg's capital was home to a US army base, there were frequent evening events with the GIs. I was called Harry, because Herbert sounded too German to their ears. I liked this nickname, which stayed with me until the end of my studies. We visited a kindergarten during advent, and one of the soldiers spent Christmas Eve with us. I was 17 at the time and managed to learn an enormous amount of colloquial English.

I was sent to Freiburg im Breisgau for the last six months of my apprenticeship, after two and a half years of generally interesting work in Stuttgart. I passed both the written and oral examination for sales clerk with the top grade of "Very Good", for which I received a prize from the local chamber of commerce, and was praised in my local Nürtingen newspaper. I still have a binder standing on my bookshelves reminding me of my wonderful three-year apprenticeship at Shell. It contains the reports I had to write on each station I went through. The reports amount to 200 type-written pages documenting the apprentice Henzler's progress.

After I passed the exam, Shell hired me as a sales clerk for the southern Black Forest region, at a salary of 550 marks a month. From time to time, I was allowed to use a Volkswagen to visit the Shell gas stations and provide them with promotional items, for example an antifreeze mixture which went by the name of Glysantin® (a premium-grade coolant). Placards (Wintertime: Glysantin®time) were designed to remind motorists sufficiently before the onslaught of the cold season to not only take gas at the Shell station, but also fill their radiators with Glysantin®. One of these tours, in the winter of 1961, led me to Domenicus Federer, the tenant of a gas station in Hinterzarten. He had been told that I was going to deliver Glysantin® placards and he wanted to see them immediately. However, we had not received them on time in the branch, and I tried an excuse probably heavily in use with salesmen who fail to deliver: "The guys in Hamburg, at Deutsche Shell's company headquarters, failed to deliver the goods on time so I am standing in front of you empty-handed." I muttered a few more accusations about the lack of efficiency of big companies in general and the carelessness of Shell in particular. But Domenicus Federer grabbed my tie and hissed in my face: "My dear Henzler, as far as I am concerned you are Mr. Shell! I only know you in the entire company, and if you have issues with the gentlemen in Hamburg, please sort them out amongst yourselves. If you can't do this you're the wrong man." I was only 19 years old, and this dressing down shocked me profoundly. But he was correct: I was the only person he saw from Deutsche Shell AG, and I had to deliver the placards that he wanted. I was grateful for this lesson.

The next winter turned out to be extremely cold, and heating oil had to be rationed in South Baden. If someone ordered 15,000 liters, he could get a maximum of 3,000, and I, having barely completed my apprenticeship, had to decide: "You will get something, and you won't." But I enjoyed distributing the scarce oil as responsibly as if I were Mr. Shell. This attitude garnered a lot of goodwill from clients.

This was the case for a company in the textile machines sector in Zell in Schönau, which turned to me because they had forgotten to order spindle oil for their machines. Shell had no reserves because of the winter shortage so I asked another client: "You recently received 200 liters of spindle oil, would you mind helping out another client with 50 liters?" He accepted, and I was able to procure the spindle oil for the textile machine company and help prevent the collapse of his production. He thanked me for this help in extremis by becoming a particularly good client.

Life in Freiburg also offered new things outside the professional area. I had lived for 18 years in Neckarhausen, and now I had moved, for the first time and forever. And while I lived in a furnished room, I experienced an incredible sense of freedom. My tribe, the Swabians, are a very rooted people, striving and somewhat unsophisticated. Upon my arrival in the beautiful city of Freiburg, I discovered an entirely new lifestyle – easy, happy, enjoying the good things in life, a little bit French. Here, people liked to share a bottle of wine in the evening, and partied, whereas in my hometown, people worked if they didn't sleep. The Badeners the proud people that live in Baden, with whom they formed the unified state of Baden Württemberg since 1495 never really liked the Swabians, the Württembergers but rather grudgingly respected them: "The time it takes for a Badener to say "sausage", a Swabian will have already eaten it."

In a similar manner as in school in Nürtingen, I had a rather bad experience with the fairer sex. I shared the morning train rides from Nürtingen to Stuttgart with Sybille Walker, where she attended fashion school. She was particularly pretty. I managed to take her twice to a jazz club in Stuttgart, and I planned on taking her to the Nürtingen high school prom. Sybille accepted, and we even discussed seating arrangements. However, her father, who taught at high school in Nurtingen, and her mother also planned to attend the main prom of the year. They insisted that their girl should attend the event with a real high-school graduate. Consequently, she was obliged to ditch me. Subsequently, I stayed away from high school proms because I didn't belong.

This incident made the rounds in Nürtingen fairly quickly and contributed to my decision to move to Freiburg, where nobody knew me. It was a time when humiliation in a small town like Nürtingen could be very painful.

As I had hoped, I was a blank sheet of paper in Freiburg. And while moving from Swabia to Baden was a culture shock, it gave me a real kick. I lived life to its fullest. After work, I rode my yellow Vespa around the old town of Freiburg, found girlfriends, made trips to nearby Alsace and became active in sports. At first, I played football for the FC Freiburg amateur club, and later for TSV Alemannia Zähringen. I also joined the Freiburg Ski Club. I spent many wonderful weekends in their hut at Feldberg and I am attached to this club to this day. I am still in contact with its president, and I delivered the commemorative speech at their 100th anniversary celebration in 1995. This close relationship certainly contributed to making my time in Freiburg very happy.

Nevertheless, something kept irking me: students partied into the night, while I had to go to bed to be at work the next day at 7.30. When I met a very good-looking girl, she made it clear to me: "I am attending medical school." I immediately realized that this was not going anywhere. "A future doctor, my Vespa will not do the trick." I thought more and more frequently that I was second-class. And that was not limited to unsuccessful dating. The western side of the collegiate building of Freiburg's Albert Ludwigs University is adorned by a motto engraved in stone, drawn from the Gospel according to John: "Truth will make you free." Whenever I passed by, I thought about this inscription. "… and what greater can give man to man but truth?" Friedrich Schiller once wrote. His freedom ideals had been discussed in Middle School, as well as the works of his contemporary Friedrich Hölderlin, who like me hailed from the Neckar Valley.

When I stood in front of this university, this venerable institution bound to truth in the service of freedom, it dawned on me that this was where the highest intellectual elite was found. Compared to people like us who sold heating or spindle oil, the university played in a different league and this was where I was headed, even if I wasn't quite sure about the way.

There were two colleagues at Shell in Freiburg who disappeared for some time and returned with PhDs under their belts. One of them, my colleague Ernst Morawsky, projected a particularly confident appearance. One time, when I visited my parents in Neckarhausen, Dr. Morawsky gave me a ride in his Volkswagen to Karlsruhe, from where I hitchhiked home to Neckarhausen. During the ride, we discussed attending university and doing a PhD. He told me how things had gone for him after high school, and what the degrees meant to him. I told him about my desire to attend university, and Morawsky said: "If that's what you want to do, you should go for it." Dr. Morawsky went on to become a board member of BASF, and his example showed that no-one had to stand still. It was possible to try to move ahead.

I researched whether it was possible to attend university without a "classic" high school diploma, and came across the Higher Business Colleges, which were being set up in various locations, similar to Engineering Colleges. I applied without hesitation to the Higher Business College which was about to be set up in Siegen. I precisely met the admission requirements, which consisted of a Middle School certificate, an apprenticeship and one year of professional experience, and was accepted. I instantly gave notice at Deutsche Shell.

The departure was very amicable, and I was even assured that I could work as a holiday replacement, at my current salary.

Each new start contains some magic, wrote Hermann Hesse. When I moved from Freiburg to Siegen in Westphalia in 1962, I experienced the magic of this new start. By this, I don't mean the city of Siegen, which was a sleepy town not connected to the German highway system, whose football club Sportfreunde barely managed to play in the second league, and where people rolled their rs and ended their sentences with "woll". Rather, I was fascinated by the possibilities lying ahead of me: finally, I was able to study in an academic setting. And this at a brand new institution, which was still developing. Nothing was cast in stone, and that meant that we could contribute to shaping many things. My livelihood was secure, too: the state of Baden-Wurttemberg paid me a monthly scholarship of 200 marks because I had passed my final apprenticeship exam with the top grade of "Very good" and was thus eligible for the Talent Scholarship Fund.

Finally, school commenced. The Higher Business College (HWF) started with 60 students, who had worked for different periods of time in their respective professions. This resulted in an unusual age structure: I was one of the youngest at the age of 20, and Robert Bohrer, the oldest student, was 36. As a former Shell salesman, I regaled my classmates with real-life stories. Unsurprisingly, I was elected chairman of the AStA student representative body by my fellow students four weeks after studies commenced. Other reasons for my election may have been that I was already captain of the newly established student football team, and that I frequently took the initiative.

As AStA chairman, I organized the first big trip to Opel in Russelsheim. An expected invitation to lunch did not materialize, so we ate at a variety of food stalls. That day also provided me with a drastic experience in the democratic decision-making process. I put everything to a vote of my 60 classmates, issues ranging from seating arrangements on the bus, breaks and when and what we ate. After the fourth vote, my AStA colleagues Hartmut Sieper and Dirk Wuppermann, both sons of Westfalia businessmen, took me aside and said:

"My dear Herbert, we admire your democratic heart, but what we need here is leadership. Just tell people what they have to do." That was a helpful lesson. Many situations exist where voting is essential for the community. But there are also many situations which require clear and decisive leadership. From then on, I always tried to distinguish between the two.

Amongst other things, I used my influence when mechanical engineering students from Siegen asked whether we business students were interested in joining their student corps. I had studied their history and mindset and had read many negative things. For that reason, I took a stance on student corps and prevailed, so that they were rejected at the HWF.

I enjoyed my AStA position, particularly because a number of competent people were elected to various sections. I am still close friends with Hartmut Sieper, nowadays a businessman in his own right, who then was head of the social section. And School Director Walter Lohmann was a visionary who had precise ideas about the development of our institution. For him, being a businessman meant to be far-sighted, to take risks at the right time and to run a business holistically. To him, the image of a businessman as a moneygrabber was in need of improvement. Lohmann thought that the new breed of HFW business graduate could contribute to that, and that he would be successful in the job market, because of the combination of theory and practical applications. He quoted Goethe, who wrote in *Wilhelm Meister's Wanderjahre*: "to really know one thing and to practice it is a higher state of knowledge than hundreds of things done by halves."

Lohmann and I got along well and worked together closely, with respect to both the academic curriculum and the social life on campus, and even beyond that. I spent many breaks in the staff room because there were always things to discuss. I also wasn't shy in telling the director which instructors were good and which weren't. Business is not a highly scientific subject, but rather a systematic and applied collection of processes. The college emphasized such a practical orientation. I liked studying and learned a lot during those five semesters, but it was easy for me. Therefore, I was able to spend a significant amount of time on initiatives around our studies. When the Franco-German Youth Organization (DFJW) was established, I was there right from the start. I wrote to DFJW headquarters in Bonn in order to find a partner school in France. Thus, for the first time in 1963, twenty Siegen students visited the Ecole des Arts et Metiers in a city that was then called Chalons-sur-Marne. Now it is known as Chalons-en-Champagne. We received the French guests in the following year, and an active exchange started.

However, we frequently lacked the money for such field trips. In that case, I went to see Bernhard Weiss, president of the local chamber of commerce. We would discuss this issue and I would usually receive a donation. Weiss was the owner and CEO of Siemag, a world leader in steel-mill technology, and helped our college as best as he could. In the course of numerous discussions, we developed a strong relationship, which later led his son Heiner Weiss to appoint me to the supervisory board of Siemag.

Bernhard Weiss told me that Basic School graduates could barely attain a position in middle management, but that Higher Business College graduates could go further. There was a big mission ahead of me!

One of the few projects not supported by the Chamber of Commerce was my idea to establish a jazz club in the cellar of the castle sitting above Siegen, as I had seen done in Stuttgart. The project was discussed by the relevant committee but received a negative reply. The reason was explained in the minutes of the committee meeting: they did not want "negro music" in the local castle's cellar. I was disappointed that we didn't receive a grant. But above all I was shocked that such a way of thinking was still exhibited in Germany in 1963, and specifically by dignitaries in the local business self-administration, the Chamber of Commerce.

Eventually, the final written and oral exams for the Higher Business Graduate degree were given at the end of the fifth semester. When report cards were handed out, we discovered that I was the only student receiving the top grade. When the announcement was made, the entire room broke out in applause. This degree was not only pleasant to have, but also useful. The final grade was combined with a high school diploma, which now recognized by many universities. The doors to a real A alma mater now stood open for the former sales clerk and current Higher Business Graduate Herbert A. Henzler.

Before studying at university I went to the Unites States. It was summer, and I had saved for a Lufthansa student ticket. I used the three-month holidays to discover the country of endless opportunities. First, I went to visit my aunt Emma on the East Coast. Emma was my mother's sister and had emigrated from her native Swabia to the US in 1922, as a 15-year-old girl, together with her brother Karl. Since that time, she has been living in Watertown, NY. She helped my family with care packages in the post-war period, and also visited us once, which was a big event in our village.

I was received very affectionately in Watertown, and was generally very impressed by the Americans' friendliness. At the same time, they appeared a bit strange when they asked whether I'd rather stay in the US since we didn't even have cars and fridges in Germany. After all, this was 18 years after the war ended, and we had long found prosperity, with American support. Thus, I explained to the startled US citizens time and again: "Sure, we have fridges in Germany. Sure, we have cars, and I even own one."

America also appeared strange with respect to politics. I moved around in Republican circles – that is German Americans who had become modestly wealthy under very difficult conditions – who decidedly disliked John F. Kennedy. The young president was revered in Germany but almost hated by many of his fellow Americans. His Democratic Party was dubbed "Demorats", and he was catholic to boot. I went to the movies a few times and watched movies featuring "The German Nazi" – at that time all Germans were considered national socialists in the US. This country with its numerous witless inhabitants didn't tempt me at all. I was not interested in living there.

Then I bade goodbye to my aunt and the East Coast to visit her brother on the West Coast. Uncle Karl lived in San Diego, CA. Prior to my trip, he sent me a Greyhound bus ticket for $99, and I traveled across the Continent. It took three days and three nights to cross the US from east to west, and I realized that the country's dimensions were enormous. Arriving in San Francisco, I changed my mind and thought that I could probably stay in the US for a longer period of time.

I flew again to the US two years later, this time for work. I had organized an internship for an American student at Karl M. Reich, a family-owned company in the wood technology business in Nürtingen. His family returned the favor by organizing an internship in the US for me.

I stayed with my aunt Emma again and worked at Stebbins Engineering and Manufacturing Company in Watertown, which made concrete tanks. My first project was a cost analysis, which showed that the company lost significant amounts of money on half of its tanks. One of the reasons was the syndicate structure. A construction worker wasn't simply a construction worker, but there were bar benders, bricklayers and lining technicians. Each profession had its own powerful syndicate, which resulted in lack of flexibility and increased salary costs. A second project I worked on introduced a simple project-cost analysis, which enabled Stebbins to determine where they made and lost money. At the end of this internship, I traveled again to California to see my uncle. This time again, I had mixed feelings. On one side, I felt like a guest in a wonderful country. On the other side, the country appeared to be a bit too full of itself: whatever America did was automatically good and right. 'The Land of the Free and the Home of the Brave', as the national anthem says, lived this dream.

CHAPTER 5

SAVING A RESTAURANT AS A TOUR GUIDE AND FINDING LOVE

A utumn of 1964 arrived and I was living my dream. For the first time, I studied at a "real" university. In Siegen, we had worked with Wolfgang Kilger's *Introduction to cost accounting*, with Wolfgang Stützel's works on banking and corporate finance or with Gunter Wöhe's *Introduction to general principles of Business Administration*. Here, in Saarbrücken, on the university's campus near the forest, we saw these and other economics luminaries in the flesh.

The subjects offered few new aspects, so I started to look for challenges elsewhere. I passed the intermediate exams at the end of the first semester, including statistics and accounting. During the course of the second semester, I attended operations research seminars for students who were about to graduate. In addition, I studied law up until the intermediate exam and also looked at other fields of study so as to broaden my horizons. I improved both my theoretical and practical knowledge of French by taking classes at the university (which in those days had also a faculty of letters in French), but also by making field trips with classmates in my used Citroen 2CV ("Duck") to nearby France.

I had gained valuable experience working occasionally as a tour guide when living in Freiburg. One time, I worked for the Stuttgart-based Ruoff travel agency, accompanying a group of tourists in a bus bound for the Austrian Kleinwalser Valley. We drove through the night and a lady seated in the back end of the bus came to see me and said: "Back there, everyone is smoking and drinking. I can't take this any longer, I can't continue sitting there." What could I do? I was only 17 years old and much younger than most of the travelers. I felt that I probably wasn't going to get anywhere trying to issue orders regarding smoking and drinking on the bus. But then I had an idea. I offered the lady my tour guide seat right next to the bus driver and used the emergency seat myself. The lady later sent a commendatory note to the travel agency praising my decision: such a young tour guide would go far in life. I was very pleased and settled the question of smoking on subsequent bus trips right at the start by putting it to a vote.

I liked dealing with people, which is why I looked for a job as a tour guide in Saarbrücken as well. I found a job with International Section of the German Student Association (DSR), which, amongst other things, organized ski trips to Austria. I led several trips to Westendorf in Tyrol. My primary task was to keep people entertained, although they always found a fly in the ointment, such as bad weather, a hangover from the previous evening, or the snow. Being a tour guide was a crash course in people leadership. I discovered that a group of 50 students could be affected positively by initiative and constructive feedback. In particular, they had to fill out "feedback forms" at the end of the trip, where I received top grades. I heard of that at the occasion of a visit to DSR headquarters in Bonn.

My Westendorf trips typically lasted from late February to early April. The local branch of the Tyrolean ski school checked out my skiing skills and I became a ski instructor during the day – at that time I was the only German among 40 instructors. I had a great life, also owing to my red pullover, which identified me as a ski instructor: I received free food and drinks in the café, enjoyed special status in the bar, and at teatime, the latter being coupled with dancing activities.

My groups stayed at the Maierhof, a beautiful old Tyrolean guesthouse, which had quite visibly fallen on hard times. The source of the trouble was obvious: for example, the menu was way too long. Therefore, I suggested: "Just offer five dishes, and that only from 19.00 to 21.00, after which there will be ham, cheese or sausage sandwiches." Frequently, guests left deckchairs behind in a sorry state, and I recommended introducing a utilization fee of six shillings. The hotel owner implemented my recommendations and soon there were positive results. However, the crisis became acute again after the brewery stopped beer deliveries. The reason was unpaid bills.

What is a guesthouse and restaurant without beer? The hotel owner and I drove to the Gösser Brewery in Wörgl to discuss a solution. Finally, one of the brewery executives told me: "If you participate and dedicate yourself to saving this business, I will give it another try." Beer deliveries to the Maierhof continued, and after four weeks I personally delivered the monies due to the brewery. From then on, things went back to normal. I liked this type of business consulting, and the Maierhof is still in existence.

I met the woman who was later to become my wife at the occasion of my second trip to Westendorf. Rosemarie Zens had arrived with two friends, and the trio made a significant contribution to the cheerful mood all around. I noticed immediately that she was a good skier. She told me that she didn't want to attend a skiing class because she considered it boring. I liked her answer, and I started to look at her more closely.

When the two weeks of vacation were over, it was hard to say goodbye. She attended university in Munich and studied to become a Middle School teacher for History and English. I went back to Saarbrücken. We wrote many letters over the following weeks, but only met once for a weekend, after which she told me: "Our relationship will only work if you come to Munich." I didn't object, but dodged a clear response: "Sure, maybe, but then maybe not." Being that vague in my response, I of course didn't take any steps to arrange my transfer. Saarbrucken University was excellent, I had many friends there and she made that suggestion very shortly after we had met.

Rosemarie didn't accept my indecision and did everything to make sure that my Saarbrücken certificates were recognized by the Ludwig Maximilians University in Munich. I was impressed. Had she not done that, I would have probably stayed in Saarbrücken. But due to her efforts, I was able to enroll at the university in the Bavarian capital, as a third semester student.

I knew nothing about Munich, but felt immediately attracted to this lively city with the southern flair when I moved there in 1965. Rosemarie and I lived in Schwabing in separate quarters and had a wonderful time. I also liked the university. Compared to Saarbrücken, it offered yet another dimension. We dealt with interesting professors, such as Edmund Heinen, who had founded the Institute of Industrial Research. I learned a lot from him, as well as from his colleague Erich Preiser, the legendary economist.

All the same, I continued my habit of pursuing other interests in addition to my studies. In winter, I frequently taught at the university's ski school on the weekends, and in summer I traveled the world. I had already been to the US twice, in 1963 prior to attending university, and in 1965 when I worked for two months at Stebbins in Watertown. But the continent to the south of the US was a blind spot on my personal map. Thus, I decided to travel to Latin America. I took Spanish classes at university, and the Konrad Adenauer Foundation in Bonn, and looked for contacts to a company where I could potentially work. In the end, I found a family-owned company in Uruguay. The salary they offered was sufficient to cover my cost of living, and I earned the travel money by working for the iron and sheet metal forming department of the Alfred Gnida Company in Nurtingen. I also worked on a couple of projects in their offices.

I boarded the *MS Louis Lumiere* which took me from the French port of Le Havre to Latin America. I had booked a place in a six-bed passenger cabin in tourist class. Three of the travelers were sick most of the time, with all the unpleasant by-products generally accompanying such a state. The stench was unbelievable. But upon my arrival in the Uruguayan capital of Montevideo, an immensely interesting period of two months began. This was the first developing country I visited – immense social discrepancies, enthusiasm for football, and tremendous corruption which manifested itself in broad daylight and for all the world to see. Parking offenders would buy their way out of parking tickets. I was very impressed by the Latin Americans' particular temperament, simultaneously cheerful and melancholic.

I worked for a textile company, Textil Uruguaya SA, which was owned by the Belgian Steverlynck family. The company made cloth from cotton, for example for shirts and bed linen. They had no cost-accounting systems, and my task was to introduce such a system within two months. The timeframe was generous, so I decided to use a particularly granular cost-accounting model called work-center costing. This model relies on determining each material's processing location and time, by man and machine, and then cost markups are determined. I developed forms, which were distributed to workers. Their task was to record which material arrived at which work center at what time, and the time it took to be processed and leave the work center. But when I went to collect the forms the next day, I was in for a nasty surprise. No-one had recorded a single position on my forms, they simply didn't care about my ambitious cost-accounting project.

I decided to tackle this task differently. I sat down and analyzed the production process using technical literature and dictionaries, until I understood how the process worked: here narrow materials were used, and there, broad materials. Here, the materials were rolled three times because they were used for a certain type of product; and there ten times, because this was required for a different type of product. Subsequently, I discussed my findings with the production manager. Thereafter, I had all the information required to determine appropriate cost markups taking into account the specifics of each production stage. The final result was the equivalence numbers showing how costs were allocated to product groups.

My efforts were worth the trouble, as we realized that the current crude average cost accounting showed losses with respect to certain products, and profits with respect to others, but was largely insufficient. Consequently, we completely reworked the price structure. Later, the company CEO wrote to say that the business was profitable as never before and that they even exported to Chile.

Grateful for the interesting time in a foreign country, I returned home. The passage with the *Eugenio* C of the Italian Costa shipping line went from Montevideo via Buenos Aires, Rio de Janeiro and past Madeira to Genoa, where I took the night train home, across the Alps. I came home almost at the same time as Rosemarie, who had worked as an au pair in the US while I was in Uruguay.

The academic environment in Germany had seen a few changes in the meantime. The precursors of the 1968 student insurrection could be seen in the Bavarian capital. Protests were held against the Vietnam war, emergency laws, the Springer publishing company, against the so-called "Establishment" including the universities and their hierarchies ("Under the gowns - muff of a thousand years"). I once joined a protest march through Schwabing and shouted: "Protest, march with us and don't stare at protesters!" The closing rally in Königsplatz Square in Munich was a big event. But as a general matter, I had difficulties sympathizing with the student movement as it had in my view little to show in terms of concrete goals, with the possible exception of educational policy. Rather, it was the creation of sons and daughters of well-heeled parents looking for adventure.

I found it much more interesting to participate in the Konrad Adenauer Foundation's debate clubs, discussing for example the so-called emergency constitution, the laws enacted in May 1968 dealing with the state of emergency, the state of defense of the Federal Republic. I had read a notice on one of the university bulletins that the Konrad Adenauer Foundation was on the look-out for highly skilled individuals, and that interested parties should apply by sending a hand-written CV, accompanied by grades and two references. It was understood that only a few applications would be accepted. I read in a newspaper that Bruno Heck, the former German family minister, had been the head of the foundation since May 1968, and was looking for young people interested in the political development of the country.

I said to myself: why not file an application? No sooner said than done. A selection session was held in the Black Forest, and I felt honored to be among those chosen. As Konrad Adenauer scholars, we had annual political training courses in Eichholz near Bonn or West Berlin. We met the future hopes of the Christian Democratic Party and experienced how the Adenauer Republic slowly tested the Social Democrats as future coalition partners. At one time, I even managed to shake hands with Konrad Adenauer (the first post-war Chancellor of Germany), at the occasion of an awards ceremony of the Germany Foundation held in Munich. This was a major event, but I soon realized that almost all of the other scholars had set their sights on a political career – Uwe Barschel amongst them. There were also Bernd Kränzle and Ursula Männle, who became members of the Bavarian government. However, the more I dealt with them, the more I became convinced that I just wasn't like them. That may have been because I felt intellectually much more independent. Many of them already knew local politicians and were members of a variety of organizations, which wasn't for me.

Barschel and I happened to share a room on the occasion of a meeting of the Konrad Adenauer scholars in Eichholz. Back then, Barschel was an active member of the Young Christian Union and had a well thought-out plan for his political career: he wanted to become a member of the local parliament in his home county of Lauenburg at the age of 28, then a government minister in the state of Schleswig-Holstein at 31, and that of course wasn't going to be the end of it.

I didn't harbor any such political ambitions, even if the Christian Democratic/Christian Socialist party fascinated me as a people's party, rooted in conservative values, and not prone to concepts of redistribution of wealth and income. Such sympathy grew stronger over time as I started to work more closely with Lothar Späth, Edmund Stoiber, Horst Seehofer, Wolfgang Schäuble and Annette Schavan, all of them acting with utter conviction.

My lack of affinity for a political career notwithstanding, I became the first speaker of the Munich Konrad Adenauer scholars and in that way established regular contact with Otto B. Roegele, publisher of the *Rheinischer Merkur* and our faculty student adviser. I benefited hugely from this contact. In my speaker function, I organized monthly meetings to which I frequently invited Christian Socialist Party dignitaries.

I then sat my final exams. In 1968, I wrote my Master's thesis on the recognition of principles of group taxation in the Federal Tax Court, located on Ismaninger Street. When I found out that the court had a special library for the Federal judges, I wriggled my way in and was allowed to work there and use its resources. I still remember a discussion with the Federal judge Hugo von Wallis who explained in short that taxation of intragroup profits should not be deferred "*ad calendas graecas*" ("until the Greek calendar"), because the Greeks did not have a calendar in the Ancient Roman era. This insight contributed to the grade of "Very Good", which I received for my thesis in business taxation. The oral exam had to be moved to a neighboring building as there was a strike in progress at the university. Finally, after a total of seven semesters, I received my Diploma in Business Administration with the grade of "Very Good".

CHAPTER 6

GO WEST

BERKELEY, GREAT STATISTICIANS AND PROTEST MARCHES AGAINST VIETNAM

H aving gained great experience in Uruguay, I contemplated working for a big international company. I liked the thought, as I spoke English well, and knew French and Spanish to some extent. But I was also considering an academic career. In any event, my immediate goal was to do a PhD. in Munich and to get a job as a research assistant. Irrespective of that, I also applied for a US scholarship with the German Academic Exchange Service (DAAD). I managed to obtain the scholarship, and when my favorite university Berkeley accepted my application, I started to look forward to a year of studies in California. It suited me well that Rosemarie had just passed her teaching qualifications. She was able to postpone her practical teacher training and thus we were able to go to the US together.

Rosemarie and I got engaged in June 1968. When I received a letter from the DAAD confirming my scholarship and we knew that we were going to California, we decided to get married prior to the great adventure. On July 19, we went to the civil registry office with our parents and witnesses and celebrated this lovely day with a small circle of friends and relatives. After this, we were ready to take off. We boarded the *Bremen*, the flagship of the Norddeutschen Lloyds, at the Columbuskaje, a shipping pier in Bremerhaven, in order to cross the North Atlantic in seven days, destination New York. The passage was calm, and only on one day did we have a wind speed of seven, which made for turbulent seas. Our fellow passengers were mainly German Americans who had visited relatives in the old home country and were now heading back to the US.

Rosemarie and I met many people on board the ship. A guy from Chicago who was in the steel business quizzed me about my background and offered me a job. He was prepared to pay a monthly salary of $5000 to get me to join his company as a manager. But I had different plans and wasn't ready to change these. He kept at it and continued to be annoying until we reached New York.

It was fascinating to watch the proud *Bremen* arrive in Manhattan harbor and dock at the pier. The maneuver took two hours. Since then, I have visited New York numerous times, but always by plane, in a hurry. I frequently thought about the arrival by ship in the summer of 1968 because it was the most beautiful way to approach this unique city with its breathtaking skyline.

Some practical aspects of life in the New World posed challenges. What is an appropriate tip for the porter carrying our six suitcases and bags as well as two pairs of skis from the deck of the ship to the pier? I thanked him profusely and gave him two quarters, which in those days were equivalent to two marks. He screamed: "I am a rich man" and threw the money in disgust on the street. I then doubled the amount for the cabdriver taking us to the Greyhound terminal. But he wasn't satisfied either, as the ride was just about six blocks.

We took the overnight bus to Watertown, NY. to my Aunt Emma's house. I had already visited twice, and we spent a few carefree days with her and her family. Rosemarie and I had met a couple of students on board the *Bremen*, who had brought their VW Beetle on board and intended to sell it at the end of their US trip. That gave us the idea to get a car to go to Berkeley and to visit a few states on the way. In the end, we found an old Ford Falcon in Watertown and we bought it for $250, and were on our way.

First, we drove north to Canada. We took the Queen Elizabeth Way across Quebec and felt independent and completely free, as it was described later by Dutch documentary filmmakers Peter Delpeut and Mart Dominicus in *Go West, Young Man!* When returning to the US we took the famous Ambassador Bridge, which connects the Canadian province of Ontario with the US state of Michigan, and arrived in the car metropolis of Detroit, where we looked for a motel room. However, my wife didn't sleep a wink because we had watched Alfred Hitchcock's movie *Psycho* a few days before. Anthony Perkins played the psychopathic serial killer Norman Bates, who struck terror into people's hearts in motels.

Our journey then took us through Nebraska to the Denver area where we stayed with Agnes and Harry Bitterman. We had met them at the Munich Oktoberfest, and they invited us to see them in Evergreen. They threw a party in our honor to which they invited many of their friends. One of them immediately called his in-laws in Alameda near Oakland when he heard of our plans and organized accommodation for a night. Once more, we experienced American hospitality.

As planned, our Go West ended in Berkeley. We found an apartment on Francisco Street, and after a few disappointing experiences Rosemarie found a job in a kindergarten. I took up my studies at Berkeley, University of California. Berkeley had a reputation as one of the world's elite universities. Famous professors of economics and statistics taught there. I was hoping to meet luminaries such as George Danzig, West Churchman, Norman Blackwell and Jerzy Neyman, and expected to receive first-hand knowledge and experience. I had changed the topic of my PhD dissertation while still in Munich and decided to tackle a statistics topic instead of taxation, since the great statisticians of the time taught at Berkeley, and I hoped to benefit from their teachings.

Ernest "Ernie" Königsberg was one of them, a protagonist of "Operations Research", which combined applied mathematics, economics and computer science. The goal of this was to support the decision-making process with the aid of quantitative models. Königsberg once told me after an exam: "Next time I'd suggest you have a whisky before the exam." I asked why. "It was obvious that you were very nervous." The rapport between students and professors was very straightforward and direct, which was unknown to me from my time at German universities. This model is what I still use today in my teaching at Munich University. I address students in class by their first names and am open to questions not directly related to topics covered in class.

Berkeley was impressive in many respects for someone hailing from a German university background. I sensed early on that a number of people were more than matching me with respect to intelligence and efficiency. I will never forget the Taiwanese operations researcher and the Indian statistician – they played in a different league. The vibe was more creative and intense than what I was accustomed to. At the same time, the university was incredibly well equipped. I had never seen such libraries, some of them open until 2 am, and a stadium that had been built exclusively for the Golden California Bears, Berkeley's football club, which housed 70,000 spectators. The university was not only rich, but also a living institution. Its students felt that they were the chosen ones. Their professors were unique. In addition, I was given a key, which granted access to this alma mater at all times. I was not the only one studying and it was particularly hard to return this favor.

At that time, the Vietnam War was in its final stage, and America was shaken. Protest marches had been virtually unknown until then, but now they were taking place all across the country. They were particularly intense in California, to the considerable chagrin of then governor Ronald Reagan. In Berkeley, thousands took to the streets. Protests were not only launched against the Vietnam War, but also in support of a Black College, for public parks and so on. It was hard to believe, specifically with respect to normal conditions in the US, but the establishment and unruly students didn't speak the same language any more. When students rededicated a parking lot as a "People's Park", the university administration countered: "You cannot just steal other people's property!" But the students retorted: "You stole the land yourselves, from the Indians."

Rosemarie and I also planned on joining the protest marches, but university publications warned that foreign students could be subject to arrest and deportation when taking part in unapproved protest marches. As a result, we desisted. When police arrested more than 480 protesters in May 1969, some foreign participants, specifically Swedes, were registered and deported. "Never break the law": the government made this very clear, and participation in an unapproved protest march was considered a glaring violation of the law.

Americans were not only shaken by the hippie movement and student unrest. They were deeply concerned about whether America could maintain its role in the world as an unquestioned moral point of reference, , when thousands of young GIs died in Da Nang in South Vietnam, when North Koreans captured an American ship and held its crew captive for a long time, and when in Europe protesters burned American flags. I knew students who tore up their draft notices sending them to Vietnam. One of the neighbors in our apartment building fled to Canada to avoid the draft. No one wanted this war anymore, but young people in their early twenties were sent to Vietnam to risk their lives! It was clear even to us that mainly African Americans were sent to Vietnam to bear the brunt.

When Richard Nixon was elected president in November of 1968, all hopes for a quick end to the war were dashed. How could a firebrand such as Nixon extract the US from such a convoluted situation? Today, we know that Henry Kissinger brought an end to the war in a manner frequently used in history: he simply declared victory and withdrew the troops.

Numerous companies were present at Berkeley's Placement Center and competed for future graduates. They posted bulletins as to when company representatives would be on campus to conduct interviews, and interested students were invited to sign up. I had read about General Motors, Arthur Andersen and many other companies with an international reputation, but McKinsey somehow escaped me. I only heard about them having been on campus from my classmate Franz Scherer, who had met them, undergone the interview procedure and received an offer.

I had talked to a couple of companies. But I was still interested in an academic career in Germany, and none of what I encountered in the Placement Center could have deterred me from that goal. But what Franz Scherer told me about McKinsey appealed to me – a young, dedicated group of professionals, a great atmosphere, interesting clients, international work. This confirmed my impression that McKinsey had to be a very special company. In fact, I often found that the most important articles I analyzed at Berkeley with respect to management topics, had been written by McKinsey professionals. Wherever multinational groups made strategic decisions, McKinsey consultants appeared to have a finger in the pie. And by all accounts, McKinsey paid fairly well, too.

I hadn't abandoned my plans of pursuing an academic career, but wanted to see whether this firm could be an option after all. I applied to McKinsey's San Francisco office and was invited for an interviews. The first meeting with Ted Demosthenes, head of support staff, was remarkable. He knew my CV, knew Berkeley and thus made candidates feel right at home. I went through several rounds of interviews, and the last interview took place at lunch with Tim McNamara, a McKinsey partner. I don't remember what we discussed, but I will never forget how it ended. As we said goodbye, Tim said: "My dear Herbert, it would be fantastic if you joined McKinsey. I think you would be an exciting colleague."

To this day, I don't know how I managed to convince my interviewers. But all of a sudden the door was open to a firm which attracted people from all over the globe. I was inspired by the great feedback, and possibly caught the McKinsey virus, which would never lose its hold on me. I didn't accept the offer, but I knew that I had an excellent opportunity up my sleeve.

While at Berkeley, I continued my career as a ski instructor during the winter months. Rosemarie had never taught skiing before but she received permission to do so and we went to the California ski resort of Squaw Valley on the weekends, teaching skiing for four hours on Saturdays, for which we received $8 per hour.

Finally, the intense year in Berkeley came to an end, but we decided to see a few countries before returning home. Rosemarie had received a scholarship for her work on the "Intellectual interests of the early Nobility". Thus, our tight budget wasn't that tight anymore. We had managed to save $3000 in the course of that year, and traveled to 12 countries.

We took the Japanese airline JAL across the Pacific Ocean, and stopped in Japan, Taiwan, Hong Kong, Indonesia, Malaysia, Singapore, Thailand, Nepal, India, Afghanistan and Russia. After eight weeks, we were back in Munich, in September 1969. We celebrated our church wedding in November; when we went to Berkeley in 1968, we barely managed to arrange for a civil ceremony – allowing Rosemarie to come with me as my spouse. Our church wedding with family and friends took place in November 1969.

While in Berkeley, I worked on my PhD dissertation entitled *Optimizing the stratification in random samples*. The idea was to set limits to pure chance by way of methodical analysis, so that the result (eg of surveys) was as certain and precise as possible, and not just an arbitrary reflection of reality. It may sound boring to the layman, but a closer look revealed its relevance.

While my dissertation took shape, I worked as a research assistant to the chair of statistics held by Professor Hans Kellerer, and taught junior students. I liked teaching statistics seminars, but harbored some doubt during these two semesters about whether I was suited for an academic career. I had certainly enjoyed my studies and continued to be fascinated by the academic atmosphere. I admired great scientists, such as Eberhard Schaich and I got to know him as an extraordinary statistician, but he appeared to be caught in the daily grind of university life. A job in academia had always appeared to be an attractive option. But being a research assistant was the litmus test, and it became clearer from seminar to seminar: faces were different, but everything else remained the same. The same formulas, the same content, the same "aha" moments for the students – all of that until retirement?

In addition, I felt that academic life had little to do with real life, about which I was passionate. Professors appeared to enjoy a significant amount of freedom and also free time, but I didn't find this appealing. I wanted to help shape society, to move the needle even if I had to go to my limits. Nothing could be more appalling than a standstill. While I couldn't be lured with freedom and free time, money was a different matter. But a professor's salary wasn't exactly pushing the envelope in terms of financial opportunities. I was soon to receive a letter stating that McKinsey's starting salary was roughly equal to a professor's final salary. That was a compelling argument.

But before that, on February 9, 1970, I received my PhD in economics, which constituted the first step towards an academic career. As far as I was concerned, it was the first step towards a career which I didn't take, for fear of boredom. I sounded out options, for example at Deutsche Shell where I had apprenticed, at Siemens and of course at McKinsey. The San Francisco office had made the verbal commitment that I could start at any time. I would have to go through the recruitment procedure once more, but they considered this a mere formality.

However, saying goodbye to an academic career wasn't that easy. It dawned on me that I was still undecided when I received an offer to become the main research assistant in statistics from Professor Ingeborg Esenwein-Rothe in Nürnberg University. I didn't want to reject the offer out of hand and traveled to Nürnberg. I even took Rosemarie with me.

Shortly thereafter I received the university's firm offer, but in the meantime I had also received a formal offer from McKinsey Germany, which tipped the scales. During the course of a long evening, I discussed various options such as an academic career, Siemens, Shell or McKinsey with my classmate Eberhard Kriese, who had joined Siemens, and a couple of other classmates. The decision was clearly for McKinsey.

I sent a letter to Ingeborg Esenwein-Rothe and included the terms of McKinsey's offer. The salary was approximately three times as high as the position at the university. I was probably trying to get her to understand why I rejected the offer, by showing how far apart the terms for the two jobs were. It was a mistake. Mrs. Esenwein-Rothe replied in bitter terms that I was clearly a slave to rotten money and didn't understand that profession had something to do with vocation.

CHAPTER 7

———

START AT MCKINSEY

PSYCHOLOGICAL TESTS, THE FIRST TRAIN SMASH AND BECOMING A BATTERY EXPERT

Upon hearing that I hadn't accepted the offer immediately, Irene Scott, Head of HR at McKinsey, said in a slightly indignant manner: "We believed you would have given it some thought beforehand!"

I had done all the interviews, and even flew to London where Dr. Cabot, a dire psychologist, tested me for an entire day. I had to answer a never-ending stream of questions, amongst those some rather abstruse ones, such as: "How can you live with the conscience of being likened to Hitler's son?" I was quite tired, having gone through test after test, as Dr. Cabot asked all of a sudden: "Imagine that a tribe invents some foodstuff which causes its members to become twice as tall and twice as strong as members of other tribes. What would be the consequences?" I responded, exhausted: "These members of the tribe will need bigger cars, bigger chairs and new clothes." The psychologist looked at me vividly and said: "But think about those who remain small, too." After that, he tried to goad me to enter a fantasy world à la Thomas More. But I wasn't ready for that after so many hours spent with him.

Subsequently, he prepared a psychological analysis report, in which he stated that I had an enormously appealing charisma and that I kept my cool under pressure, but that I had remained superficial in borderline situations, which I hadn't fully penetrated. In addition, my career choices remained unclear. In the end, Dr. Cabot concluded, nevertheless, that I was a good fit for McKinsey because of my disproportionately high social skills. Afterwards, when I read the report, I was rather surprised since my impression after the day with the psychologist was that I better not join McKinsey. Later, I learned that Dr. Cabot's aggressive demeanor deterred many potential candidates from joining McKinsey. In the end, McKinsey made do without the psychologist's services. By the way, my response to the Head of HR's offer was as follows: "Thank you, I will think about it." I was quite serious. Rosemarie and I discussed it at home a number of times, since we would have had to move to Düsseldorf. We had just returned to Munich after a year in California and this would mean that we would have to leave Munich again, while Rosemarie was still in teacher training. McKinsey Germany didn't appear too attractive; they had only one office in Düsseldorf. To us, the Rhineland almost seemed like exile. Rosemarie and I liked Munich and had no intention of moving. And did I even want to move to a world of intense competition and the "up or out", as McKinsey called it? Joining this firm meant to leave familiar terrain for uncertain, unknown territory. I had no concrete idea what a professional working for a big consulting company actually did.

Nevertheless, McKinsey's attraction proved irresistible. As a student, I had done a few consulting projects and always enjoyed analyzing issues, developing concrete action points and observing their successful implementation. In the end, we decided to accept McKinsey's offer in Düsseldorf.

I started work on July 1, 1970, together with Peter Schlenzka who had attended Stanford University. Together, we looked around the Düsseldorf office and were not quite sure whether to be proud of our new job or rather intimidated and filled with awe by household names such as VW, BASF and many others, who were clients of the firm. Up to now we only knew these companies as consumers or from reading the press.

Work started in the afternoon. We were dealing with Hans Heinrich Thyssen-Bornemisza ("Baron Heini", as he liked to be called) and his more than a hundred companies, domestic and foreign. I received materials so as to get up to speed. That's what a McKinsey study looked like! In this study, my new colleagues recommended selling a few companies, merging a few and taking stakes in others. A management information system had to be established and I was part of the team which was assigned this task.

After one week I was already traveling to the Netherlands and other countries where Thyssen companies were located. I worked with Henk Harkema and Buie Homan, both of the Amsterdam office, the London project manager Paul Henderson, and Max Geldens, the relationship director. We worked flat out to develop a concept, to more efficiently manage Hans Heinrich Thyssen's maze of companies. But after two months, "Baron Heini" stopped the project for political reasons, which had nothing to do with us. That was the end of my first McKinsey project, and Geldens told me when we bade our farewells: "Herbert, whatever you want to do, you can do it with this firm." As of that moment, I knew that I had arrived.

But not everything went according to plan. I suffered my first train smash on my second project. I was assigned to implement budgeting and long-term planning at Boehringer Ingelheim, a pharmaceutical company. Unfortunately, I was rather clueless but had to put on a brave face. I found a McKinsey guidebook on PPB that is "Programming, Planning, Budgeting", and adopted whatever appeared relevant for my assignment. I then presented my work to the client, suggesting this and that measure to achieve this and that goal. When Boehringer CFO Folkert Bellstedt read my recommendations, he simply said: "Are we supposed to pay good money for a piece of amateur work?" I had egg all over my face, but fortunately I managed to make amends quickly. The project went well, and I experienced for the first time how McKinsey prepared an economic analysis of a company. We took the company's numbers, analyzed them, compared them to market and competitive developments and drew them up in a conclusive format. Then, conclusions were drawn and communicated in typical McKinsey style that is in diagrams and clear statements. In stark contrast to academic tradition, results were presented first: we almost ambushed the client with the dramatic quintessence and thus created the requisite attention for our suggestions, which were then presented.

Boehringer Ingelheim was a family-owned company with business interests all over the globe. It produced mainly in Germany, but its revenues were generated mainly abroad. This constellation provided an opportunity to learn how German drugs had to be positioned with medical schools worldwide, how marketing support had to be given by the head office and how various international inputs had to be bundled for purposes of German research. The legendary Karl Diehl was Head of Controlling for Boehringer Ingelheim and the power behind the throne. He controlled the information flow between head office and subsidiaries. We worked together so well that they tried to recruit me. After six months work on the project, they offered me, a twenty-eight year old management consultant in his first year, a job as director of their Argentinean subsidiary. I felt honored but turned the offer down.

My next project revolved around sorting batteries. Herbert Quandt, one of the great industrialists in post-war Germany, had hired McKinsey to develop a new management structure for his group (Varta, Byk-Gulden and a few others). My job on the McKinsey team was to develop a concept for the Varta battery division, which was part of the Quandt Group. It took us six weeks to present the results of our analysis and our suggestions for the future.

Our contact person was Hans Graf von der Goltz, Quandt's close ally, who went on to become president of the Supervisory Council of the Quandt holding company, and who also wrote works of fiction. Herbert Quandt himself was also in attendance at our presentation, as the battery business was one of his personal hobbies. He had a special charisma, which was almost physically felt in the room, probably because he was almost blind due to a lifelong eye disease, or perhaps because he was curious as to what these "American management consultants" had to offer. When I met him for the first time, I greeted him with a timid "Grüss Gott". He immediately started to laugh loudly. When he had calmed down, he told me that he had heard this greeting after the war in Ellwangen, and had spontaneously said that this had been the first order in months, that is to greet God. That broke the ice.

This was the first time that McKinsey had been hired by Quandt. After thorough analysis of the situation, we suggested forming Battery AG as a holding company, with four subsidiaries dealing with different areas: start-up batteries, dry cell batteries, industrial batteries and batteries for outside Europe.

I was no battery expert and thus had to conduct intense research so as to determine the best way of sorting such energy storage devices and how to best define the scope of each subsidiary's activities. McKinsey had already tested the principle several times, among others with BASF and with the industrial company KraussMaffei, and called it a divisionalized structure.

The reason for such divisionalization was the vigorous development of German companies. Typically they were set up along functional lines: production, the purchasing department, research, sales, each function headed by one person. But the post-war period saw significant growth, and companies expanded their activities and acquired other businesses. Thus, they became a sort of centipede, which could not be efficiently managed under a centralistic functional structure.

McKinsey's concept of divisionalized structures targeted this phenomenon. Groups which had become too big and unwieldy were broken down into manageable parts, so as to enable them to correctly allocate profits and losses. To that end, we divided groups into single businesses (generally along product lines), that is divisions receiving their own management structure and clear rules with respect to dealing with headquarters.

Varta was one of the last significant divisionalization projects for McKinsey. It marked the end of a phase for the so-called Germany AG (a small group of companies of international standing), during which they established a new and more manageable structure after the tremendous expansion of the post-war era. I was glad to be able to experience and contribute to this process with respect to Varta. We were enthusiastic when Herbert Quandt accepted all of our suggestions for Varta and implemented them 100%. Our team's plans called for the consolidation of the businesses of CEAG Dominit AG (heavy current switches, electronics) and Byk Gulden GmbH (cosmetics, drugs, food) under the roof of Quandt's holding company, Varta AG. Bayerische Motoren Werke (BMW), Industrie-Werke Karlsruhe-Augsburg (IWKA) and a few other companies were excluded because family ownership still required restructuring.

The Varta project was more than an interesting assignment for a young management consultant. It was an incredible experience working directly with one of the most impressive industrialists of the old Federal Republic. At any time, we sensed the strategist capable of taking risks, but also his long-term view, as he had for example demonstrated with BMW. Quandt had rescued the car maker, made a risky investment and orchestrated its turnaround, turning it into a company that thrives to this day.

When Herbert Quandt visited Varta in Hannover, he first stopped by the office of Alfred Borsum, the labor representative. He asked for a report , after which he went to see management to get their version. In my entire career as a management consultant, I have not seen many business leaders such as Herbert Quandt, who possessed an extraordinary entrepreneurial vision, combined with an eye for his managers and a steady hand in dealing with the rank and file.

Quandt implemented McKinsey's suggestions. He limited himself to running the holding company in Bad Homburg, and the Batterie AG board in Hannover was responsible for managing the business of the battery division.

CHAPTER 8

MANAGEMENT CONSULTING

A PROFESSION, NOT A BUSINESS

Marvin Bower had retired as Managing Director a long time before. But the man who had succeeded the founder James O. McKinsey and put his stamp on the company like no-one else was the right person to convey the McKinsey way to us rookies. To that end, I interrupted one of my first assignments as a management consultant and traveled to New York. Together with 30 other McKinsey newbies from all over the globe, I attended a two-week induction training. Marvin's evening seminar on professional ethics was the highlight of these two weeks.

We were given case studies, which we discussed in teams and then presented to experienced McKinsey staff, under considerable time pressure, just like in real life. In addition, we underwent interview training (this was videotaped, even back then), and attended courses on how to deal with hard and soft information. Hard information was defined as that which was quantitatively measurable (revenues, costs, market share, operating income, cash flow). Soft information was defined as qualitative, such as specific skills, cultural skills and attitude towards new techniques. However, the core of the induction training was to acquaint us with McKinsey's philosophy. Bower preached: "We are a profession." Just like lawyers exercise their profession according to certain rules, Bower's view was that management consultants also had certain values, procedures and techniques. A rite of initiation was celebrated, which did not disappoint: we had the impression of belonging to a unique organization.

After two exciting and inspiring weeks, I went back to the daily grind in Germany. Normally, life as a management consultant had a fixed rhythm. From Monday through Thursday, we worked with clients. The team consisted of an engagement manager, a senior consultant and two "normal" McKinsey associates, such as myself. A typical study started by trying to understand a company's numbers. One of us analyzed sales, another production and a third one controlling. In addition, we conducted detailed interviews with management. To the extent available, we used external information with respect to market developments and competitors. Using manuals, we asked what happened in a corporate division, which changes had occurred and were about to occur, which major challenges they faced. For example, after speaking for one and a half hours to a sales manager, we knew that quality issues existed with respect to certain products, that other products were mispriced, that competition was particularly tough in certain areas or that the organizational setup was particularly challenging in other areas. We then wrote down our findings and passed them on to other team members. The days were pretty charged, and we frequently worked into the evenings. Then we went to our hotel, sat down and discussed the day's events.

McKinsey wasn't stingy with respect to travel expenses. We took flights to see clients, which in those days was considered a luxury, and we generally stayed in comfortable hotels. Life at McKinsey included the best hotels as well as considerable salaries. But it wasn't just the salaries and perks which made the job attractive. I greatly appreciated working in small teams of like-minded people, roughly of the same age, all of whom were similarly motivated and committed.

Even back then, Friday was traditionally an office day for management consultants. We met in the Düsseldorf office to discuss the week's events but also to maintain contacts and networks. What happened in the McKinsey organization? What happened with respect to comprehensive projects, with respect to future trends important for our work? Who were the new guys? Who left the firm and why? And numerous internal discussions also took place on Fridays when everyone typically was in the office. For example, reviews. Normally each consultant received a so-called engagement performance review (EPR) every three months, where the following items were discussed: What was the quality of the analyses? Did he make good use of McKinsey's resources? What was the client feedback? What was the team members' feedback? What was the project manager's feedback? Which improvements were necessary and how could these be implemented? All that feedback found its way into a ranking and consultants were evaluated after a period of six months – with respect to development of their analytical and social skills, with respect to client communication and commitment. McKinsey's evaluations were merciless and I observed very early what it meant not to get anywhere or even to fall behind. This meant that the McKinsey career was over. The organization parted ways – generally without causing a stir- with consultants who didn't move ahead. Typically two evaluations below standard were enough for that.

Fortunately I did not have to worry. Right from the start, I was in the lead and I was already considered outstanding and a rising star in whom the company had high hopes after a short period. I received my first salary increase after six months from 4,200 marks to 4,800, and after a few more months I received another raise. Compared with conditions in normal German companies, the degree of increase was rapid. It was mainly based on my excellent EPR results. At the same time, I also got involved with McKinsey's internal affairs. Düsseldorf, the German McKinsey branch, was a relatively small office. If one was interested, there were numerous opportunities to apply oneself. For example, I worked on our training programs and as of my second year taught courses in statistics, cost accounting and controlling. All of that gave me the great feeling that I wasn't an ordinary employee but I contributed actively to this office and to this firm! In those days, there wasn't any separation between professional and family life. Quite the contrary: Marvin Bower said again and again that there was a successful partner behind each successful partner. Bower was also of the view that no-one could achieve a management position without a "strong woman" – he hailed from another era. But I could only agree with his first conclusion because Rosemarie was such a "successful partner" for me. In our early years in Düsseldorf, she was amongst the few wives of McKinsey professionals who worked. She taught middle school in Meerbusch-Osterath.

We partied together almost all weekends, with other associates including wives or girlfriends. We all knew each other. It went without saying that wives were invited to attend the partner conferences in the Bahamas, in Monaco, Florida, Arizona or Hawaii – this included only spouses in the 1970s, but this changed later on. Rosemarie accompanied me when she had school holidays. It was a wonderful thing for the women. McKinsey was one big family, which was demonstrated time after time. Marvin Bower himself is considered to have shaped the history of McKinsey. The founder, James O. McKinsey, had hired the corporate lawyer in 1933 as a partner – allowing James O. to accept a CEO role in Marshal Fields in Chicago When McKinsey died in 1937 of pneumonia, Bower became the sole head of the company, which grew in leaps and bounds because of his unique approach to consulting. Bower has left his indelible mark on McKinsey. He formulated the principles which still determine the company's philosophy. Part of his heritage is McKinsey's set-up as a partnership, i.e. McKinsey is owned by active partners. In addition, the goal is to attract the best and to pay the highest salaries. Marvin Bower was also behind the "obligation to dissent", that is the duty to not simply accept things, not to be economical with doubts, but to dissent. When I saw Bower as a young associate at my induction training, he did not hold an official role at the firm any more, but as an elder statesman, he embodied the spirit and style of McKinsey like no-one else. He was omnipresent and ensured that no-one violated the McKinsey spirit. I was going to feel the force of that on several occasions. In 1976, the international partners conference was held in the Bahamas and while I was only a newly minted partner, I was tapped to make a presentation on strategic concepts.

To that end, I had read a lot about Carl von Clausewitz, the great Prussian war theorist and strategic thinker. For my presentation, I used the parallels between military and business strategy. I analyzed the campaign of a German group (Siemens) waged against French competitor (Schneider) and described various strategic phases based on Clausewitz's theory. It became apparent very quickly that it wasn't a good idea to discuss Clausewitz at the occasion of this international conference. Applause was rather moderate. I was ignored during the coffee break that followed and here and there I picked up comments such as "looks like the Germans never change." Marvin Bower, then director emeritus, reacted to my presentation with a written rebuke: there was no room for anything military in a McKinsey consultant's toolbox, and I was to remove it from mine as soon as possible. This first appearance in front of the highest McKinsey committee (the international partners' conference) was a fiasco.

Eighteen years later, this time as head of the strategy committee, I gave another presentation at a partners' conference. It was in the spring of 1994 in Phoenix, Arizona. I presented a paper on our strategy. I described how we recruited, trained and promoted talent and called this our "business system." I had barely mentioned this term when Marvin Bower got up at the back of the hall. He was about 90 years old, but still had his penetrating voice. He almost screamed across the hall: "Herb, this is not a business!" What we did was not a business but a profession! He had advocated this all of his life and told me numerous times: "This is not a business!"

This intervention from the last row made me helpless. Each of us consultants used the term "business system" each day with our clients. I had used it purely technically in order to describe what we did to ensure our own performance. But now I stood as a heretic, as one who deviated from McKinsey's pure doctrine or, even worse, had never really understood it in the first place.

Nobody helped me. McKinsey's great old man had reprimanded me in front of everyone and many a partner will have thought that this was what Henzler deserved. During the following break, I tried to explain to Bower that I just intended to use a technical term, as opposed to delivering a creed, but he didn't want to talk to me.

I heard some time ago that I lost any chance of becoming a successor of Fred Gluck, then managing director of McKinsey in Phoenix. I don't know whether this is correct, but I consider it a possibility. However, I had no ambitions for the job. I did not want to travel across the globe to have dust thrown in my eyes by local offices saying "everything is fine and what is not fine will be fine tomorrow." I rather wanted to build the German practice and thus had never considered throwing my hat in the ring. I took a page from General William T. Sherman who fought for the Union during the American Civil War. "If nominated I won't run. If elected I won't serve." This was his saying when they tried to convince him to run for President of the United States.

My relationship with Marvin Bower gradually stabilized after the Phoenix episode. My last encounter with him came in 2000, a year before his death. I visited him in a rehabilitation facility in Florida in order to get his advice. This was the time of internet euphoria and big IPOs, which had raised the aspirations of a lot of McKinsey people. Many partners saw a possibility of forcing McKinsey's IPO. I was a staunch opponent of this plan and hoped to get arguments and backing from Mr. McKinsey himself. Marvin had transferred two-thirds of his then 60% share in McKinsey to other partners at the occasion of the set-up of the partnership in 1950 at book value and not at market value. It was estimated that he could have made at least $25 million then.

Why didn't he seize this opportunity? I asked that question and he replied: "Herb, I was never motivated by money. I wanted to create an institution." He certainly succeeded in that goal. This sentence was quoted at his memorial service in Lincoln Center. And the status quo remained. McKinsey wasn't listed and is still owned by 1,200 people around the globe, the big family.

Because I wanted to belong to that big family, I organized events as a young associate in my free time for this family, especially sporting events. I introduced the Saturday McKinsey football game at the Dusseldorf Rhine meadows. People liked to participate because they were in a similar situation to me. We had moved to Düsseldorf and were not socially established so McKinsey was a temporary home for us. Once I organized a football game between staff of the Dusseldorf and the Dutch McKinsey offices. Then we organized a skiing competition with the Swiss McKinsey people. This "winter retreat" became a regular, large-scale event for 25 years between February and March, with children included.

I was particularly motivated by praise, which was for me the main driver. I required it and my success depended upon it. When I was in school and during my Shell apprenticeship, I was motivated by praise. This was the same for me at McKinsey. I was constantly motivated by appreciation for my performance and commitment. I function the same way as Bastian Schweinsteiger and Thomas Müller, who play all the better the more that the trainer and fans appreciate them. More money was a sign of appreciation and was good. But probably more important was management trust in excellently evaluated staff and the more interesting studies that resulted, the more appealing challenges, the greater responsibility. McKinsey and I was a marriage made in heaven, a happy association.

I increasingly learned what made McKinsey people tick. I had been at McKinsey for only three months when all European consultants went to a conference in Rome in October 1970. We discussed our firm's engagement in Africa. Previously McKinsey had only done sporadic projects for the government of Tanzania under its President Julius K. Nyerere. The question now was whether to increase our activities in Africa and to attack a new market on the black continent? The Tanzanian politician George Kahama sat on the podium at the Hilton hotel, which hosted the conference, and talked about the significant challenges for the African continent. He warned us against doing business in apartheid-ridden South Africa (although some of our American and European clients would have liked us to do business there).

The conference leadership divided us into teams of ten members, with each team featuring one Senior. What should and could we do in Africa, what was the theme on this Continent? There was a wild discussion in my team where everybody spoke at the same time. Nobody listened to the others and a lot of nonsense ensued. After one-and-a half hours, Senior Terry Williams rose to speak: "Let me recapitulate what we just talked about. There are three things resulting from our discussion: first, we shouldn't look at Africa in general but rather initially focus on two countries of choice. Second, we need to find people who would live in Africa for a longer period; that is a minimum of ten years. And third, if we decide to go ahead we wait for one or two years to see how things are going before we decide on a more extensive strategy for Africa."

Terry Williams' way of summarizing our discussion was instructive in two respects. One was "the three things", which I encountered time and again at McKinsey. That's how we went to the heart of the matter and how we presented our work product – in clear, unambiguous and catchy terms, in order to generate the maximum effect for the client presentation. I learned how to quickly get down to the essentials at McKinsey.

But even more interesting with respect to Williams' summary was that it did not give an account of what had been discussed at all. It described a plausible and reasonable position, which unfortunately had not been worked out in our windbag forum. Terry Williams nevertheless presented the position to the plenum and received a lively round of applause. For me, it was an impressive example of leadership through communication. If the right person said something at the right point in time, everyone followed suit without a significant degree of resistance, unless someone took an entirely contrarian position.

To succeed at McKinsey, a combination of analytical and social skills was required. We had to be able to understand and analyze facts quickly, and to draft diagrams with content and depth at short notice. In addition, the diagrams had to be presented to the client in such a way that he actually liked them.

In those days, many McKinsey people were more analytically inclined and only learned the absolute minimum of social skills. They wanted to prove their value through the contents of their slides, but were less interested in connecting with the client on a social level. The opposite scenario existed as well, but very rarely: some people were barely able to connect the dots but went down very well at each client meeting.

My skillset was somewhere in the middle. If in a coordinate system analytical skills were entered on the y-axis and social skills on the x-axis, my position would be near the bisector of the angle, which was a recipe for success at McKinsey. I had the reputation of a pragmatic and productive consultant, who built great client relationships. However, McKinsey demanded not only thorough analysis and social competence of its young professionals. Whoever wanted a professional future at McKinsey had to bear the following principle in mind: "Always give the clients more than they expect." McKinsey's standard was to surprise clients by increased efficiencies. A consultant who knew how to exceed client expectations fitted the bill and could count on a fast career track. In this respect, I was also happy to receive very good evaluations.

As much as I enjoyed the work and the success it brought, Rosemarie and I were unable to get used to Düsseldorf life. Four years in exile was enough. The mountains were far away. Lake Baldeney was the only lake in sight so it was completely overcrowded when the weather was good.

The Hinsbecker Schweiz was considered hilly for local purposes, but was a small consolation for us, as we loved nature and the mountains.

Munich was our home and I would have liked to work from there. I constantly suggested to my colleagues that McKinsey should open an office in Munich, but my suggestion fell on deaf ears. Office manager John G. McDonald who headed the German McKinsey branch said: "We don't have a single project in Bavaria. Why should we open an office there?" But I didn't give up and drove my British boss up the wall so that he finally caved in and we set up a working group which was to provide an unbiased review of the Munich idea and to make a recommendation. At the outset, the team's position was completely undecided. The team was headed by George McIsac, an American senior partner who had no geographic preferences in Germany. The two other team members held contrarian views: my colleague Juergen Zech himself hailed from the Niederrhein and was against a Munich office. I was a staunch supporter of the office because that is where I wanted to go. The working group held meetings but I was the one who really worked on this matter while the others limited themselves to providing comments to my drafts. This project taught me that one can make one's points in a task force by not hiding in the group and by fighting vigorously for one's beliefs. In any case, we unanimously recommended that as an experiment and subject to cancellation, McKinsey should transfer one floor of the Dusseldorf office to Munich. In 1974, my colleagues Helmut Hagemann, Armin Timmermann and myself moved into a five-room office in Koeniginstrasse 28 in Schwabing, ideally located between the university and the English Garden. The Munich office developed into by far the biggest office of the German McKinsey branch and today it is the largest office in the whole firm. The first client was Siemens. When this group hired McKinsey, I was chosen to manage the project as engagement manager. Former Siemens CEO Gerd Tacke had considered management consultants a waste of time. He thought they needed six months just to get to know a company and then they made suggestions which the company could arrive at itself by reflecting on its own. Tacke's views were similar to the views of my mother, to whom I once explained the job of a management consultant, and who simply said: "Then you do the job for which the management gets paid a lot of money."

Professionals having worked successfully for six or seven years for McKinsey are nominated for partner positions by their country offices. An international committee met regularly in New York and discussed the nominations. I was honored to be made a partner only after four and a half years at McKinsey. The financial arrangements were such that a partner then had to invest 180,000 marks in the company. Ninety percent of the amount was credited and I paid the remaining 10% with most of what I had saved up for a rainy day. In return, I received an increase in fixed annual salary and a bonus, which was distributed at year-end. Much more important for me was the fact that I now was a partner. A partial owner of McKinsey. At the age of thirty-three, I could now have my own clients. I was now the Engagement Director who negotiated projects with the clients. I managed the teams working on these projects, sometimes two or three projects with respectively two or three teams at the same time. I was now able to do as I liked, whereas many former classmates of the same age fought with academic bureaucracy or worked in other companies still hoping to move ahead. For me, the job as a management consultant was the right choice. McKinsey showed its high esteem for people by appointing them to Firm Committees. Such working groups deal with the inner workings of McKinsey. For example, early on, I was appointed together with colleagues from San Francisco, Chicago and London to a committee looking at the associates' situation, that is the 90% of consultants who were not yet partners of the firm. We organized a big survey and the result was that these young colleagues felt very bad as a general matter. We presented these shortcomings to the Shareholder Council without sugar-coating them and managed to fix a few grievances. Among them, we instituted a training program for engagement managers and put in place an ombudsman in all McKinsey country offices that is some type of mediator to whom employees could pour out their troubles.

I had been at McKinsey for only eight years, three-and-a-half of which as a partner, when I was elected director. After that, I received the honor of being appointed to the PCEC, the Principals Candidates Evaluation Committee. This position came not only with significant influence but also insight into the overall organization. As a PCEC member, I was assigned four offices whose partner candidates I had to evaluate. These were the West Coast, Dallas and Mexico offices. I visited these offices twice a year for a week each, took a close look at the candidates and drafted an evaluation.

The PCEC normally met twice a year in New York. Each member presented his/her views after which we collectively voted on the candidates. There were three possible results: "Elect now" which meant a direct partner promotion at this time. I would estimate that five out of ten candidates were elected to partner on their first try. The second variation was "Not yet": in such cases, in the committee's view, these candidates had not yet shown sufficient performance, for example, with respect to client work or as to development of methodology. They could try again within six to twelve months. The worst case was "Never" and this signified the end of the working relationship within six months.

I really enjoyed the PCEC work, even if it was difficult to make time for it in addition to the daily grind and even if it was an unpleasant duty to convey bad news to failed candidates and their office managers. But this committee, which elected partners worldwide, actively built the platform for McKinsey's future. I spent three years on the PCEC. In those days, five to seven partners were elected every six months (nowadays this is 35 to 40). I participated in the election of the first female partner, Linda Levinson in New York, and the election of Rajat Gupta, the future firm-wide managing director. I also spent two years on the PRC (principals relations committee), which reviewed the performance of principals and elected directors. After that I spent five years and subsequently again three years on the DRC (Directors relations committee. The DRC evaluated the directors and determined total compensation according to evaluation categories. The differences between the top category and the lowest category amounted to 3.5 to 1. Colleagues who spent more than two years in the lowest category were encouraged to leave the firm. I was also a member of all other 'standing committees' at McKinsey during my active time there.

CHAPTER 9

THE 7S MODEL AND OTHER CONSULTING DEVICES

G
ermany was a difficult place for management consultants. In the fifties, Georg S. May, founder of the
eponymous consulting firm, had sent his semi-skilled
consultants from Chicago to Europe, where they made
a lot of money with empty promises from mainly small companies
and finally left scorched earth behind. Big companies were led by
boards who considered themselves responsible for the German economic miracle, and many of those saw no need for consulting.

McKinsey's first European client was the Dutch/British mineral oil group Shell where I had done my apprenticeship. Shell com-
missioned a big organizational study from the consulting firm which
back then was purely an American company. As a result of this,
McKinsey set up an office in 1961 in Geneva and from there
opened up shop in Germany. The first office was opened in 1964 in
Düsseldorf's Koenigsallee. Clients were not exactly queuing up to
see the original three McKinsey professionals, but enough German
managers wanted to try out what these Americans had to offer. After
all, America was Germany's most important ally. The US was the
most important economy in the world and several global brands such
as Coca-Cola, Kleenex or McDonald's had originated from the US.
Consequently Americans had to be knowledgeable about business
and, with increasing frequency, German companies wanted to better
understand the management philosophy of the New World.

When I joined McKinsey in 1970, the wave of divisionalization
was about to subside. In a next phase in the 1970s, management information systems (MIS) were the big topic. McKinsey offered ideas
on how to efficiently manage, steer and control companies. Because
under German law, boards held collective responsibility, MIS were a
required tool for all board members.

On the one hand, it was a challenge to obtain current group-
wide information because data systems were still in their infancy.
On the other hand, our system had to deduce from many facts the
few meaningful ratios which top management really needed. MIS
were in demand and McKinsey successfully set them up in many
German groups.

A typical McKinsey product of the 1980s was the 7S model. Tom Peters, Robert H. Waterman and other colleagues had asked the question to which no systematic answer was available to date: why is one company successful and not the other, although both have the same structure and follow an identical strategy? What are the real factors upon which success and failure depend?

Tom Peters worked out of McKinsey's San Francisco office and was remarkably talented, but also remarkably unconventional. I liked his thoughts and approach and invited him several times to Germany, for example to the legendary partner's meeting in 1979 in Vienna, legendary because it featured a performance of *Tosca* in the Vienna Opera House, a visit to the Lippizaner horses, the Vienna Choirboys and a gala evening at the Palais Schwarzenberg, including fireworks. His speeches were always brilliant but the essence of his theses wasn't easy to understand. His partner Bob, on the contrary, was a great simplifier. He was capable of writing down Peters' complex ideas combined with his own in a clear and comprehensive way.

Both studied company histories and management methods and compared cases from the Western cultural environment with Japanese cases. In total, 43 top companies received the label "excellent". Finally, on the basis of their findings and the common features they had analyzed they developed a model based on the seven elements, which in their view were relevant for success. Three "hard factors" played a role. First, the strategy had to ensure a competitive advantage. Second, the structure had to turn the company into a functioning organization and third, the systems had to provide the framework for corporate procedures. The four "soft factors" in this model were special skills, which distinguished a company, the permanent staff, the style which expressed itself in a company's culture and finally the way a company saw itself, its shared values and visions. Tom Peters and Bob Waterman wrote a book about the 7S model (*In Search of Excellence*), which was published in 1982 and sold more than six million copies worldwide. The seven elements making up the model were very useful for McKinsey because they named the factors which provided a starting point for external consultants in order to increase performance for the company. At the same time, the model marked a modified trend in management science: the human factor received much more attention and weight than before. The model was called 7S because the English expression for the seven elements started with the letter S: 1. Structure, 2. Strategy, 3. Systems, 4. Style of Management, 5. Skills, 6. Staff and 7. Shared Values.

In addition, they developed another model with eight features which defined successful companies and which in this combination quickly became established as "company culture": 1. Primacy of Action, 2. Proximity to clients, 3.Freedom for Entrepreneurial Action even inside the Company, 4. Productivity of Staff, 5. Visible Value System, 6. Commitment to the Traditional Business, 7. Simple and Flexible Structure and 8. A Loose-Tight Management Culture.

It sounded better in English: "Do it, try it, fix it."

The topic "excellent, successful companies" was new for McKinsey and we developed questionnaires on the basis of which we surveyed our clients according to the 7S model. In addition, we tested along the eight basics – whether companies were close to their clients, acted according to the motto: "Let the cobbler stick to his last." In total, our surveys of management produced a number of helpful starting points, even if the Stuttgarter Zeitung ridiculed Daimler, saying that the board in a fit of grass-roots democracy was trying to feel the pulse of company culture.

We also tried to get a couple of European companies to participate, but to no avail. All attempts failed and frequently we were told that most companies who had hired Tom and Bob for their studies had been American companies. In addition, in their view, we had limited knowledge about these companies' internal mechanics and had not been on the ground.

The most interested company was Siemens AG but we never got beyond a two-day workshop in Rottach-Egern on the Tegernsee. The legendary Max Guenther and his head of corporate development Hermann Grabherr wanted to know what this concept was all about. Employees of Siemens, known as Siemensianer, were not quite sure whether they were such an excellent group or not. Finally, it also appeared that the successful companies all of a sudden were not that successful. Amongst those having been graded as excellent by Tom and Bob, some companies such as Apple, Hewlett-Packard or Delta Airlines all of a sudden hit trouble.

But that didn't put us at a disadvantage. McKinsey had expanded the range of tools designed to evaluate companies and, compared with competitors in the management consulting business, had a much broader approach. It remained Tom Peters' and Bob Waterman's undisputed achievement that they had toppled the old model of the rational human being in business and showed that top performance in a company was frequently closely related to its culture. Frequently, we pointed out to a company, which we advised that it did not foster a culture corresponding to that of an "excellent company". This caused consternation and often we worked on culture building programs thereafter.

Even if Tom and Bob later left McKinsey and chose a different path, they had a lasting influence on both McKinsey and McKinsey clients.

Inspired by these two, we further developed tools and concepts for our clients. For instance, we invented benchmarking, that is we analyzed what the best of breed did better than our client: who had the best purchasing department? Who sold goods at the highest price? What were the reasons for that? To this day, Siemens maintains a benchmark calendar, which contains all-important comparative data on rivals. One result of such analyses was for example that certain components were purchased as opposed to produced, or we developed a comprehensive process to catch up with the competition in order to get to the top.

In addition, we introduced overhead value analysis to clients – overhead includes all administration and costs of functions ranging across the company. Overhead value analysis provided frequent and significant cost savings, and helped to position McKinsey in the areas of operations.

We developed concepts as early as the 1970s which enabled us to adapt entire companies in such a way that marketing became the focus of the clients' thoughts and actions. West German businesses had been spoiled with success during the reconstruction years and I frequently experienced that Production was the center of attention: they developed and manufactured a product, and sales was then supposed to see how to best sell it. But this strategy proved unworkable once international competition intensified.

The transformation of a product-oriented company into a market-oriented organization with consultants involved for 12 to 24 months turned out to be a big project each time. Programs developed to that end ran for three to five years. We employed 30 to 50 consultants, and the client's team of employees numbered even more. This type of project management was referred to by Antonella Mei-Folter, an Italian partner of the Boston Consulting Group, when she wrote to me at the occasion of my departure from McKinsey saying that I had revolutionized the consulting scene.

Be that as it may, no two cases are exactly the same, and no issue concerning a company can be solved by simply using a stencil. But when analyzing individual cases, similar questions emerge which tend to be the heart of the matter. As a result, it is useful to have a few basic principles and points of reference at one's disposal. In the course of my career, I accumulated a wealth of theories and laws, which I use in my daily work, just like a toolbox.

Adam Smith takes a prominent place, with his theory of free market economics. The free market produces the best results – whatever obstructs the free market is bad for the economy. If a single person maximizes his benefit, the benefit for the overall market is also maximized. This theorem of the Scottish economist is used as an argument in consulting practice to critically analyze established practice and never-examined creeds.

For example, I discovered that many companies employed the bad practice of offsetting transactions. For example, an IT company sells software to a carmaker and in turn buys its company cars from them. That could hardly be considered in conformity with Adam Smith's theories, as offsetting transactions rarely maximize mutual benefit. At the very least, it should be checked whether cars could be acquired more cheaply elsewhere.

Another typical case, which I remember well: we had been hired by a company which tested materials in-house and charged an internal hourly rate of 110 marks. We obtained a quote from the German Technical Inspection Agency (TÜV), which was equally up to the task. This quote amounted to 50 marks per hour. According to Adam Smith, it would have been in all participants' best interests to shut down the expensive internal department and hire the TÜV. A number of big companies realized quickly that it didn't make sense for them to carry out certain tasks themselves. Some outsourced IT services because they could be obtained more cheaply and in equal quality, others outsourced catering or transport services. In my experience, Adam Smith's teachings can also be made fruitful with respect to companies' internal relationships. Even in that area, maximization of personal and company benefit go hand in hand. A common thread existed with respect to particularly excellent and successful companies I got to know, be that Shell, Bertelsmann or Daimler: they paid their employees significantly above the pay scale and trained them better than their competitors. This resulted in employees identifying themselves more with "their company" and in their willingness to work harder.

McKinsey itself applied these principles. Employees' personal development ranked very highly. We paid significantly more than our closest competitor. Thus, we attracted the best people who, in addition, were significantly more motivated. Once an employee reached partner status, he could act almost as if he were self-employed – to both his own benefit and that of the organization.

In addition to Adam Smith's teachings, my toolbox contained the teachings of another great economist, the Englishman David Ricardo. His theory of comparative advantage, which he put to paper in 1817, reads today like an early manifesto of globalization. If a nation focuses on the products which it can produce more cheaply – in relative terms – wealth in each nation should increase. For example, Portugal should produce good wine, and England good cloth, and both nations should trade with each other. Such international division of labor today has reached dimensions which he probably couldn't imagine. Obstacles to trade have disappeared, and at the same time mobility of capital, know-how, information and goods have increased immensely.

I have seen many cases in the course of my long career as a management consultant where Ricardo should have been taken to heart early. When we went to Eastern Germany in 1989 after the wall fell, we were proudly shown a computer chip practically handcrafted by a collective of the workers and peasants state. It was only partly serviceable and more importantly had been produced at a cost many times of what it would have cost to buy it for example in Japan, a country specializing in these products.

Our experience was similar when we drafted economic studies for Argentina and Brazil. These countries frequently tried to produce their own goods, e.g. automotive parts or personal computers, with a view towards gaining economic independence. But our calculations demonstrated that their economy was effectively weakened if they produced goods which could be acquired at half the cost in the global markets.

I rated productivity comparisons quite highly and used them frequently in my work, because they allowed me to gauge future developments. The McKinsey Global Institute (MGI) is an internal economic think-tank which I helped to set up in 1990. It developed a method which made it possible to establish an international comparison of the productivity of specific industries or entire economies. MGI produced analyses with respect to the international competitiveness of the automotive and retail industries in Germany and France, on the one hand, and the US on the other. Certain European industries had to fill productivity gaps of up to 30% compared with their American competitors. Amongst the most important tools – with varying degrees of emphasis depending on the industry – figured the product mix, the faster and broader implementation of innovation with respect to products and processes, but also regulation.

The productivity gap of the economy as a whole for Germany and France with respect to the US amounted to 15% and was less than the gap in certain key industries. But after Germany and France had almost closed the gap in the mid 1990s, the study showed that the Europeans had again lost ground and that specifically Germany had lost ground to France in the nineties. Later, voluminous studies showed that in some key areas like retail and logistics, Russian industry lagged behind the Western productivity standard by a margin of 70%.

Such analyses are particularly attractive with respect to strategy consulting for international companies. Over time, differences in productivity will lead to differences in wealth for all trading partners. These analyses show where to reduce cost disadvantages and they also show migration of productive capacity. The migration of Eastern European workers to Germany and other western European countries serves as a prime example.

Cost accounting was another important tool in my toolbox, and included calculations of cost types, cost centers and cost units. We calculated gross margins by product group, product category, by factory, by local markets and by many other criteria. This methodology played an important role during my early days at McKinsey. If we could show to management that the gross margin of certain branches did not cover the headquarter's fixed costs, and if a sensitivity analysis demonstrated that an increase of 5% of material costs brought the gross margins in many product categories down to zero, then the client would pay attention.

We caused surprises for managers who hadn't heard much about gross profits when we demonstrated, in the case of retail businesses for example, that a bottle of whisky which could be turned around in three months generates much less income than a toothpaste which can be turned around in three days. One of the reasons for SAP's early success was that they developed software capable of carrying out German cost accounting, thus enabling companies to draw conclusions much faster as to their situation.

German cost accounting has been called too complex and not sufficiently meaningful in an international context. I tackled this issue early in my career, for example in a 1975 article for *Manager Magazine* ("Grandpa's cost accounting is dead"), assisted by the legendary Winfried Wilhelm the co-editor-in-chief at that time. Notwithstanding justified criticisms with respect to our system of cost accounting, for me as a young consultant it was something akin to a crutch, which helped in analyzing the cost structure of a company.

I had learned a lot about Operations Research (OR) in Berkeley. Working with my classmate Thorlef Spickschen, I had even solved the particularly thorny Plywood problem, which consisted of finding an optimal product mix in a multi-stage production process with several bottlenecks. We solved the issue by using a linear programming approach (LP). But at McKinsey, OR was still in its infancy. When we had to solve a problem involving optimal product mix for Dynamit Nobel AG's Trovidur factory, we put together the first significant LP study, led by my partner Hasso von Falkenhausen. Out of a total of 3,000 products running through calendars, molding presses and cutting machines, we chose 2,250, thereby increasing profit by 30%. At a later stage, I also tried to use this type of optimization.

I found that the highest rate of return is achieved where capacity limits are reached and consequently eased. I felt that this new form of management science opened up new doors for both companies and consultants.

Because I had done my PhD in statistics, on the theory of sampling, I was pretty much considered the chief statistician of my associate class at McKinsey. Wherever insights could be gleaned from sampling, I was up to the task: a quick analysis of customer satisfaction, of late payments or laboratory results – thanks to my statistical expertise, I always had enough diagrams handy in order to analyze and explain seemingly complex facts and relationships. Sampling was my secret weapon, which never ran dry.

To this day, I enjoy studying correlation analysis, non-parametric tests, or new statistical theorems.

Richard Foster, a former McKinsey director, published a remarkable book on the advantages of technological offensives entitled *Innovation: The Attacker's Advantage*. He describes how all technologies develop slowly, how significant innovations occur during the course of their growth, but then become outdated with a declining rate of innovation and finally are replaced by new technologies. He described this process as an S-Curve. The fine art of management is to recognize the turning points on the S-Curve and to draw the consequences at the right time.

For example, communication engineers were still backing analog technology when digitalization had already appeared on the horizon. Or certain carmakers still used traditional braking systems when the new anti-blocking system (ABS) had already been tested successfully. The list goes on and on. It is certainly not easy to try to anticipate the next technological trend, and it remains a risky proposition notwithstanding all of the facts available for analysis.

But it is also dangerous to simply project the current technological status quo into the future. Shannon Airport in the west of Ireland provides a classic case study. Formerly, aircraft crossing the Atlantic towards North America stopped in Shannon for refueling. Because of increasing trans-Atlantic travel, Shannon Airport was expanded at considerable expense, but once the giant airport was completed, engineers had developed new jet engines making a stop in Shannon redundant. I always had the case of Shannon in the back of my mind when advising management relying on continuation of the technological status quo.

CHAPTER 10

A BUSINESSMAN'S CALENDAR, OR PROPENSITY TO ESCAPISM

Simple organizational analysis figured amongst the techniques I used with clients. Using a detailed organizational chart, we broke down the organizational structure at different levels. We frequently counted seven to ten levels between the board and the operational activities such as research and development, production or sales. As a consequence, messages traveling from level to level were of course subject to modifications, which took a lot of time to correct. It is not difficult to imagine how long it took for messages from the bottom of the chain to reach the top, and vice-versa. If it snowed in Bavaria and the need for gloves was communicated to the glove-purchasing department, the snow would have pretty much melted by the time everything had been coordinated by the central purchasing department.

McKinsey's conclusion was that having more than four levels was generally a bad thing. By the way, the Catholic Church makes do with four levels. The industrialist Herbert Quandt, with whom I worked with during one of my first assignments, considered that even in the case of four levels, too much of a gap existed between the man melting lead for the battery production and management.

We frequently used the so-called portfolio model, which segmented businesses according to their respective market position and market prospects. To that end, McKinsey had developed a nine-box rating matrix. At the same time, I maintained a table, which listed, with respect to each business, the client's competitive advantage, his toughest competitor and the respective management champion. Thus, we were able to instantly recognize where the issues were. The portfolio model was particularly useful in order to analyze whether financial resources for investments, research and personnel had been meaningfully deployed. It provided a benchmark for deploying resources on a forward-looking basis, as opposed to continuing to do things the way they had always been done. In this manner, many a poor decision was avoided, particularly in the case of companies with diversified businesses.

With regards to Lead Customer Analysis, I analyzed why major customers bought the client's products, in what amounts and over which time periods. Such analysis was frequently the key in better understanding the client's business. But at times it made sense to also provide softer analysis, e.g. when dealing with HR issues: what was the relationship between acceptance and rejection of offers by first-rate candidates? How many internal promotions occurred compared with external hiring? What was the company's ranking with respect to being an attractive place to work?

In addition to benchmarking analysis, I introduced another calendar-type analysis. I got my team to analyze diaries of both senior management and board members in order to detect wasted time and tendencies of escapism. It came to light that roughly 80% of all appointments had been booked far in advance. This implied that little time was left for spontaneous client visits, reflection about competing products or ad hoc feedback for employees. Time was reserved for speeches and meetings with the press. In addition, meetings were generally set up by personal assistants. The result was that many managers were cornered by their own surroundings. For those affected, the message we conveyed could be difficult: we told them that such diaries didn't leave room for reflection about innovation, and that innovation was a company's life-blood. A company could die if no room was left for reflection. If we determined that board members spent 20% of their time to respond to incoming mail and to sign letters, remedies were available. But a number of senior managers were disinclined to give up, i.e. to delegate such activities. But in most cases, a rather high degree of willingness to change their attitude existed once I made it clear that the board's time was a scarce resource for the company.

Furthermore, I checked with rank-and-file whether management specifications were actually carried out. A striking example was provided by Mipolam, the floor covering division of Dynamit Nobel AG. Mipolam applied a concept of exclusive distribution: 42 floor covering distributors were permitted to call themselves "Authorized Mipolam Distributors", and as a general matter Mipolam products were to be sold to end customers exclusively through them. I harbored certain doubts as to whether this set-up really worked in practice, and on the Friday preceding the Monday client presentation I decided to conduct a reality check. I randomly chose 12 non-authorized floor covering distributors in Düsseldorf, called them and asked whether they could deliver 2,000 square meters of Mipolam 220 for our new office. Not a single one said: "Sorry, but we are not authorized, why not call an authorized distributor?" All 12 non-authorized distributors were able to supply Mipolam.

Our presentation was due the following Monday. I inserted a slide stating: "Mipolam's exclusive distribution doesn't appear that exclusive after all!" Management, who clearly had been clueless, were flabbergasted. The result of this reality check was that our project for Mipolam was realigned and that my office manager was duly impressed by my practical approach.

In the early eighties, my observations in the executive suites of German companies, but also in our own office, lead me to write a memorandum to our partners and consultants. I warned of a phenomenon, which since then has run rampant. I called it: "Propensity to escapism": there is so much to do that no time is left for real work.

There are the important calls, which come in dozens, although there should only be a limited circle of people to be put through or having one's mobile number. Nevertheless, important and urgent items to be discussed on the phone occur on average 20 to 30 times per day. Each call means an abrupt change of subject and mostly turning away from a task, which was in the company's best interest. A study by management guru Henry Mintzberg showed that top managers have to deal with different topics every nine minutes. Many important questions don't fit this rhythm and may easily not get their fair share of time.

Or take the example of important meetings. They occur on all levels, and meetings are held with respect to each and any topic. The agenda, the last meeting's protocol and the distribution of tasks will be discussed, and while conflicts are to be avoided, everyone feels like showing off. These meetings rarely produce tangible results. Important meetings go by the title of "Workshop", and really important meetings are called "Retreats". Those discussions don't always generate real and feasible results, but are extremely time-consuming: members of management are absent from the company for the length of the retreat.

Travel is another variation of escapism. I rarely experienced managers or board members who avoided travel, even if the destination was far away and the travel arduous. But I also frequently experienced that visits to foreign subsidiaries resembled state visits: form and atmosphere are friendly, and substance is close to zero. Local management pulls the wool over the eyes of visitors from their headquarters, and the latter leave them alone. Time and energy are scarce in any event, and who doesn't prefer a harmonious farewell.

Meetings with the press also distract management from its core functions. They have gotten out of hand over the last few years. One reason for this is that public interest in business and the economy has increased and that more media than ever exist. Failure to communicate with the press can be very dangerous in a crucial phase of a company. But leaving that aside, more and more managers like to appear in the press, radio and TV. I have experienced very often that they try to emulate politicians and rather unabashedly ask after the program: "How did I do on the talk show?" Or: "Did you read my comments in the newspaper?" Modern media communication and wasting time because of vanity remain two very different animals.

Many managers view conferences and symposiums organized by industry groups or political players as mandatory events, but they also detract from real work. Only rarely will such events result in essential insights. The number and prominence of participants are more important than the actual content.

Industry group events, supervisory board meetings, social and cultural engagements – there are numerous important activities which can also serve as a wonderful means of avoiding the tough issues of daily management activities. It goes without saying that managers need to make calls, attend meetings and travel; of course they should engage in social and cultural activities. But the dose makes the poison. A good manager needs to lead his people, master the technical basis of his product, and actively contribute to its further development.

He knows his suppliers' capacities as well as his customers' requirements, and actively analyzes the competitive situation. He constantly encourages debate with colleagues and subordinates. Whatever additional activities he undertakes must be compatible with these tasks.

Today's managers need to spend more time on strategic issues. Indeed, numerous factors contribute to accelerate the need for decisions. Setting the strategic course takes less time than in the past. But those who don't recognize when decisions have to be made will inevitably cause issues for their companies.

My observation is that several types of managers exist with respect to escapism. The prevalent type is the manager who constantly receives promotions until reaching a level of incompetence – also known as the Peter Principle, i.e. the hierarchy of the incompetent. They mask their flaws by attending important meetings, projecting an aura of activity and significance.

There is also a type of competent manager who over time has become so important that he is constantly in demand and accepts everything because he considers himself irreplaceable. This type of escapist is keen on attending all kinds of meetings as he considers them flattering. Finally, an El Dorado for escapists is provided by organizations and companies linked to politics, such as transport, energy and manufacturing. In this case, the question of whether the meeting is meaningful or whether it has anything at all to do with major topics of a company is not even asked.

There is also a third type who continues to develop with the tasks assigned, from the perspective of both technical knowledge and leadership. Frequently, this type learned his trade in smaller subsidiaries, which enabled him to subsequently manage larger divisions. This type of manager focuses up to 90% on his job and thus doesn't fall victim to trends of escapism.

Those who don't want to neglect important things, and avoid getting bogged down in trivialities, must exercise tight control over their diary. I provided a yardstick in my memorandum: management should allocate 90% of their time to the core activities of executive leadership, that is product development, quality control, sales, human resources, internal and external representation of the company. Anything outside the company's core activities should take up at a maximum half a day per week.

I thus advised clients strongly to thoroughly check their scheduling and work plan according to whether the most important tasks are appropriately considered. My advice was both aimed at my partners and colleagues, so as to sensitize them to the issue with respect to their own conduct. This was also aimed at client work, because the risk of escapism looms large over people in exposed positions. Then, they will not ask themselves whether what they focus on is an important task, but rather believe that whatever they do is important by definition.

My paper bore fruit with Hans Lutz Merkle, the former CEO of Bosch. He made my warning about the propensity for escapism an assigned topic at Bosch management seminars. However, he told me that its impact had been limited.

Herbert Hainer, CEO of Adidas AG, is a good missionary of these findings. At one time, when he observed the numerous media appearances of the CEO of a telecommunications company, he asked bluntly: "When do you actually do any work?" He is a classic example for a non-escapist, and Adidas management have the same attitude.

My toolbox grew from year to year, and using it became easier as I became more experienced. Such a toolbox is indispensable for a management consultant.

CHAPTER 11

HEADING THE GERMAN OFFICE

WITH MORE WOMEN

We were on the rise. McKinsey Germany had grown to 80 associates and 17 partners. Friedrich Schiefer and myself were considered the strongest partners. We belonged to the circle of partners whom the Office Manager John McDonald, in consultation with Ron Daniel, considered potential successors. We enjoyed a very good working relationship. The Englishman who had lead the office in Dusseldorf – and later the Munich, Hamburg and Frankfurt branch – from the start was a noble and low-key man whose quiet demeanor was well-liked by German managers. He advised Franz Heinrich Ulrich, then CEO of Deutsche Bank, and Flick manager Dr. Herbert Rohrer.

John McDonald was almost obsessed by quality. He scrutinized each slide, and let no presentation pass until it had been practiced to perfection, until the early hours of the morning should it be necessary. His high standards with respect to McKinsey's presentations and materials stood me in good stead. His quality standards left their mark on me for my entire professional career.

McDonald had always supported my career, for example by assigning me interesting projects or delegating responsibility as to McKinsey internal matters. He was certainly successful in his role, but Friedrich Schiefer and I wanted more of a say. One day, at a German partner meeting in Sylt, we suggested a new management structure for the German office. From now on, an executive committee instead of a single person would control the fate of our company – the Office Manager who headed the German branch would be a member "by birth"; in addition two members would be nominated by the New York head office and two members would be elected by the partners from the circle of directors.

Our model actually won the day, although it was a first for McKinsey. Directors Helmut Hagemann and Michael Roever were elected to the committee; Schiefer and I were nominated by New York, with the understanding that one of us would succeed the current boss John McDonald as Office Manager when he retired after 22 years of service. When the day arrived in October 1983, John McDonald joined the UK office, and Friedrich Schiefer had shortly before joined Allianz as its CFO. With no-one standing in the way, my rise continued. I was promoted to Office Manager at the age of 42 and became the Head of McKinsey Germany. I still remember one helpful piece of advice: "Treat it like a family ship." I tried to take it to heart.

We organized a big farewell celebration for John McDonald and sang "God save the Queen" for him. The man who had established McKinsey's profile in Germany moved back to London. He intended to establish himself as an active Senior Director in the London office, but never really gained a foothold again in his native country. He left fairly soon thereafter. He may have raved too often about Germany's beauty for his English colleagues' liking.

My inauguration took place in November 1983 in Munich. Henry Kissinger was the guest of honor. The great old man of American foreign policy explained the world from a business perspective to 20 top German managers invited by McKinsey: South Africa wasn't recommended because it would never overcome apartheid; Russia – a hopeless case; China – the great market of the future. I enjoyed sitting next to the prophet while the top managers wrote down each word coming out of his mouth.

For the moment, however, the great time in Munich was over, as I had to also set up office in Dusseldorf. I inherited my predecessor's personal assistant Gisela Ludorf, and all kinds of documents typically found in desks and drawers of an office manager. I was particularly interested in my colleagues' personnel files, including CV, starting salary and reviews. I realized however that these files didn't exist. The only document I found was my psychological evaluation, prepared in London at the time.

I quickly established a working group headed by a partner in order to sort out the personnel situation. The model soon proved its worth, such that further committees were set up to deal with internal matters such as training, but also organization of office parties. The committees were a pillar of support for me as a young office manager, and the other pillar was Ina Weber. She was a colleague in her mid-50s who had been at McKinsey for such a long time that she knew all the ins and outs of the company. When I brainstormed the idea of a Christmas Party on a large scale, she told me: "Don't even touch it, someone already tried this two years ago…" She provided advice when colleagues entered my office, for example to ask for a loan to fund the purchase of a car. She warned: "This guy is just exploiting the fact that you are new in this job." When I had to make a speech at one of the numerous internal events, she gave me a short briefing: "Today, your turn is after the soup. You have exactly five minutes, and don't make the same mistake as last time when you mentioned three colleagues by name, but not the others!"

Ina Weber was particularly useful during my first years at the helm of the office. She helped me to avoid rubbing people up the wrong way for no good reason, not to behave like the proverbial bull in the china shop, and prevented me from making avoidable mistakes. Of course, I did make mistakes. Today, I count amongst these my attempt to reform the support staff compensation system. McKinsey was doing very well, and I felt that members of support staff should also participate in our success, since they had also made a meaningful contribution. I made funds available, and we agreed that each department should rank its members' work as above average, average or below average. According to this ranking, bonuses of 1,500, 1,000 and 500 marks would be distributed.

It was an attempt at creating fair results on a case-by-case basis, and it lamentably failed. We had barely distributed the bonuses when chaos broke out. Those ranking in the lowest category couldn't understand why they had been ranked so low, those in the middle category couldn't understand why others had been ranked higher, and those ranked top ducked for cover for fear of resentment. In any event, no one was happy about receiving the bonus, but rather people were frustrated because they believed they had been wrongly ranked relative to colleagues. And so we completely missed our target. The following year, I agreed with department heads to make a uniform bonus payment of 1,000 marks for support staff, and that principle remained in place during my time as Office Manager. While the amount increased over the years, it increased uniformly for all support staff.

The focal points of my position were of course somewhat different, and allocation of resources played a prominent role. Qualified consultants make up a consulting business' capital, and an Office Manager's job is to find the optimal allocation: how should they be allocated across projects? And what to do if the volume of mandates and resources were not balancing each other, which was a common occurrence. In that case, I might have to withdraw an associate from an existing project, and while he might be indispensable for a study, he was needed even more elsewhere. Or sometimes I had to replace an experienced top performer with a rookie.

My main task as Office Manager was the constant balancing of projects with resources, and it inevitably lead to conflicts. In addition, I had HR responsibilities such as employees' performance reviews and the consequences thereof: I organized promotions, but I also had to deal with employees who had not met our requirements and received poor reviews. My task was to advise them to leave McKinsey, but also to find a modus operandi for the time after McKinsey. With the benefit of hindsight, I consider it a success that we never ended up in Employment Tribunal, a popular destination for German employees.

My third domain as Office Manager was our representation and contribution to the McKinsey organization. I got heavily involved in New York, and joined international working groups, task forces and committees. I even managed to get elected to McKinsey's highest committee, the Shareholder Council (which at that time consisted of 11 members), in the record time of ten years, and got re-elected for twenty-three years. I believe that I always had an eye on the overall firm. In that sense, I was more of an international resource for McKinsey than a country representative.

I had a lot of work as Head of Germany, but I didn't hand over any of my own clients, but continued to work with them and even managed to expand the mandates. I had experienced a few times that Office Managers disappeared from the scene once they stopped working with clients. But consulting was my passion, specifically with respect to clients such as Siemens and Daimler.

Both groups were my clients and for that reason I was a heavy user of McKinsey's resources. Because I was also in charge of allocating resources, a number of conflicts sprang up in the Executive Committee with which I had to coordinate most things. My colleague Friedrich Schiefer and I had originally helped to create this management model, but I found it increasingly annoying. When I was accused of making use of the scarce resources first, I went to see McKinsey's global head, Managing Director Ron Daniel, in New York, after ten months and presented him with the following choice: "I will either become a real boss or you'll have to get someone else!" Daniel abolished the committee, established me as Office Manager with old powers, but allowed me to keep the title of Chairman.

Right after starting in my new position, I issued the challenge that the German office was to rise to the absolute top within the McKinsey organization. I wanted us to not only become the biggest office with the best partners serving the most important clients, but also with the highest intellectual standards. My most important tool to promote the German office was our staff. We were the first to train apprentices and recruit scientists, and we also boosted the recruitment of women. In addition, we provided internships so as to get more young people interested in McKinsey. At the same time, I endeavored to create a new climate of more openness and better communication. The first measure I introduced was an open-door policy. Whenever possible, I tried to be accessible for my colleagues on an ad hoc basis. I also participated in as many internal events as possible, for example in associate or project managers' meetings, or when it came to welcoming new hires. Theo Weimer, the current CEO of HypoVereinsbank – UniCredit – and formerly one of my associates, once told me how much he was impressed by our welcome and that he tried to emulate this in his current position. Similarly, Barbara Kux, later Head of Central Purchasing at Siemens, one of the few female board members of a Dax company, traces her personnel management style back to me.

Gradually, I began to realize that specifically younger colleagues tried to copy my style such that the intended hierarchy-free communication became more and more a reality.

I complimented each associate on promotions with a hand-written letter. With the help of our assignment coordinator Jutta Weider-Pipping, I collected information as to individuals' contributions to studies. I also tried to memorize people's family situations and certain other personal matters. I used these items in my congratulatory letters, which typically had to be written every three months and frequently took half a day to complete.

I also involved our support staff. Each quarter, I met with the department heads in order to take stock of what had happened in important support functions, but also to make sure that they actually felt part of the family.

After three years, I set up an Operating Committee to both relieve me of certain tasks and to get others involved as well. It was made up of my colleagues Wilhelm Rall, Axel Born, Klaus Droste, Michael Jung, Thomas von Mitschke, Guünter Rommel and later Andreas Biagosch and Jürgen Kluge. We discussed the major office issues on a monthly basis: allocation of resources, recruitment experience and preparation of various events. We would not have been able to manage our office successfully without this committee and the engagement of these colleagues.

The number of clients increased, but also the dimensions of our projects. We were tasked to reorganize entire companies and had to set up comprehensive transformation processes, uncharted territory even for McKinsey. In these cases, where formerly three consultants had spent six months with the client, now thirty consultants spent three years on the project. The only way to handle such significant projects was to increase staff. For that reason, we started earlier than usual to deal with partner candidates. We put them under the microscope eighteen months prior to the date of the partnership vote, and agreed a personal development program with each of them. All things considered, this strategy produced the best partners for the German office and contributed to its strength.

After four years, we caught up with McKinsey's biggest office, New York, and after eight years we were bigger by 25%. Germany became McKinsey's flagship office. At my departure from the firm, we had extended our lead to 50%. We were the benchmark for the entire organization. Our success was based on a team effort, and I considered it a privilege to be the leader of this outstanding team.

My job also presented its fair share of challenges. Traditionally, young partners were entitled to question McKinsey's current strategy at the occasion of our annual partners' meetings. Frequently, discussions about the right strategy lasted until the small hours of the morning. This tradition almost backfired when we held our 1995 partners' meeting in Marrakech. I had just returned from New York where I successfully represented our office, as we had managed to clear the hurdle for seven new directors and five new principals. I was looking forward to a quiet meeting in the old Moroccan City of Kings, and had invited Fred Schmid, a Swiss psychologist, to observe and analyze our conflict management.

A rather aggressive group led by Klaus Droste suggested a number of controversial items, amongst other things that partners reaching the age of 55 should pass on their client relationships to younger partners, and the introduction of paid sabbaticals lasting for several months. We had distributed small "consensors", that is little hand-held computers in order for each of the 40 partners to express their votes on each item. The partners voted using their "consensors" and expressed support for each item, with a majority significantly in excess of 60%.

Young partners expressed satisfaction, older partners shock – and I was dismayed since I didn't think any of their suggestions could be implemented. In the evening, I sat down with Fred Schmid and my colleagues Wilhelm Rall and Axel Born, and we debated how to best deal with these issues. Fred Schmid sensed the harbingers of a revolution, Rall thought we had to take it very seriously and Born grumbled that it didn't make sense that each newly minted partner was entitled to express his views.

Undecided, I went back to my hotel room. I sat down and worked until dawn on a ten-point plan which I hoped would accommodate young partners and also avoid fatal resolutions. At 7 am, Ina Weber and I went to the conference room and collected the "consensors".

We packed them up and stowed them away. When the partners arrived, I explained why no "consensors" were available on that day, why I had changed the program and that I was going to make a statement right away.

I presented my ten points with a lot of emphasis. They were geared towards pragmatic changes, which we could actually implement but which didn't shake the foundations of the organization. With the exception of two, I still remember these points well: 1. Client service teams would be expanded by two younger partners, who received a significant amount of responsibility. 2. In addition to client work, each partner should get involved in a practice group. 3. We were to speed up the introduction of an early retirement system, under which partners did not have to work until the age of 60, but could take early retirement at 55. 4. Each partner should take on one pro bono client. 5. We were going to make targeted investments in our regular clients. 6. We would introduce parental leave and other types of sabbaticals. 7. We would specifically promote the development of young colleagues. 8. We would "export" people to other McKinsey offices.

The last point resulted in more than 15% of our partners working abroad after one year. Unfortunately, this was not fully reciprocated by our foreign offices as we only welcomed a small number of foreign colleagues in Germany. In addition, 12 consultants took paternity leave after this "revolution". After Morocco, the Client Service Teams generally felt energized, and some really took off. The Practice Groups also produced more output.

I was relieved to see that my attempt at avoiding this conflict was successful. Martin Blessing, the current CEO of Commerzbank, called the insurgence in Marrakech a "revolution of the dwarfs". I learned a lot from it.

We were going in the right direction after all. I felt encouraged to continue to lead McKinsey with heart and mind, to which another event also contributed.

I felt very sad at our autumn conference in Istanbul in 1996. Our partner Martin Niederkofler had fallen critically ill and sent a letter, which was read to the audience. He described how much he missed us and how we gave him strength to conquer his illness and that he would be attending next year's conference in April.

On Easter Monday 1997, his brother Paul called to say that Martin was now very ill and that he had asked for me to visit one last time. Thomas von Mitschke and I drove to Austria where he had been admitted to the Regional Hospital in Hochzirl. We sat on the edge of his bed and discussed the useless Austrian football players, and Gerhard Berger's Formula 1 successes. He died the next day, and the next week we accompanied him to the cemetery in Wörgl where he found his final resting place. When I spoke at his final farewell in the Wörgl church the words escaped me. I have rarely been as affected by someone's death as in his case. I later visited his mother who told me how much her son had appreciated our community.

I liked to hear that, as it confirmed that my approach wasn't all that bad. If I was later called a people person and some even spoke of me as some kind of Pied Piper, there was something to it. Part of it is the conviction that humans are the focal point, combined with a couple of basic technical rules. Former Mannesmann CEO Egon Overbeck, who had been a member of the general staff during his time in the German army, once told me that he had three guiding principles of leadership. First, only criticize in private. Second, praise so that everyone can hear it. Third, if someone complains about someone else, it says more about the former than the latter. I adopted these principles and added a fourth: "Let others shine!" I put others on the pedestal as much as possible, even if I had contributed to the success. It was gratifying to see how people grew if their performance was acknowledged and praised.

I experienced this as well when I became a major sponsor of female associates. Be that Rotraud Nusser for the co-op studies, Barbara Kux for the Siemens study or Clara Streit with respect to the Dresdner Bank projects – I learned to appreciate their analytical brilliance, their extraordinary team spirit and their high degree of acceptance by clients.

When I took over as Office Manager, we had only five female associates, and it appeared difficult to increase that number. Once I realized that the situation was different in McKinsey's US, UK and Scandinavian offices and that about 25-30% of their consultants were female, I set the goal of reaching a similar level.

We targeted female hires, tried to project a less male aura, made sure that our few female colleagues made more public appearances and were interviewed by the press. We also started full-page ad campaigns in business journals, showing our consultant Ulrike Michel and two of her female colleagues. We tried to reach young women through this publicity campaign, asking them to drop their prejudices against McKinsey and to give us a fair hearing. We also talked about the exciting projects the three consultants were involved in.

However, progress was slow. Ours was a downright macho image, as confirmed by a study. Boston Consulting Group had a reputation as a more lifestyle-oriented consulting firm, which helped in recruiting more female associates. Which, at that time, was hard to compete with.

The other reason was that our best women didn't project a lot of credibility as female role models in interviews. They worked hard together with male consultants in their respective teams and, not to put too fine a point on it, some of them exhibited rather masculine traits. If they didn't like something, they thumped the table, and the language they used sometimes even made me blush. Unfortunately, this wasn't doing the trick for potential female hires with less masculine demeanor.

There was also a third reason, rooted in society. Our republic wasn't particularly adapted to the combination of work and family life. Christine Bortenlanger, then CEO of the Munich Stock Exchange and a board member of Bavarian Stock Exchange AG, once told me that she had to defend herself wherever she went. She was instantly confronted with the question of whether she didn't love her children. She was considered an uncaring mother, and I believe it will probably take decades for this type of thinking to disappear, and for a sufficient amount of day-care facilities to appear. Women hailing from former Eastern Germany, as well as French and Scandinavian women, had the least amount of issues with respect to criticism as to being uncaring mothers.

It was a shame that the proportion of women only increased rather slowly. I always enjoyed working with female consultants. I remember assigning a female consultant, Maike Braun, who was a biologist by training, to a project in Daimler's truck production plant in Worth. I was asked whether it was a good idea to assign her to a project dealing with 16 ton trucks in the production plant, as opposed to a marketing or sales project. But I was adamant and simply said: "Ms. Braun will remain a member of the team at the production plant. After six weeks, you can still tell me whether she should stay or not." After six weeks, everyone at the plant loved Maike Braun.

We experienced similar reactions in the case of construction companies, such as Bilfinger and Berger. In the end, female consultants never caused issues, specifically if they were positioned so as to convey to the client that they wanted to work with them in order to solve their issues. For me, one of the most important items was to walk and talk. Working with Siemens or at the Daimler truck production plant, team members, male or female, had to identify both with the client, as a general matter, as well as with the specific products. I still find myself talking about clients using "we": "We Siemens guys", or "We Daimler guys".

In my experience, compared to their male team colleagues, women were much better at understanding the clients' emotional state. In the early days, we criticized our clients in one-on-one interviews, by hook or by crook: "You have no clue about the market. Your competitors are much better. Your staff are sleepy heads! You don't make any money! Your situation is very bad and will only get worse if you continue that way." If we had a woman on the team listening to our never-ending criticism, she would frequently tell us afterwards: "Do you actually have any idea of the effect on the client? If you continue like that you might lose the client. There's only so much negative feedback they can take." And of course the female consultants were right in that respect.

I will never forget our first presentation to Werner Bahlsen, an entrepreneur in Hanover. After concluding our analysis, we said: "Your purchases are too expensive, you produce too many rejects, other biscuits taste better, and your advertising is no good ....". After the presentation, Werner Bahlsen told one of my colleagues that he had vomited, as we had trashed his life's work in one and a half hours. That was an important lesson. I believe things would have turned out differently with a woman on the team.

After that event, I paid close attention to giving the client's staff an active part in the presentation. I gave much more thought to the wording of certain things. At Siemens, no presentation took place with less than 20 managers present. And since there's not always much love lost between managers, we had to take a great deal of care, for example, not to criticize the Head of Production in front of the Head of Sales, or else he would not have been respected by anyone else (specifically if he wasn't that well liked to start with). Extra care had to be taken with respect to the relationship between headquarters and operating entities. To that end, consultants also received psychological training.

Back to women: as stated before, a proportion of 30% was out of the question. Within 14 years, we only managed an increase to 11 percent. Today, the proportion of female consultants in McKinsey's German offices amounts to a respectable 20%.

CHAPTER 12

MISSION IMPOSSIBLE

EARLY DAYS AT SIEMENS

Siemens was a self-referential company. A third of the best electrical engineers of each class in Germany started their career there. If someone had found a job with Siemens, he never left, even if competitors offered more money. But this group was managed in a democratic way – the plant manager in the Regensburg equipment plant could award million-mark contracts without having to seek board approval. Ulrich Glasemann, commercial director of Siemens' installation equipment division, described its typical functional self-image cynically as follows: "We develop and produce first-rate products, and our sales function damn well ought to distribute it."

They didn't really notice that competitors offered more shapely products, and they also failed to realize that installation equipment was increasingly sold through hardware stores and other DIY channels. That was how I got my first project at Siemens: I was tasked to analyze the installation equipment division, in the Regensburg plant, as they were on reduced working hours. It was 1974, the year of the football World Cup.

We made a huge effort for the "Siemens 01" study, as we knew that this was a test. The company had a second-supplier policy, and they had engaged the Boston Consulting Groupin parallel. Their representatives were sent to Erlangen. While BCG dealt with medical technology, we had to look at products such as switches, electrical outlets and automats. In other words, these were not exactly the most exciting products. But that couldn't matter for carrying out our task.

We had six weeks to come to an evaluation of this line of business and of its future prospects. I considered this short timeframe a "mission impossible" and as an afterthought told the Division Head, Jürgen Knorr: "We didn't even get a chance to speak to you in person, and I don't really think I want to work with Siemens again." We had dealt with managers two or three levels below the board, who had significant authority at Siemens, but didn't really know what to do with us and also had little time for us. In addition, controlling information and specifically market information was in short supply. Nevertheless, we tried to do as good a job as possible to convince these managers, so that they could tell their colleagues and superiors that McKinsey had done a great job and should be hired again.

"Siemens 01" became a great success, difficulties notwithstanding. We succeeded in explaining to management that switches and electrical outlets could be purchased in department or mail-order stores, or in hardware stores, but Siemens wasn't present. Their first reaction was that this couldn't be true and that they didn't believe that installation equipment could be sold by hardware stores. But the DIY business had passed Siemens by, and they had never taken a closer look at their competitors' products.

Siemens' view at that time was as follows: "We manage research and development, and we produce in our German plants, according to Siemens standards. Subsequently, products are passed out, either to our German branches or to foreign Siemens subsidiaries." Unfortunately, they had overlooked the independent wholesalers whom they didn't supply. Siemens staff had to be well and truly woken up and they had to understand that they couldn't continue to be self-referential.

After my giving Jürgen Knorr a mouthful, Siemens' perception of McKinsey changed. We won a follow-up assignment right away. From then on, we received project after project. None of our team members (sometimes three, sometimes four) were overly familiar with their business, but everyone contributed knowledge and skills. We took an interdisciplinary approach, and our mantra was to learn together and to learn faster than the others.

I considered it a privilege, both for myself and for McKinsey, to work with Siemens. In those days, Siemens was Germany's most international company, since it made first-rate products and was geared to customer value, although at times it was in danger of being overly technocratic. The company was steeped in engineering, thus engineers had the final say and business people took a back seat. Siemens claimed technological market leadership in over a hundred areas, which probably wasn't exaggerated.

Siemens' success was based on its highly qualified staff and excellent working conditions. Employees received reasonable salaries and had a prospect of life-long employment. The company reflected the tradition of its founder Werner von Siemens: "The money we make would burn in my hands like red-hot iron if I didn't give my loyal employees their due."

Jurgen Knorr, head of the installation equipment division, and Karl-Heinz Preising, CFO of the division, showed me the ropes and taught me the company's language and culture so as to make sure that I navigated around the institution better and better. Our projects were dealt with at increasingly higher levels, until I started to operate at eye-level with the management board. McKinsey had become a constant companion of a leading German industrial group which until recently had considered external consultants a waste of money. This breakthrough had ripple-on effects far beyond Siemens: as far as Germany's industrial elite was concerned, we had arrived.

In the end, our consulting engagement at Siemens was about showing the firm that market conditions and competition were subject to constant and increasingly rapid change, and that the original Siemens concept – see Ulrich Glasemann – was proving less and less workable. At a number of occasions, I traveled to the US with Siemens board members and division heads, for on-the-ground observation of product innovation. We wanted to see with our own eyes how GE, one of the world's biggest conglomerates headquartered in Fairfax, Connecticut, sold goods not only via its own distribution channels (GECSO), but also through independent wholesalers. In addition to comparing market activities, the goal was to evaluate whether it made sense for Siemens to look at a US acquisition.

Traveling with clients, which I had done since becoming a project manager for Varta, and later with the co-op board and then Reinhard Mohn, was always particularly fruitful and became one of my specialties. By travelling together, the distinction between client and consultant became meaningless as we both simply turned into students. Also, I was able to introduce my McKinsey colleagues in other offices to my clients and thus implement the "One Firm" concept.

Our Siemens engagement nevertheless didn't go off without a hitch. When we had to make an important presentation, I discovered that we hadn't been given all relevant data required to produce a good study. Once again, I complained to the division head, Jürgen Knorr, this time even more fiercely: "We don't sell shoelaces! We are not auditors ticking boxes! We don't simply move around boxes in an organizational chart! We are different, we help define strategy. But if we're not important, if Siemens is not interested in listening to us, then why go through all this trouble?"

It was risky confronting a client in that manner. Siemens was one of our main clients even back then, and in this moment the entire client relationship seemed at stake. But Jurgen Knorr kept his calm and said: "I am sorry if we didn't do things the way they should have been done. I admire your courage to bring this to my attention in such a clear manner." No break-off ensued, we received further assignments and Jurgen Knorr and I became close friends.

One day in 1978, Siemens board member Dieter von Sanden called me and asked for help. I had met von Sanden in 1977 when he was responsible for Siemens' telecommunications division. Having evolved from the old Siemens & Haske Company this was one of the biggest of the three divisions, apart from the components and tele-type divisions. He had lost a leg owing to a skiing accident and looked like Kurt Schumacher, former head of the Social Democratic Party. I perceived him as a man combining three rare features: he was a visionary technician, at the same time very pragmatic and also a top manager equipped with an unusual sense of humor.

When the IT specialists at ITT Corporation, a large competitor, complained about high R&D expenditures for a new automatic telephone exchange system 12 for the German Postal Service, he showed them his calculations: of all R&D expenditures, 30% were attributable to the German Postal Service, 30% to the French, 40% to the British and 20% to the Belgian Postal Service. Dieter von Sanden asked: "Is it possible that this amounts to more than 100%?" Roaring laughter ensued. Siemens, ITT and Philips managed to get their R&D expenditures fully paid by the Postal Services.

"UB N" as the telecommunications division was called back then in Siemens shorthand, was the main revenue generator and the second most important of a total of six divisions, right after the energy technology division ("UB E"). Dieter von Sanden was considered a powerhouse in the board members' internal competition and a potential successor to the then CEO Bernhard Plettner.

During the late seventies, McKinsey conducted a business segment analysis for measuring the device segment in "UB N". Von Sanden took to our analytical approach, and he and I developed a relationship of mutual trust.

During our 1978 conversation, he told me that he and Plettner had been called in by the Postal Service, which was requiring an electronic telephone exchange system for the German telephone network, as the current analog system was outdated. There was a significant risk that Siemens might not be invited to tender for the next telephone exchange system. CEO Plettner was upset as he had been lead to believe that everything was going fine. He threatened von Sanden with the loss of his job and asked for detailed monthly reports on this matter.

Dieter von Sanden hired McKinsey in order to pull the chestnuts out of the fire for Siemens. While it was true that Siemens was a major player in the telecommunications market, they had missed the change from analog to digital technology. The German Postal Service threatened to buy from foreign suppliers if Siemens were unable to provide digital telephone systems. Siemens had just about two years to get into digital technology and to develop the electronic telephone exchange system EWSD, which was to be installed in South Africa and to serve as a reference for the German Postal Service. McKinsey was chosen to manage this crucial project.

It appeared impossible, but I accepted the challenge. I assembled the best people I could get in Germany, the UK and the US and formed an excellent team, which at times had 15 members. They started project work simultaneously in many areas, just like a Siemens division. They managed processes, made sure that the right decisions were made at the right times and that technological development occurred with costs remaining manageable.

Von Sanden received weekly reports and provided the team with crucial feedback: "Check how many encoding mistakes we make when developing the new software! Check how many program modifications will occur and their repercussions on complexity!" It was an enormous effort, but this exchange system was introduced in South Africa in 1980 and then sold in over 40 countries.

Von Sanden reestablished his reputation as the great developer, and McKinsey's reputation as consultants was strong as never before, six years after our very first project for Siemens. We had demonstrated that we could manage a dicey situation, and that we were capable of not only producing studies, but also directly working with the Siemens organization in a very difficult process, thereby creating real value.

My personal relationship with Dieter von Sanden also grew during this time. When he became president of the Munich Rotary Club, I became his Secretary. We provided input when he had to give important speeches on economics. And when I suffered a complex leg fracture, he was one of the first to visit. We met on a weekly basis, and there was rarely a weekend when we didn't discuss the entire world.

His technological vision enabled him to predict the coalescence of data and voice networks. Unfortunately, he was unable to impose his views that Siemens should develop appropriate components and to rather discontinue telex technology, then a big revenue generator. He didn't find much acceptance for his views, but a few years later both divisions were combined into the communications technology division, which showed that he had been right.

Dieter von Sanden had retired from UB K (the communications division) for barely a year when he suffered a fatal heart attack while delivering a speech in Bonn. I lost a great mentor way too early. When advising Siemens and other high-tech companies, I frequently asked myself: "What would my mentor Dieter von Sanden say to that?"

After the South Africa project, Siemens board members took to recommending that their children start their careers with McKinsey. All of them had to pass the rigid recruitment process. We had become a premier address, and to me it was the ultimate accolade.

All the more regrettable was the fact that Siemens had entered the digital era with our help at the last minute, but failed to conduct a follow-up. Then, all participants had sworn to high heaven that the company would never again miss any technological development in the telecommunications area, but unfortunately that didn't turn out to be the case. With respect to telecommunications, Siemens is today dependent on its partner Nokia.

During my time at McKinsey, I worked on Siemens' projects for more than 27 years. But the worst difficulties we got ourselves into were none of my doing. Siemens looked at acquiring Plessey, then the second-biggest British electronics company, and the English press turned out to be rather critical of the matter. A reporter of the London *Financial Times* called McKinsey's office in London and asked director Bill Pade what we thought of Siemens swallowing up Plessey. While Plessey was not a client of ours, he was quoted as saying: "Plessey does not need Siemens", which was reported the next day on the front page of the newspaper.

Siemens headquarters in Munich were not amused. I was summoned to a meeting with Siemens CEO Karlheinz Kaske, and when I entered his office I saw the *Financial Times* on his otherwise empty desk. Kaske said: "Mr. Henzler, one point on the agenda for tomorrow's board meeting is to terminate all of McKinsey's project engagements. I think that will be the end of our cooperation."

At that time, almost one-sixth of our associates worked for Siemens. The company was our most important client, and Siemens was extremely well connected in the German marketplace. If we were fired, everyone would know about it right away. Other companies had followed Siemens' lead and had become our clients. The pattern, it seemed, could work in reverse: if Siemens wanted nothing to do with us, others might follow suit.

I had not been the Office Manager for that long, but was already confronted with a catastrophe with respect to my main client. What was I to do? I felt helpless and simply told Kaske: "This is a quote from a clueless colleague which I strongly regret. I apologize profusely, but I can't make it undone." Kaske replied coolly: "It has been put on the agenda, and there's not much I can do for you."

After the meeting, I called Hermann Franz and asked for advice. He was my main contact on the Siemens board, and we were on excellent terms. Franz told me: "You didn't serve in the military, that's why you don't know how this works. There's only one thing you can do in such a type of situation: hide in the trenches until the storm blows over." I asked: "And what about the current studies?" "Just finish them, and the world looks different in four or five months."

We discussed internally whether to send an apology letter to Siemens or to release a statement in the press – or what else we could do in order to avert the impending doom. In the end, we decided to follow Hermann Franz's advice: duck our heads and see what happens. There wasn't much imagination needed to see what could happen if the media made much of this issue or if an internal competitor used it against me. Or, if all of a sudden one sixth of McKinsey's projects fell away: my career would have been finished.

But none of that happened. I was lucky and Hermann Franz was right: the issue went away and we continued working with Siemens as per usual.

I loved working with Siemens. Without fail, we worked on exciting projects, we loved our clients and we were recognized as consultants. I was invited to many special gatherings and birthday parties? of Siemens management, and I knew all the board members and many members of level two and level three management personally. Since I had done projects in all areas of the company, Hermann Franz once greeted me at a private reception in Erlangen with the following words: "Mr. Henzler is the best-informed person at Siemens AG."

Allow me to mention the corruption affair, which resulted in extensive US Department of Justice and SEC investigations, targeting 40 former Siemens managers. One heard again and again that bribery was common practice when it came to infrastructure installations and services, and one of Siemens main business areas was the production of infrastructure equipment for telephone systems, hospitals, transport and energy companies. This appeared to specifically be the case when "dust-and-desert" countries were customers, and the number of competing companies was small. This tendency increased significantly after the first and second oil crises, in 1973 and 1979, since the Middle Eastern states entered the arena as purchasers of goods and services. We heard again and again that significant "useful charges" were required in order to secure a mandate. Nevertheless, I still think that this wasn't a genuine German specialty. The Americans, Italians and the French had all developed their own skills in this area. I don't believe there is a single defense contractor not subject to a case of corruption over time. A discussion with Martin Walser in *Manager Magazin* focused on the Siemens corruption affair. I expressed the view that Heinrich von Pierer knew nothing about it and relied on the statements of the Audit Committee.

But in the end corruption is corruption. The common view was that either top management knew of the affair, in which case they were fired for all the right reasons. Or they didn't know about it, in which case they were not qualified to run a giant group such as Siemens. And the stereotypical question of the Audit Committee as to whether signs of irregular or unlawful actions had been detected was answered with No. Another fundamental question is how a giant company with more than 400,000 employees can be managed and controlled at all.

I would like to say a few words with respect to Heinrich von Pierer, the CEO: he found it very challenging to establish himself at Siemens during his early years, that is around 1991 and 1992. Internal critics didn't mince their words. Once, when visiting the Rhine and Ruhr region, I heard that a steel executive had been asked whether he would consider taking the top job at Siemens. I could no longer hold my horses and immediately flew back to Munich. I managed to put myself in his diary on the very same day. He had to attend a board meeting, but I nevertheless asked for ten minutes of his time. I told him that Siemens was so dissatisfied with his performance that they were looking for an external successor. That hit home. Heinrich von Pierer tells the story himself.

He developed a ten-point action program and recovered the initiative. Today, he half-jokingly says that he owed his job to me. Later, he grew with the task – he was called "Mr. Siemens" – and was even perceived as a presidential candidate. He was the "foreign secretary for German business" for more than two decades and many were happy to walk in his shadow. Looking back, the fact that his name in retrospect is mainly associated with the corruption affair shows once more how the media shape public perception.

As a management consultant, I loved to solve issues, but was also ready to delve into the heart of the client's business. We certainly needed to know the products we dealt with, understand the competitive situation, and the customers and suppliers. And we needed to have in-depth knowledge of technological and industrial developments, which were prone to rapid change.

In today's world, sleeping through technological development can be the end for a company. Ignoring certain types of mobile phones caused losses worth millions for Siemens. Customers don't buy mobile phones any more just because of the Siemens or Nokia brand. Klaus Kleinfeld, who later became CEO of Siemens, had no choice but to exit this line of business. Companies are ephemeral, and the faster the pace of technological change, the faster a company must react to it. Once, my fear was that Daimler might suffer a similar fate, in the sense of simply continuing to do the type of business they understood, which had generated their revenues to date. This kind of thinking can quickly lead to missing developments. History is rife with many great companies which went downhill: Karstadt, Neckermann, Schiesser, Borgward or Quelle.

We started working with Karstadt (a German chain of department stores) during the early eighties. It was an arduous course, as department store executives had been like pampered children. They were very well paid, purchased goods cheaply all over the world and offered thousands of goods under one roof to German customers in the heart of cities – this business model appeared hard to beat. Walter Deuss, one of the industry's institutions and probably for the longest time the only university graduate holding a PhD amongst department store executives, warned me that a consulting project in his company could only succeed if he himself set a good example. Therefore, we devised a narrow project for his own area. This type of "Self-Accusation" worked – once Deuss agreed to a critical analysis of his own area, other functional areas such as purchasing or sales had no reason not to put themselves to the test. The other board members followed suit.

Subsequently, we played a key role in developing a refined strategy for Karstadt's various types of department stores. This covered outlets ranging from "Highlights" (department stores worthy of a metropolis) to "Spartans" (simple department stores) and was a successful strategy for more than a decade. Walter Deuss was promoted to CEO. While at that time he was still a vehement opponent of extended opening hours, he was open to learning something new and subsequently changed his mind. Press reports described the Karstadt-McKinsey relationship as extremely beneficial.

Karstadt's merger with Quelle, orchestrated by Deuss, was generally considered a strategic masterpiece. Unfortunately, the success story didn't last. Market conditions changed drastically in favor of suburban shopping malls, discounters and high-end specialty stores. Karstadt had to fight for survival.

I was always shocked by economic crises. I still remember the shock in 1973 when the oil price quadrupled. A McKinsey team returned from BMW saying: "They don't need us anymore, they have to cut costs." This statement didn't leave me entirely unaffected.

The second oil crisis followed in 1979, and after that shockwaves followed every three to four years. The last shockwave I experienced with McKinsey was the 2001 internet crisis. It was very dramatic, as was the global financial crisis in 2008. I lived in London at that time, and it was disheartening to see many people looking for a job.

Unfortunately, the next crisis is already approaching.

CHAPTER 13

OUR CLIENT DAIMLER

NOT JUST A FOOTNOTE IN HISTORY

One Saturday in October 1983, Gerhard Prinz died on his exercise bike, and Daimler-Benz had to look for a new CEO. Traditionally, this task fell to the chairman of the supervisory board, who hailed from Deutsche Bank. But because of the latter's stake in Daimler-Benz, which at that time was worth more than the entire Deutsche Bank itself, and after discussions with the seven board members and his fellow supervisory board members, Chairman Wilfried Guth's choice fell on Werner Breitschwerdt. An engineer by background, Breitschwerdt was a top developer of vehicle bodies and the company's Head of Development, which compared with the CEO position, was the job from hell. Thus, many questioned the decision. Breitschwerdt's fellow board members Edzard Reuter (CFO) and Werner Niefer (Head of Production) considered themselves as better candidates for the job. In other words, they felt left out. The press speculated about whether Reuter, son of the legendary social democrat politician Ernst Reuter, had the wrong party affiliation for the top job.

We were hard at work on the first project optimizing overheads in the Dusseldorf transporter plant, when Breitschwerdt called me and asked me point blank whether I could imagine becoming a Daimler board member. He felt that I was qualified both from a technical as well as an age perspective, and I would have become the youngest board member, together with Manfred Gentz.

Certainly, I felt honored but suggested waiting until our project work was completed. I had a good working relationship with Breitschwerdt, although he requested time and again that "his guys had to work more" and should not exclusively rely on McKinsey consultants.

However, my relationship with Reuter and Niefer had another dimension. Both thought that I could not only help with the daily business, but also contribute to restructuring the company when the time was ripe. For example, they were discussing a combination with the communications company SEL (Standard Elektrik Lorenz AG). But prior to discussing this or other important strategic measures such as the acquisition of AEG or of the defense contractor/aeronautics company MBB (Messerschmitt BolkowBlohm), a lot of fighting amongst competitors for the company's top job took place, and I was involved more than once.

When Daimler celebrated a big jubilee in 1986 named "100 years of automobiles", a big gala event was organized in Stuttgart. Representatives of all the main automobile companies in the world were present, and German president Richard von Weizsäcker, US ambassador Richard Burt and the Chairman of the supervisory board, Alfred Herrhausen, sat in the front row next to Breitschwerdt.

The gala was broadcast on prime time TV, and there was no lack of prominent names. Michael Pfleghar was the director, and with his wife Wencke Myhre, he took the spotlight for a song. Niki Lauda dabbled in anchoring a portion of the program, and many others followed suit.

It looked like absolutely no rehearsals had been conducted. Nothing seemed to work, everything was too long and before the eyes of the entire Republic the gala looked like a failed graduation ceremony: someone is trying to sing a song but forgot the music sheets. The teacher is supposed to praise the students but pulls them to pieces. Everything is taking too long and people just want to leave. The *Bild* newspaper wrote the next day: "What a disgrace!"

Apparently, Daimler had not taken care of the event, but rather left the organization to the show business people. I couldn't understand how a CEO could accept that. Guests had come from all over the globe, and he didn't make use of the opportunity? I called Alfred Herrhausen the next day to discuss a broader agenda. But he wasn't interested: he was furious about the jubilee celebration and asked me what I knew about it and why I hadn't done anything in the run-up to the event. I responded, clearly happy about this vote of confidence: "I am sorry, McKinsey is working on a project for Daimler in Düsseldorf, but I knew no more about the 100-year gala than you did." The jubilee fiasco spelled the beginning of the end for Breitschwerdt. However, while the supervisory board was clearly unhappy with the new CEO, they were not quite ready for a change at the top.

One evening, I received a call from Herrhausen, who had become sole CEO of Deutsche Bank and as per tradition had also assumed presidency of the Daimler supervisory board. He had heard that something was brewing at a board retreat in Rome: apparently, Niefer and Reuter had decided to leave the three-day event on the morning of the second day. Herrhausen told me in his inimitable way: "As far as I am concerned, the gentlemen's reputations will not improve if they leave prematurely because they have better things to do than to participate in a board retreat." Herrhausen couldn't keep his frustration to himself and knew that I was close to both. I sprang into action and called Edzard Reuter the next morning at seven in his hotel room. He didn't like being troubled that early, but I explained: "Mr. Reuter, there's something you need to know. Don't ask me where I got the information, but you are planning to leave today. If you leave the board retreat early, it will be tantamount to an insult. You will have to pay for it."

I am sure that Reuter, a gentleman from head to toe, well read and spoken, very conservative for a social democrat and in my view on his way to the top of Daimler, realized immediately that Herrhausen (informed by Breitschwerdt) was behind my call. Reuter asked: "What would you do?" I said: "I would stay, leaving would be detrimental to your career." He followed my advice and both he and Niefer stayed in Rome until the end of the retreat. I was relieved.

In July 1987, Reuter succeeded Breitschwerdt as Daimler's CEO. He had a vision of an integrated technology group, which would develop the car of the future, but more generally make sure that the automotive business would continue to prosper. Reuter saw two areas of pressure for the car market: first, he thought that the market for luxury cars was saturated; second, cars were increasingly demonized by environmentalists. In his previous position as CFO, he had already worked on realizing his vision of a global group, claiming market leadership in important technologies, using technological synergies, and becoming largely independent of economic cycles.

In my view, Daimler's acquisition of the Dornier aircraft business and of the remaining 50% stake in jet engine manufacturer MTU in Friedrichshafen/Munich was a good idea. I thought it made sense to carefully build the corporate base by expanding into areas at least technologically compatible with Daimler's core business. Dornier's medical devices business worked well for Daimler, as this technological area was viewed as particularly positive. After the first year post acquisition, Dornier's operating results were already equal to the purchase price.

AEG was acquired the same year. According to *Spiegel* in April 1988: "Daimler's great feast continues. Electronics company AEG will be fully integrated into the group." Initially, I thought it was a mistake, but why wouldn't it have worked? Conceptually, the combination of an aircraft and aerospace business with electronics and software made sense. General Motors (GM) had set the tone and made a lot of money with Hughes Aircraft and Hughes Electronics. Nevertheless, I knew quite a few things about the old-line company based on my work for Daimler's competitor Siemens, and saw reason to intervene with Reuter. In my view, AEG was in a catastrophic condition. Only three of its fifteen business areas could be considered top. In addition, execution of the strategy by the rank-and-file could hardly be supervised by top management, and AEG's CEO Heinz Dürr could be counted on to make sure that Daimler wouldn't ask too many unpleasant questions.

I met Edzard Reuter for a working breakfast at the restaurant "Post" in Stuttgart-Plieningen and explained why I considered the acquisition a mistake, arguments to the contrary notwithstanding. He listened attentively and said that the streamlining of AEG's portfolio of businesses was certainly required, but that some pearls within the electronics business contained significant potential for synergies with the car of the future. I could only issue a stern warning.

In my view, the new situation was barely manageable for Daimler. Even this new part of the group took a life of its own. All of a sudden, not only the promising growth potential of the civil aviation business mattered, but Daimler also became dependent upon whether some defense minister decided to build a certain type of helicopter or not, or whether governments acquired a space shuttle. These were businesses that had nothing to do with the group's core competencies.

I remained in close contact with Alfred Herrhausen during this period of integration. He was also skeptical as to Daimler's foray into the defense business, in addition to the civil aviation business. His fellow Deutsche Bank board members frequently queried him about Daimler's large presence in the aerospace sector. I advised him best as I could, and he formulated the goal of developing a European solution for the aeronautics business. He had followed this route together with Edzard Reuter during the decisive meeting at the Bavarian Chancellery in 1988, where Franz Josef Strauss, Gerhard Stoltenberg and Martin Bangemann insisted that this venture was a "license to print money", that contracts for the space shuttle "Columbia" as well as anti-tank helicopters and electronic equipment for the military were done deals. Thus, the aeronautics business was concentrated within DASA (the aerospace subsidiary of Daimler-Benz).

Herrhausen and Reuter worked together well, were respectful of each other and constantly exchanged views. Working with Reuter always presented an intellectual challenge, and I still remember fondly the host of management topics and McKinsey's potential role that we discussed. I consider it an honor that Reuter asked me to help Götz Friedrich with the Deutsche Oper, an opera company located in Berlin. After Herrhausen's assassination in November 1989, Hilmar Kopper became president of the supervisory board.

During the early nineties, Reuter's strategy was harshly criticized. He was blamed for the acquisition of AEG and Fokker, and also the development of software house Debis. The more the public took offence at Reuter's strategy, the more I became the target of criticism. Stefan Baron, then editor-in-chief of *WirtschaftsWoche*, wrote in 1992: "How is it possible that the best manager (Edzard Reuter), advised by the best consultant (Herbert Henzler) and controlled by the best supervisor (Hilmar Kopper) wiped out so much value, as expressed by market capitalization?" This sentiment was also rooted in the general economic crisis.

Reuter's analytical abilities were brilliant, and working for him was a challenge. I still hold him in high esteem. Nevertheless, it was likely that the transformation from a pure car company into an integrated technology business might have been too fast, and operational grounding may not have been sufficient. Car guys produced the best cars, and they were now supposed to stabilize AEG, a company close to bankruptcy. Too many reservations existed with respect to the new company, and it didn't appear possible to approach it free of prejudices. In addition, AEG's wily CEO Heinz Dürr complained that the car controllers from Unterturkheim prevented "his guys from doing their work" each time they arrived at his Frankfurt headquarters. Later, Daimler dissolved AEG and Edzard Reuter admitted that the integration had failed.

We frequently advised the Daimler board with respect to group strategy and structure. During Edzard Reuter's tenure, we discussed establishing a holding company in Stuttgart-Möhringen, bundling various components of the group from AEG via Debis to DASA, physically separated from the production facilities in Untertürkheim. I wrote a paper for Reuter, which I had to defend a few days later in front of Herrhausen in Frankfurt.

But we were also involved in decisions with respect to Daimler's core car business. On our advice, Strategic Business Area Planning (SGP) became a compass for long-term car and truck development, and time-consuming testing of new models was improved by establishing testing bays and computer simulations. In addition, truck product specification was reorganized. We made sure that hundreds of Daimler managers were schooled in McKinsey techniques during the course of our projects. For each McKinsey consultant, three to five Daimler managers were attached to a project, which lasted approximately six months.

During the early eighties, driven by the introduction of the Fleet Tax in the US (a specific tax on cars), it became necessary to introduce fuel-efficient models to the product range. Daimler asked for McKinsey's views with respect to the introduction of the successor model to the first C Class, the "Baby Benz", as the W 192 model was called. Pricing for this model was hotly debated within Mercedes. Should it be less than 40,000 marks? Mercedes CEO Helmut Werner asked for our views. I thought that Daimler shouldn't become the "cheap jack". The company shouldn't feel the need to sell its products by means of low prices. It was best to charge a higher price and, in case of doubt, improve quality. Daimler's motto "The best or nothing" was in line with my philosophy: "Better 10% of additional quality for a 20% higher price".

The entire McKinsey team got together to discuss this topic. We debated the appropriate price for Mercedes' C Class for a whole day. In the end, it appeared that most of my colleagues, led by Jurgen Kluge, didn't share my views. They thought that even Daimler had to learn how to cater to a mass market and to make its production more cost-efficient. I went to see Helmut Werner and conveyed the result of our discussion. Our recommendation was to price the car below the 40,000-marks threshold. He considered our input significant, and that was what happened.

Who was right in the end remains to be seen. It is exceedingly rare that a provider of high-quality products succeeds in imposing upward adjustment of lower prices. It appears however that the roaring success of the "small" Mercedes class is in part due to its low price. It is a fact that all luxury car manufacturers have difficulties making money with small or medium-sized cars. Daimler's highest earning always occurred when they produced about 500,000 cars and delivery periods were long. It is also a fact, though, that Japanese car makers, who were generally thought not to be able to produce luxury cars, have in the meantime managed to produce respectable models such as Lexus and Infiniti.

Another Daimler project consisted of establishing contact with the Japanese automotive group Mitsubishi. I had great expectations for this project. McKinsey helped in developing a concept of strategic partnership between the two companies. American media fought this alliance in a somewhat polemical manner, describing it as a new edition of the partnership between a Zero fighter and a Stuka, that is fighter aircraft produced by Mitsubishi and Junkers, with which Japan and Germany had caused a lot of suffering during World War Two.

While Edzard Reuter was bothered by such negative press, he nevertheless pressed on and the project continued. There were many indications that the project would be successful, and my Japanese colleagues agreed. Mitsubishi had no convincing luxury car, with the exception of the "Galant" which looked as if it was modeled according to the rather heavy Gelsenkirchen Baroque style. That meant that we had an ideal Japanese distribution partner for the S Class. In return, Mitsubishi Diesel generators could have been used for Mercedes transporters.

In practice, the partnership didn't work because the Japanese stonewalled. I remember one encounter at the Konstanz Insel Hotel. Both Daimler and Mitsubishi had sent 15 managers to discuss potential projects for the strategic partnership. While Daimler managers from a variety of areas made substantial proposals, their Japanese counterparts produced reports, financial statements and profit and loss statements from a variety of Japanese Mitsubishi subsidiaries. During the whole morning, we scraped by under the most difficult conditions. During the lunch break, Gerhard Liener, the Daimler board member in charge of the project, and I decided to terminate the meeting and postpone the project indefinitely. My experience was that a balanced joint venture with Japanese companies wasn't feasible at that time. Siemens had a similar experience with Fuji.

Reuter's favorite to succeed him as CEO was Jürgen Schrempp, who was certainly the strongest man on the board and who epitomized the power-conscious manager. He appeared to be the most suitable candidate to succeed Reuter. But Reuter showed last-minute misgivings. He reacted in an ambiguous way when external parties brought the successful Mercedes CEO Helmut Werner into play. Ferdinand Piech, who had just become Volkswagen CEO, even wanted to place a bet that Werner, as a successful car boss, would get the top job. Because all of a sudden, Reuter and Werner were addressing each other with the familiar "Du", and speculation in the press ensued that the Mercedes CEO could become Daimler CEO – and such speculation was not discouraged.

In the end, Jürgen Schrempp became the new Daimler CEO in May 1995. Edzard Reuter, who believed that he had been promised the Chairmanship of the supervisory board, did not get that job. It can only be speculated how business would have gone with the tandem of Schrempp and Reuter in charge. Schrempp soon developed a close relationship with the Chairman of the supervisory board, Hilmar Kopper.

I knew Schrempp well from shared mountain tours, as I had invited him to join the annual meeting of the Similauner, our club of top business people interested in mountain climbing. During the first two tours – he hadn't been promoted to CEO by then – he realized that this group presented a challenge.

I had asked him to join us, as he told me that he jogged so I thought he might be interested in mountain hiking and climbing. He was very enthusiastic and contributed actively to our discussions. At that time, he had decided to build the Smart car. Wolfgang Reitzle, then Head of Development at BMW, advised against the move: "Don't even bother. You make more money with the sun canopy of the S Class." Schrempp argued that it made sense to build small cars. In the future, urbanism would increase and the cities would be filled with cars so that only the Smart was a useful car, for the sake of finding parking space. Of course, all other members of our group gave their views. In any event, Reitzle was proven right. Once, we hotly debated board compensation, and opinions diverged strongly. I am certainly not divulging any secrets by saying that the spectrum ranged from 100 (basic value) to 500 (ideally). Schrempp was always an enrichment of our group, and I regret that he didn't find time to participate during the last years.

Because we considered ourselves friends, I was disappointed that he didn't breath a word about the greatest coup of his life once he became Daimler CEO. When the Daimler-Chrysler merger became public, he justified his silence: he had been unable to talk to anyone since he was obliged to treat the matter with the utmost confidentiality. Schrempp had sold all the companies which didn't suit Daimler's strategy – "Back to the roots" was the new strategy. Daimler was back to being a car company, albeit a global one. Secret talks about an alliance had also been held between Daimler and Ford, but they went nowhere.

Now that the "marriage in heaven" had been decided, he asked *en passant* for my views. I gave it to him straight: "First, Chrysler went bankrupt twice during the last 25 years. It is unlikely that the exclusive reason for that was the sluggish automobile business. Rather, I think there are many issues specific to Chrysler, such as research and development, production and the entire value chain. Second, Mercedes spends 5% of its revenues for development of new cars, Chrysler only 1%. What do you expect in terms of innovation?" Chrysler cars were indeed metal boxes, prettied up from time to time, and given the low R&D spending, no change was in sight.

At first, the numbers appeared to contradict my views. In the area of procurement, synergies were increasingly realized at the Chrysler head quarters so the finish of Chrysler cars improved. Two years after the merger, Chrysler reported profits of $ 5.5 billion, more than Mercedes.

I watched Jürgen Schrempp and Bob Eaton presenting their story of the "World AG" at the World Economic Forum in Davos. Some 1,200 of the most important managers in the world got up and applauded. Schrempp could feel like an incarnation of the global business leader. His example led other German companies to consider combinations with US companies. At that time, rumor had it that Siemens could combine with Motorola, or that E.ON was the ideal partner for the US energy group Enron.

As high office changes people, Schrempp was changed by Daimler's top job. The friend from older days, who showed up in Kitzbuhel with his dictating machine and constantly absorbed new ideas and inspirations, became CEO of a global company, surrounded by aides and appeared to reflect less and less. He moved in the sphere of big CEOs, discussed his organization with them, advised on the acquisition of Mannesmann by Vodafone, and very openly maintained his independent management style. Such was his surprise when the board refused to support the further development of his strategy, that he went to the supervisory board's personnel committee to discuss early termination of his employment contract.

Our personal relationship continued to be friendly. He helped me with a presentation at the McKinsey senior partner meeting in

Barcelona in 2001, and I helped him with the presentation of his first biography in Frankfurt. But he appeared more and more lost in reverie, and barely accessible to external advice.

As a result, Schrempp, who had been treated kindly by the press, was named one of the 20 worst global managers by *Business Week* and threw in the towel a year prior to his scheduled retirement. Daimler shares promptly gained a couple of percentage points. A rather nasty surprise for Mr. Shareholder Value.

Schrempp was succeeded in 1996 by Dieter Zetsche, who sold Chrysler a couple of years later. Zetsche himself had been CEO of Chrysler and knew best why the global marriage wasn't blessed. In my view, the divestment was helped by the fact that Schrempp had not become Chairman of the supervisory board. He deserves respect for his decision not to accept the Chairmanship, which he had been offered. He wanted to give Zetsche free rein and didn't want to wait for a corporate governance commission to give Zetsche the green light. He would have probably tried to prevent the divestment, to the extent possible. He was too much part of the system he had created. If I were to ask him about DaimlerChrysler today, he would probably say that the project hadn't been properly managed and that those responsible hadn't realized its great opportunities.

After the failed strategic grand projects of "integrated technology group" and "Automobile World AG", Daimler today, in my view, is the best carmaker in the world. It's mix of excellent developers, dependable production based on the German culture of master craftsmen, and confident but client-oriented salespeople is unique, both in Germany and abroad. It is and will always remain a synonym for Made in Germany. I have known Dieter Zetsche since our early Daimler projects, and visits to Auburn Hills and Brazil. He impressed me with his ability to listen carefully. He still remembers the content of our discussion during a three-hour flight from Marrakech to Stuttgart after a Daimler event in 1993, which is testament to his capacity to absorb, and his fantastic memory.

CHAPTER 14

EXPANSION TO THE LAND OF PELE AND TO GLOBAL DAVOS

I had been Head of McKinsey's German office for a year and a half when I looked for another challenge. Today, I would say that I was restless. I wanted to open an office in Brazil and asked our New York head office whether they saw any arguments against my plan. Chairman Ron Daniel's response was clear: "Herb, you are a young office manager, there's enough to do in your office. Focus on Germany!"

I would probably have reacted similarly had a young country head of 43 years told me that he wanted to go to Brazil. Daniel's announcement was a quasi-prohibition to start any activities in Brazil. But prohibition presented a challenge and stoked my ambitions. I wanted to demonstrate that there was a creative solution.

I had met Werner Lechner in Stuttgart, at Daimler. He headed Mercedes Benz do Brasil, the biggest foreign subsidiary of the group, and needed our help. But that wasn't the only reason. Ever since my youth, I viewed Brazil as the country of the great soccer player Pele. The country had fascinated me during my first visit in 1966, and I went later, in 1976, with Rosemarie while working on a Siemens study for McKinsey. We had been fascinated by people's joyfulness, and captivated by their optimism. The Austrian author Stefan Zweig, who emigrated to Latin America after the national socialists took power, wrote in *Brazil* that a trip to this country was a cure for the soul. And that was what I wanted to put into practice.

I quickly assembled a team of three motivated colleagues. They were Thilo Mannhardt who spoke Portuguese, as did Stefan Matzinger, whose wife was Spanish, and Heinz-Peter Elstrodt, who took a crash course in the local language. Roger Bell and Wolfram Nolte later bolstered the team.

Thanks to the fantastic support provided by Werner Lechner, the head of Mercedes-Benz do Brasil, we established what was practically an annex of the German McKinsey office under the roof of Mercedes-Benz do Brasil in Sao Paulo, sharing office staff. We were successful from day one, a novelty for a newly established office, but it is hard to go wrong with a client such as Mercedes. After a year, the trio moved to their own premises in the heart of Brazil's biggest city.

Nothing is more powerful than success: of course, I invited our head honchos from New York, Ron Daniels, Fred Gluck and Don Waite, to show them what a fabulous country Brazil was and what a great team I had assembled, working for McKinsey locally. I had circumvented his prohibition, but there was nothing he could say given the setup and success of the local operation.

In addition to Mercedes, we counted other subsidiaries of German companies such as Volkswagen or Siemens amongst our clients. But we also advised Brazilian companies such as the Private Bank Itau, Companhia Vale do Rio Doce (CVRD), one of the biggest mining companies in the world, publishers, insurance companies, and big construction and retail companies.

We benefited from having first mover advantage: all of the management consultancies, including McKinsey, had quit Brazil in the early eighties because of hyperinflation and the uncertain economic outlook. But we were back, and now we had an edge. After ten years, the Sao Paulo office was decoupled from the German office and elevated to the status of Brazilian office. The office nowadays boasts more than 300 consultants. I, as the founder, had the pleasure of celebrating a grand jubilee with them.

My successful adventure in Latin America – in addition to setting up offices in Stuttgart, Berlin, Cologne and Vienna – encouraged me to pursue further foreign expansion plans. I always followed the proven pattern: we took top talent from our office and sent them to countries where the local consulting market was still underdeveloped. We gave them great latitude, provided help where necessary, made sure they could work undisturbed and protected them from bureaucratic interference by New York headquarters.

I have never had a single disappointment applying this method. It worked in Istanbul, Moscow, Warsaw, Prague and later Budapest. We always started with a core team around a German partner, bolstered by partners fluent in the respective local language. At the start, we usually had a reputable client serving as a reference and contributing to our ability to recruit top local talent.

This resulted in the establishment of successful offices. Staff quickly absorbed the McKinsey culture and our offices were considered as great employers, such that they attracted the best talent. They quickly developed a great reputation in the community, certainly also aided by pro bono projects.

These have a long tradition at McKinsey. In the US, they can be traced back to Marvin Bower, who had even studied the specific requirements for management of non-profit organizations. Once the German office was firmly established, after its early stage, we took up the tradition and did a number of studies free of charge: for example, taking stock of the Bavarian Protestant Church's position, devising a plan for the Olympic Games in the divided Berlin, a merchandising concept for the FC Bayern soccer club, a study on the cost of the German reunification for the German government, support for cultural institutions and much more.

The general approach was to analyze complex situations and present the results in such a simple manner that appropriate conclusions could be drawn. Thus, we helped non-business actors to make correct decisions. But we also met decision-makers whom we ordinarily wouldn't come across, and our consultants broadened their horizons by moving into unknown territory. For example, our new Moscow office enhanced its reputation by providing valuable studies free of charge for St. Petersburg's Ermitage and Moscow's Bolshoi ballet.

The German variant of McKinsey became more and more dominant, and I suffered gladly being called "Herb the founder" at that time within McKinsey. According to *manager magazin*, the number of consultants increased six-fold and revenues rose eight-fold during my time at the helm of McKinsey Germany. In 1998, we were the uncontested flagship within the McKinsey organization; one in five consultants worked in a German office. One of the reasons for that was certainly that German exports were in demand all over the world.

In retrospect, innovation was one of my favorite topics at McKinsey. Not only had I set up the first foreign office from a German office, but I had also set up the first office outside of Düsseldorf long before that. And I was amongst the first in East Germany, and founded our

Eastern European offices. Perhaps this is due to my agility, or perhaps just a sign of the times.

My years at McKinsey were years of expansion, years of awakening and change. And our presence in Davos was part of it.

Each January, the World Economic Forum (WEF) takes place in Switzerland. Founded in 1971 by the manager and economist Klaus Schwab, it was originally conceived to train up-and-coming European managers in the recently built – and underutilized – Davos Congress Center. Three years later, Schwab transformed it into the World Economic Forum, designed to provide a platform for business leaders to discuss current global developments and network with colleagues. Heads of state and government first participated in 1982, after which the WEF gradually took on its current format. Managers, politicians, but also trade union leaders and heads of NGOs show up for a huge gathering in this small winter sports resort. For five days, it is all about see and be seen, official programs and unofficial meetings, networking and business.

But it took time for Davos to develop its attraction. During the eighties, Swiss companies at best sent an authorized representative to Graubunden in case a client might show up. Many shared the views of Fritz Gerber, then CEO of Hoffmann-La Roche, the chemical and pharmaceutical company: "People who like to go skiing to Davos should pay themselves." McKinsey had similar thoughts. We stayed away from the Davos circus, as there wasn't much we could have used for our clients. When Klaus Schwab made initial contact in the early nineties to sound us out for possibilities of cooperation, his approach became the subject of a controversial debate. Richard Burt, the former US ambassador to Germany, had become a McKinsey partner and was in favor of cooperating with the WEF. Our Strategy Committee nevertheless considered once again that we would give more than we took, and thus we declined.

Interestingly, however, our client Siemens had a strong presence in Davos. In the end, we sent a reconnaissance group to Davos, analyzing contents and participants. Subsequently, we took up negotiations with Klaus Schwab to do a "diagnosis" project and won the mandate.

The study, led by Ted Hall, produced a number of critical results: the WEF program was out of hand, and doubts existed as to composition of the panels and a thin layer of internal management. Klaus Schwab, to whom we presented the study in the presence of WEF senior leadership, was disappointed. He thought we had been overly critical with respect to the program and above all hadn't understood the spirit of Davos. Nevertheless, Schwab got Rajat Gupta, who had become McKinsey's Global Managing Partner, to join his committees, and hired McKinsey to analyze the WEF's internal organization in Geneva. Shortly thereafter, former McKinsey partner Mickey Obermayer was hired as the WEF's director.

From then on, McKinsey people were present in Davos each year, putting forward new consulting concepts, discussing new analyses of the McKinsey Global Institute and presenting selected topics with respect to, for example, the automotive, pharmaceutical or logistics industries. These meetings enjoyed a great deal of success, and today McKinsey events such as "CO_2 Cost Curve" or discussions of long-term interest rates attract scores of interested managers and journalists to the small conference rooms of the Hotel Belvedere. The McKinsey party held on the Thursday night has attained legendary standing.

I particularly appreciated political discussions in Davos. Bill Clinton was one of the first who presented his views on global politics on an annual basis. He used Davos quite successfully for fundraising, for example for the Aids Foundation. I listened to then US Vice President Dick Cheney trying to explain that Iraq possessed or was about to develop weapons of mass destruction and thus needed to be attacked by Coalition forces. Then Pakistan president Pervez Musharraf explained to a small circle of participants that they knew exactly where Bin Laden was hiding and that it wouldn't be long before he was caught.

In 2010, I witnessed a fuming Recep Tayyip Erdogan storming off the podium: the Turkish prime minister felt challenged by Israel's president Shimon Peres. Another unforgettable event remains an early morning session on the topic of "Islamic Renaissance".

Approximately 1,000 participants crowded the conference room, mostly managers and journalists hailing from Islamic countries. The presentation started with an impressive retrospective on the great times of Islam, its decisive role in translating Greek and Persian philosophers, the great Spanish mosques and other evidence from the Islamic past. Then, the question of what prevented an Islamic renaissance was asked. The plenary session was asked to choose from a number of answers, such as analphabetism, the huge consumption of natural resources, the historic burdens of colonial times, insufficient political leadership or the existence of the State of Israel. When the result was announced, 72% had voted for point number five, that is the mere existence of Israel. Something akin to euphoria was felt in the room: a common denominator had been found. I left the room together with a Greek friend with a sinking feeling. The fact that Arabic elites were obsessed with the fact that Israel's mere existence prevented them from becoming great (again), was a clear sign that no self-reflection had taken place. I said to myself: why is analphabetism still rampant in many Arab countries with significant oil money, why do women have few rights and why is there such a nightmarish track record of non-existant human rights? Representatives of Arab countries presented themselves as good global citizens in Davos, but were unable to provide a convincing answer when asked why women weren't allowed to drive in Saudi Arabia. They made some diffuse historic arguments. Other than that, Arabic rulers, and even the beautiful Queen Rania of Jordan, made merely soapbox speeches.

In 2010, a significant Chinese delegation visited Davos. When they heard that they should allow their currency to appreciate, save less and consume more, Prime Minister Li Keqiang responded that China had learned Western economic lessons well, according to which it was good to be productive, to learn and work a lot. And if foreign countries bought one's products, one became a successful exporter and richer. In addition, saving for the uncertain future was preferable to consuming here and now. China's debt ratio was at 12%, which was a good sign. And they had also learned that it wasn't a good idea to readily use currencies as an economic control mechanism, as this was a drag on trade relationships. Li Keqiang's statements provided American listeners in particular with food for thought.

I have been to Davos about 15 times. My second wife Fabienne who I had married in 1994, frequently accompanied me, called the event an annual intellectual update. She attended sessions from early in the morning until late at night and visibly enjoyed the international atmosphere.

In 1991 Rosemarie and I separated after 23 years of marriage. Rosemarie had been an enormous help in the McKinsey years till then – often supporting spouses when the McKinsey life of the men had become too stressful. Without her great support I would have never made the McKinsey career. Yet she wanted to enter a new life. She got a PhD in literature and is now practicing a psychoanalytic training called "Daseinsanalyse" in Berlin. Fabienne who later became my second wife, was an associate at McKinsey a native French that was born raised in Morocco. She joined McKinseys Munich in the mid eighties and we got married in 1994. She left McKinsey to join the European Bank of Restructuring/Development.

Davos normally starts for me on Wednesday evening with the North German Meeting hosted by Jürgen and Dagmar Grossmann, where all German participants traditionally meet. The evening usually ends with the Focus Night, where US actress Sharon Stone once was so smitten by publisher Hubert Burda that she continuously shot photos of him.

My diary for the following days frequently holds 40 or 50 appointments, as Davos provides the opportunity of meeting as many high-ranking managers as one normally would in half a year. Political encounters figure among the high points, such as meeting Gerhard Schroder, who in 1999 was not yet quite at ease in his new role as German chancellor, or Angela Merkel, with whom I had a discussion in 2005, when she was elected chancellor, or Ursula von der Leyen in 2010. She fought tooth and nail for a percentage of women in management positions, but no-one would agree with her, although numbers were on her side, as nothing had happened over the last ten years. I managed to show during our discussion that she still had a long way to go with that idea within the CDU party, which she readily admitted.

The official WEF program ends on Saturday night, and Sunday holds the unofficial high point for me: the giant slalom, organized by the "Weissfluhjoch" skiing club. This is a loose association around steel magnate Jürgen Grossmann, publisher Hubert Burda, Jurgen Zech of Cologne Re, former Hochtief CEO and BDI president Hans-Peter Keitel, former Lanxess CEO Axel Heitmann, Klaus Zumwinkel (formerly Deutsche Post), Heinrich von Pierer (formerly Siemens) and my good self. This popular sporting event provides a unique type of fun each year. For years, I had a monopoly on coming first, nowadays my former McKinsey colleague and current banking executive Alexander Dibelius celebrates victory after victory. As he calls me a mentor, I am thrilled from the bottom of my heart.

What is the WEF today? I would place it somewhere between the world's biggest cocktail party and the most significant networking event on the highest level. I still don't know when I will visit Davos for the last time.

CHAPTER 15

ONE-WINGED BIRDS
CANNOT FLY

Without any doubt, McKinsey is a company where people work hard, which means also that people work long hours. A number of different factors play a role. Clients want results fast and ideally at low cost, and young consultants are still insecure and try to do things extra well. This translates into huge time pressure.

Pressure increases even more when we don't receive the information necessary to advance a further step at a crucial moment, when a client executive doesn't find the time for an interview or when the project leader dismisses the conclusions to be used for the presentation. And when the team works into the late evenings it can be difficult for individual team members to get away, to go to the theatre or go to the gym.

At times, weekend work is required in order to make sure that the most urgent tasks get done. This is all the more true if consultants join internal taskforce groups. McKinsey set these up for industries such as the chemical or automotive industries, and with respect to certain functional areas such as marketing, technology or operations, with a view towards centralizing and developing know-how. Participants develop their reputations, but they certainly have to provide input or else they are selected out in no time. Making these contributions takes time and energy.

When I became a partner, my type of work changed. From then on, clients were not my only focus; instead I took on additional tasks within McKinsey's international organization, for example on the committees for training and strategy.

Transatlantic flights in Germany usually take off during the late morning. During the first years, I sat in Economy class and always had work of some type prepared which I could do, notwithstanding the lack of space. Once, a fellow traveller told me that I had worked for exactly six hours during the flight.

If on schedule, my flights would land in New York during the early afternoon and my typical schedule looked as follows: take a cab to McKinsey headquarters in Park Avenue, work in the office, participate in meetings, dinner with colleagues at 8 pm. My internal clock was at 2 am, which is why I frequently left after the entrée, being too tired. I slept until 4 am, and then dealt with urgent matters in Germany as of 5 am, talking to colleagues and clients. After that, I went jogging in Central Park and started the office day at 8.30 am, participating in discussions and meetings.

Typically, the return flights left New York during the evening and landed in Germany around 7 am, or earlier in case of tailwinds. I went home, showered and was at my desk in the office at 8.30 am. When the supersonic jet Concorde still flew the Paris (or London) to New York route, it happened that I flew to a meeting in Manhattan and was back the same day. I remember well my surprise hearing the Head of Purchasing of a big company saying that he received a day off after each transatlantic flight in order to recover from jet lag. That wasn't the case at McKinsey. I would certainly have accumulated many days off: during the course of one year, I took approximately ten transatlantic return flights, I visited Brazil three times in order to look after the local office, and there were a few intra-US overnight flights, for example departing San Francisco at midnight and arriving in New York the next morning at 5.30 am. As partner and office manager, I spent about 30% of my time travelling and working out of foreign offices. Travel became significantly more comfortable once I was allowed to fly Business and First Class.

It was hard work, but there was also downtime. I had six weeks of holidays per year, and as per common McKinsey practice wasn't disturbed very much during that time. Most importantly, I found time for sports, which has been an important part of my life since I was a boy. I had always been an avid sportsman when I joined McKinsey in 1970. Hans Widmer and I wanted to know who the better skier was, so we founded the legendary winter retreats starting in Lenzerheide in Graubünden one year later. Each time, more German and Swiss McKinsey staff participated, and participants numbered more than 80 in 1977. I took to it like a duck to water: We transported slalom poles up the mountain and staked out the slalom course. Thereafter, I skied down the slope and missed victory by a hundredth of a second. This was followed by a working session where I presented our latest projects, and in the evening we held a dance, and I participated as an entertainer. At one time, Rosi Mittermaier and Christian Neureuther were our guests. After the 1976 Olympics, we organized a cross-country skiing competition for all McKinsey staff.

I had met my Swiss colleague Hans Widmer during my second project for McKinsey. An American director headed our team, and the Norwegian Gunnar Hauge led the project. Boehringer Ingelheim, the pharmaceutical company, asked us to develop a new organizational structure designed to closely link the 125 foreign branches spread all over the world to their headquarters. Boehringer, a global leader in many areas, fascinated us.

We newbies were full of energy. Had we been asked to develop a cancer drug within six months, together with a couple of researchers, we would likely have said: "No problem, we got it."

Hans thought that no-one could work productively for more than ten hours per day. He made sure that we finished work at 7 pm, which did not always please management. One Wednesday, he even wanted to leave work at 5 pm in order to attend a handball game in Zurich. We were speechless.

The American director asked whether he was so well-organized that he could leave that early on a Wednesday. Hans didn't hesitate a moment and replied: "I was very well organized for our 9 am meeting, but you only arrived at 4 pm – and now I have to leave." I called him during the evening to discuss his behaviour, but he simply said: "Herbert, I don't let them get to me." I liked this unyielding, courageous behaviour. No consequences ensued, this time or other times. There was no internal training event without Hans stating his criticisms. It might be about the lack of career development for staff working for public-sector clients, or about clients complaining about our overhead. He was left in peace because of his outstanding performance.

Hans and I loved sports and seized each opportunity to practice them. In 1974, we participated in a winter retreat in Arosa and skipped a mandatory morning meeting in order to ski for two hours. We got back during the lunch break. I asked Hans: "What should we do if they fire us?" His answer was simple: "We just don't leave."

Hans became a director in McKinsey's Swiss office before being headhunted by Swiss chemical company Sandoz. Sandoz president Marc Moret presented him to management, calling it a historic day as he had found his successor. But it wasn't to be. Hans Widmer became a victim of internal intrigues and was moved to Wander AG, a food company, at that time part of the Sandoz group. But his management career was far from over. He became president of Oehrlikon-Bührle, a successful producer of tools, and was voted Swiss Manager of the Year twice in this role.

Swiss economic magazine *Bilanz* once quoted him saying that he would have liked to have become Pope in order to "engineer the intellectual turnaround of the Catholic Church". There it was again, the McKinsey impulse of considering that nothing was impossible.

In this spirit, we founded the winter retreats in Lenzerheide. When this event took place for the last time in Kitzbühel in 1997, we numbered 680 consultants, and an equal number of partners and spouses. This required an organizational tour de force accomplished by my colleague Thomas von Mitschke. My last "baby" was the European Olympics, a soccer, volleyball and athletics competition for the European offices. Franz Beckenbauer even coached the 1989 event in Cannes. Today, he recalls half-jokingly, we were a team of the blind and semi-blind, specifically when we played the Spanish McKinsey team. Beckenbauer considered our Spanish colleagues "half-decent players". We formed a German-style block in the penalty area. Whatever it was, thanks to his careful coaching we managed a nil-nil draw and moved on to the finals after a penalty shootout. Beckenbauer considered this a bigger personal success, even more of a success than the German national team's second place at the Mexico World Cup.

During the first half, I once disrespected Beckenbauer's orders, running forward and thus exposing our defence. He was furious, screaming and gesticulating, and then told me when we had a corner that he was going to replace me because of my undisciplined behaviour. I assented, of course. We lost the final to the Scandinavian McKinsey team, also after a penalty shootout.

A one-winged bird cannot fly – I forget where I got this maxim, but I have used it frequently to demonstrate my view that life shouldn't be too one-sided. I saw many young colleagues with a huge diversity of interests arrive at McKinsey, only to focus solely on their work after an initial eight-to-ten month period. I tried to convey to our associates that they needed to develop a "second wing" and that many possibilities existed for them to do so: running shoes can be taken everywhere, so it is possible to run while travelling. There is the Canadian Air Force's famous "5BX" exercise program, which takes all of 11 minutes to complete and can be done even in confined spaces such as the smallest hotel rooms.

But there's more to balance. I encouraged young colleagues to take up a good cause outside of their job; for example, helping a private theatre, raising funds for a museum, or doing voluntary work in schools or private associations – the possibilities are endless. My idea was for McKinsey staff to be "citizens actively and responsibly participating in community life, thus both leading a balanced life and benefiting society.

My work-life balance would not have been successful without sports and other activities not directly related to my job. Workload notwithstanding, I always tried to be available for important family events such as the children's birthdays or parent-teacher meetings. Calls from the US West Coast during dinner certainly were a nuisance, as was my doing work on the weekends at home. On the other side, there were also advantages. One of them was that we had numerous international gatherings at home because of my job. We received many foreign visitors, particularly from the US and Japan. We were able to combine a partners' retreat in Hawaii with a family vacation, where we met an American family who invited my son Oliver to stay with them in Seattle, at first for a summer and then for an entire year. My daughter Nicole spent time with a McKinsey partner in England. During those years, the foundation was laid for them to become something akin to global citizens.

Nicole was born on December 13, 1971. On this Monday morning, I had taken Rosemarie to the Protestant hospital in the city of

Mettmann near Dusseldorf. Of course, traffic was bumper to bumper on the access roads. We arrived around 10 am, and it happened at 9.55pm. Our little family's first-born was healthy, and we were over the moon. The McKinsey Christmas party took place that evening, and when I was sure that mother and child were in good shape and well looked-after, I went to the party around midnight. John McDonald took the microphone and announced that a healthy baby girl had been born. That was an unforgettable day for me.

Oliver was born two and a quarter years later, on a Saturday. Our daughter Nicole stayed with her grandparents in Bochum, where we celebrated the new arrival, after watching Germany's soccer team playing Spain (which ended with a one-nil victory for Germany). It was February 16, 1974.

Rosemarie had continued to work right until Oliver's birth, and when we moved to Munich shortly thereafter, she started to study history and German language and literature.

Nicole became a university professor and now lives in Seattle, WA, where she teaches demanding classes in philosophy, most recently dealing with the function of dreams. Her brother Oliver and his American wife live in New York. Similarly to Nicole, he didn't seek a career in business, but became an actor. I see Oliver and his two children more frequently as I visit New York more frequently. Unfortunately, Seattle is far away from the East Coast metropolis, so that I see my daughter, who also has a boy and a girl, less frequently.

My three children from my second marriage, Eliora, Ilan and Yoran have been raised as trilingual and are all avid athletes. They beat their father both in slalom and tennis. My children are everything to me, and I have a very close relationship with all of them. They always made sure that I never lost my balance.

Business and recreation merged, which was not exclusively due to my children. The same held true for our social life. We were face to face in the private sphere with CEOs of big German companies, who were our clients. We threw parties and were invited to parties, so that we spent numerous weekends somewhere in Germany, attending social events.

When subject to great pressure to perform in the professional area, personal balance can only be achieved in my view when life is lived fully during the little free time. One-winged birds have no future, but I have seen many of those. They were insecure and worked like crazy hoping to generate great, creative ideas. But these ideas only materialize if one's spirit is free, if one has a second wing. Then, one will also have the required energy to generate new ideas.

I generate new ideas through literary knowledge. In the course of many job interviews I conducted for McKinsey, I asked young job applicants which book or play they were most impressed with. German applicants generally responded with *Faust*. Whether it was the drama's great reputation or the profound questions about life it discussed – according to my own approximate statistics, about 70% thought that this classic drama was the answer to my question.

But perhaps they enjoyed reading *Faust* as much as I did. I was impressed when first reading it in Middle School, and I was excited about someone wanting to really know "what holds the world together in its innermost elements"; and someone so persistently looking for truth that he makes a pact with the devil. But even the devil was an exciting and exceedingly subtle character. As a management consultant, I frequently was tossed between heaven and hell. We felt intoxicated by certain results, and all of a sudden things changed and everything turned negative. In my profession, it was impossible to plan with any degree of certainty, rather it was clouded with uncertainty. In a way, it was close to the edge.

Former European Central Bank president Jean-Claude Trichet once said that the poems of youth are worth as much as monetary riches, and he is right. Poets' metaphors have shown new ways in many difficult situations. Poetry described feelings I would not have been able to express, and literature helped me to recognize the relativity of my issues. In order to push myself to my limits, I looked to Friedrich Hölderlin, as I did when it came to matters of close friendships, or in times of increasing distress and seeking rescue. Or I read Rainer Maria Rilke: "If you don't understand life, it will be a celebration." Or I quoted portions of Friedrich Schiller's poem *Song of the Bell*: "That the work may praise the master, but the blessing comes from higher."

I liked reading the chroniclers amongst the writers, for example Wilhelm Raabe, an 18th century realist. Rosemarie wrote her doctoral dissertation on Raabe and introduced me to this author. Raabe always wholeheartedly took sides with the starvelings, and was humorous and frequently wonderfully ironic. Even the titles of his works are an echo of bygone times: *The Hunger Reverend* or *The Stuffing Cake*.

Another interesting chronicler is Martin Walser, nicknamed the Balzac of Lake Constance. He published *Marriages in Philippsburg* in 1957, casting a critical light on the young Federal Republic and its economic order. In this book, everyone is judged by their success and their women. Later, I read with great interest the discussion surrounding his acknowledgement speech in October 1998 in Frankfurt's Paul's Church, at the occasion of his receiving the Peace Prize of the German Booksellers. He spoke about the instrumentalization of the Holocaust, and that Auschwitz shouldn't be used as a moral bludgeon. Insults and abuse ensued. Would such a debate be conducted more objectively today? In any event, Walser always has been a controversial and headstrong person, a writer dancing to the beat of his own drum. There is nothing wrong with it. On the contrary, writers are supposed to help us understand what happens around us. When *Manager Magazin* asked me to do a joint interview, together with Martin Walser, and we discussed corruption in business, amongst other things, he didn't mince his words.

Another favourite author of mine is Martin Suter. His *Business Class*, columns appearing in the magazine as part of the *Zürcher Tages-Anzeiger*, targeted the audacity, but also the human helplessness of a social class I knew only too well. Reading his columns gave me a great deal of pleasure.

I met Christoph Ransmayr by accident. Together with Reinhold Messner, we hiked in the Geiselerspitzen and the Kitzbühel mountains. During these hikes, I sensed how thoughts solidified while speaking. I normally didn't participate in these types of discussions, and I felt transported to another world. Then I started reading his books and I started to transform myself.

CHAPTER 16

"WE WILL KILL YOU"

TERROR AND FREE RIDERS

The phone rang. It was a dark night. Sleepily, I looked at my alarm clock, it was 1.30 am. What could be that important to call me at that time? I couldn't think of anything, except hoping that nothing had happened to any of my family members. My wife, who was lying next to me, had also been woken up by the incessant ringing of the phone. She picked up the receiver as the phone was standing on her side of the bed. She identified herself by stating her name. "We want to speak to Monsieur Henzler as a matter of urgency." The male voice with a French accent was so loud that I could hear it, too. My wife passed me the phone without a word. "Yes, Henzler speaking," I said, still sleepy. The male voice spoke in a sharp tone. "Mr. Henzler, listen carefully. I am calling from "Action Directe". You are on our list." All of a sudden I was wide awake. I knew that "Action Directe" was a left-wing terror organization, responsible for the assassinations of General René Audran and Renault CEO Georges Besse. "I am sure you know why you're on our list. You have an event coming up on July 23. This is the latest date when we'll get you and kill you, maybe earlier. Don't tell the police about this call." The caller then hung up, I couldn't utter a single word, or ask any questions. Receiving such a call at 1.30 am made the blood freeze in my veins. I sat trembling on the bed of my house in Grunwald, on the outskirts of Munich, thousands of thoughts swirling through my head. An unknown person had told me that I was on a hit list and could be sure that they would get me, at the latest on July 23, 1985. We had scheduled our housewarming party for that day. Finally, the caller had warned me not to contact the police. "What happened, you turned as white as a sheet?" Rosemarie asked. My voice faltered when I told her about the threat. Without debating the issue any longer, I said: "I have to call the police, no matter what the caller said." Rosemarie agreed, and I called the police right away, telling an officer what had just happened. Half an hour later, two officers showed up at our doorstep and tried to calm us down. After all, the caller could have entered our garden in the meantime. The officers called for reinforcements, and a VW Bus containing police officers was positioned in front of our house in Adalbert-Stifter Street. In the end, we received advice and instructions, most notably how to deal with our children, to keep things vague for them. Rosemarie and I decided to give them the full picture, since we thought that they should be particularly vigilant in such a situation, being the weakest link in the chain. For example, one rule was to never leave school to go home early if their school received a call to that effect. Of course, we also informed their school about the dangerous situation.

After the call, I realized that I had actually been expecting it. Only a few months before, in February 1985, Ernst Zimmermann, CEO of Motoren und Turbinen Union (MTU), had been executed in front of his wife in his house in Munich-Gauting by terrorists of the "Red Army Fraction" (RAF). He was shot several times in the back of his head, while both he and he and his wife were trussed up. It was a particularly brutal incident, no wonder that his wife has never been able to forget it. I knew Ernst Zimmermann.

I thought about the following: in 1968, two department stores were set on fire, marking the beginning of two decades of political terror in Germany. In 1970, Ulrike Meinhof, Andreas Baader, Gudrun Ensslin and a few others founded the RAF. They were a product of the 1968 movement. I had experienced the latter myself while studying at university, and it should not be forgotten that some positive aspects came out of the movement, such as scrutinizing what certain wealthy characters had actually done during the war. That had frequently been swept under the rug.

German business leaders hadn't fully understood at the time that there was a need to provide explanations, and it had certainly not been adequately communicated that business activities made sense for society as a whole. Economists and business leaders were not interested in establishing ties with journalists, and preferred to be left in peace. As late as the mid-sixties, Ludwig Erhard considered the journalistic fraternity as a waste of time.

Alfred Herrhausen was different, he wanted to communicate and follow a new path. "We have to explain what we do, over and over again," he said. "We have to say what we think, and we have to do what we say, again and again." Needless to say, his views were harshly criticized.

Further considerations came to mind. The RAF killed their first police officer in 1971. During the following years, it became clear that international terrorism increasingly targeted executives. This was true for the Italian "Red Brigades", the French "Action Directe" and the German RAF.

The first victim of terror from the business world was Jürgen Ponto, head of Drescher Bank in July 1970. Siegfried Buback, Head of the Federal Prosecution Service, and Hanns Martin Schleyer, president of the Association of German Employers, were all assassinated in the same year. Siemens board member Karl-Heinz Beckurts was assassinated in the mid-eighties. I had close ties to Beckurts; the others were acquaintances.

When I received my threat during the mid-eighties, many clients were still shaken. They used armour-plated limousines, and were accompanied by bodyguards day and night. Their private lives suffered accordingly. They could only make public appearances after consultation with the police and extensive security measures had to be adopted. I simply couldn't understand how terrorists could have that many sympathizers. How could they find shelter again and again, and generally operate without being noticed? A bad "joke" rampant at that time went as follows: What is the difference between the RAF and McKinsey? The RAF has sympathizers. It was horrible.

McKinsey was known to be on the list, and the firm reacted in exemplary fashion after I received my nocturnal call. Warren Cannon, the Head of Operations, was sent to Germany to review the situation. After that, I received a driver, a couple of trees in our garden were cut down for security reasons, and bodyguards protected me around the clock for about two months. It was also suggested that we get a dog. Werner Niefer made Daimler's security service available, which was particularly helpful during that period. I had a leaflet from them entitled *How to react when you are captured*.

The daily lives of all of those on the list were turned upside down. I still sense the anxiety when I think about those months. I lay awake at night, always thinking about the same issue: why would I be spared? They had already killed many people. I also thought about how to react in case of abduction: what would happen to my family when I got killed?

Munich police received a call from an unknown person the very night that I was contacted. He identified himself as a Frankfurt police officer and reported an assassination attempt on Dr. Henzler of McKinsey. Munich police were sceptical, particularly as their "colleague" gave a rather dubious phone number. They engaged him in a longer discussion, which they recorded.

The recording was analyzed by members of the Security Services, who thought that the RAF was unlikely to proceed in such a way. The Head of the Munich police criminal investigations department made their position clear. "Mr Henzler, I think it is rather unusual that the RAF would contact targets in advance. Typically, they kill their targets and follow up with a letter claiming responsibility." In the end, Munich police concluded that I had been targeted by an ordinary criminal as opposed to a terrorist organization. They suspected a crime of passion.

I was surprised and asked: "A crime of passion?"

"Do you know anyone who wants to settle a score with you?"

I shook my head. Who could be the offender? I couldn't think of any obvious enemy.

They gave me a helping hand: "A crime of passion can also be committed by a colleague at work having a very low opinion of you."

I could hardly believe that the offender hailed from my professional environment. Nevertheless, it appeared imperative to follow that lead. Kurt Steglich, my then Head of Operations, deserves a lot of credit for dividing all of McKinsey's employees into groups of ten and playing the police recording of the call from Frankfurt to each group. About six weeks after the fifth group meeting, several employees came to see him saying that they recognized the voice as belonging to a print shop staffer. He had printed the invitations to our housewarming party and thus knew about the July 23 date. His motive was sheer jealousy as he had to print an invitation for the higher echelons. Before that, he had had an affair with a high-er-ranking secretary. Because the affair ended badly, he harboured resentment against more senior colleagues. He was tried in court and received a prison sentence.

It was horrible to see someone so filled with envy. Since then, I have become much more careful.

Terror in Germany continued. The movement didn't end after the 1977 suicide of Baader, Meinhof and Ensslin in Stuttgart-Stammheim prison, but was continued by a new generation of perpetrators. They blew up Deutsche Bank CEO Alfred Herrhausen in 1989, and shot and killed Detlev Karsten Rohwedder, executive working for Treuhandanstalt executive.

I had met Herrhausen five days earlier, at a meeting with the then Economics Minister Helmut Haussmann and Hubert Burda. I was completely shocked when I heard the news, and could hardly believe it as I knew that he was closely protected. His car was always preced-ed by a security car, and he never took the same route twice. I thought that if the RAF had declared war on our capitalist system, it looked like a real war.

A week later, I interrupted my working week in New York in order to attend Alfred Herrhausen's memorial service. The Republic paid its respects, and our society vowed to fight terrorism. This is the gist of what Chancellor Helmut Kohl said: "If these terrorists declare war on us and kill one of our best, they should know that we have thousands more of his calibre." When I heard this, I couldn't believe it. There was only one Herrhausen.

After the eulogies, his coffin was positioned in the aisle, right next to my seat. The coffin carried the inscription "Brother Alfred". At this very moment, I became very sad and pensive. Alfred Her-rhausen lay in his coffin because hate-filled terrorists had killed him – that was what remained of a human being who had accom-plished a great deal. I sensed his vulnerability, my vulnerability, and everyone's vulnerability. It could be game over really quickly. None of this was easy to understand or comprehend, but everyone was incredibly vulnerable.

I always agreed with the government's position of not giving in to terrorists, for example in the case of Hanns-Martin Schleyer. When GSG 9 operators stormed the hijacked Lufthansa aircraft *Landshut* in Mogadishu, and the RAF responded by killing Schleyer, I afterwards paid respects to then Chancellor Helmut Schmidt's position. I agreed that the government couldn't be blackmailed by terrorists. If the government agreed to terrorists' requests, they would simply try and get the next one released. This had been amply demonstrated at the occasion of the kidnapping of CDU politician Peter Lorenz.

Of course, it is easily comprehensible that Schleyer's desire in this situation was that everything humanly possible be done in order to get him released. Peter Lorenz must have had the same desire.

When Susanne Albrecht, daughter of a university classmate and goddaughter of Dresdner Bank CEO Jurgen Ponto, got her parents to arrange to see the Ponto family in July 1977, she was welcomed with open arms. No-one knew that she had contacts within the RAF. Albrecht told her godfather on the terrace of his villa that he was about to be kidnapped and that he would not be harmed if he accepted being taken into their custody. This wasn't an option for the tall, imposing and intimidating Ponto. He defended himself, and was shot by Albrecht's companions, Christian Klar and Brigitte Mohnhaupt.

It is impossible to tell in advance how to react in such a situation. I had thought about what I would do in such a case. I think I would have become very small. One clings to life.

After Herrhausen's assassination, police discovered the "hit list" containing my name, amongst a total of some 40. As far as I can recall, Hans-Olaf Henkel and Gertrud Hohler were listed under the letter "H". I met again with police and was urged to remain cautious and vigilant. I received the all-clear after approximately a year. As a matter of fact, terror had ended after two decades of brutal attacks.

CHAPTER 17

WORKERS' PARTICIPATION

THE GERMAN ROUTE

I suddenly came into contact with politics when Chancellor Willy Brandt's government introduced workers' participation in 1972. The Konrad Adenauer Foundation had helped me to get two tickets for an event discussing the pros and cons of the new corporate governance. I went to Bonn, together with my office manager John McDonald. Germany AG (that is the CEOs of major German companies) was sitting on one side, and on the other side trade union leaders, together with Krupp executive Ernst Wolf Mommsen, had taken their seats. People's views clashed in an icy atmosphere.

A break ensued, and I thought, naïve as I was, that the big shots of German business were about to come up to me and say: "Young man, you have come together with your office manager. We would be keen to get McKinsey's views on the whole workers' participation debate. Do you think this will boost Germany's position, compared with other countries?" But no-one approached us, with the exception of Alfred Herrhausen's flying visit. McDonald and I stood alone at our bistro table, drinking coffee. We were veritable nobodies! Corporate governance rules were about to be radically changed, and no-one was interested in McKinsey's opinion? I wanted to work for an in-demand firm, a firm which had a say and whose opinions were valued. I didn't want to be part of a McKinsey no-one was interested in. At this very moment, it became clear to me that either things had to change, and McKinsey's opinion as to important issues become sought, or I was going to change sides, leave consulting and work for the real decision-makers.

After this shock, I took matters into my own hands and publicly took up position for McKinsey. In the spring of 1972, I published an article in *manager magazin*, encouraged by its editor Winfried Wilhelm. The article took a critical look at workers' participation in supervisory boards, but also proposed concrete steps for management to prepare for new legislation. In my view, it didn't make sense to reserve 50% of supervisory board seats for workers' representatives, but management had to be prepared for the event. It was the German route, and no other country in the world considered making life so difficult for management.

It should be stated that I am not and have never been an opponent of workers' participation. It is a crucial feature in the workplace, but the Works Constitution Act already took care of that. In addition, companies' economic committees are an important instrument for both workers' councils and management. But the supervisory board makes decisions as to items such as acquisitions, establishment of a subsidiary in China or whether Mr Muller or Mr Meier should become a board member. Such decisions should primarily be made by investors' representatives. In any event, one-third of supervisory board seats were already allocated to workers' representatives. My fear was that workers' representation would lead to lots of horse-trading, on the basis of the maxim that for example one party agreed to Schulze joining the board, in exchange for the other party supporting Lehmann's promotion to plant manager. Or one party supported the international strategy if domestic plant workers were allowed to work overtime between Christmas and New Year. I warned in my article that such workers participation would open the door for horse-trading at the top of the company. My article of course didn't prevent the law proposed by the then social-liberal coalition from being enacted, but I made McKinsey's presence felt.

McKinsey may have even benefited from the new rules. Hans-Olaf Henkel, then CEO of IBM's German operations, thought that the new law on workers' participation was the best thing that could have happened to McKinsey, because boards would increasingly request consultants' opinions in order to bolster their proposals in the new world of an increasingly complex supervisory board: "Look, McKinsey has analysed the issue and unambiguously concluded that there are no alternatives." Of course, I always denied his theory.

Daimler executive Werner Niefer introduced me to a number of politicians, for example Lothar Spath during the mid-eighties, who was then Prime Minister of Baden-Wurttemberg. Our first meeting took place early one Saturday morning in the Villa Reitzenstein, the Baden-Wurttemberg State Chancellery. We checked each other out and liked what we saw. From then on, I had access to Späth and provided advice if and when asked.

I also participated in the "Stuttgart Summit", which Lothar Späth and Alfred Herrhausen founded in April 1989. Approximately 15 top managers from all European countries met in Spath's state capital to discuss what business and politics could do to improve coordination. Media reports considered that Spath's ability to attract business luminaries such as Peter Wallenberg from Sweden, Helmut Maucher (Nestle) from Switzerland, Carlo de Benedetti (Olivetti) from Italy, or Maurice Greenberg (American International Group, AIG) from New York to Stuttgart each year reflected his heavyweight status.

Lothar Spath was the only top Christian Democratic politician who could have stood up to the then party leader Helmut Kohl. Because of catastrophic opinion polls, the Christian Democratic Union (CDU) had become quite agitated in 1989. German reunification was still not in sight. Non-parliamentarian members of the CDU had organized a few smaller protest marches. "Kohl has to go", protesters shouted. Spath told me at a breakfast meeting at Stuttgart's Intercontinental Hotel that more and more CDU politicians had asked him to challenge Kohl. The upcoming party congress in Bremen could offer the opportunity. That was where the regular elections of party leadership were held. Of course, Helmut Kohl wanted to run for office again.

Heiner Geissler was the organizer of the Bremen coup. Conflicts between Kohl and Geissler had escalated in the context of the party congress. Geissler had been forced to resign from his position as the party's secretary-general, and now Kohl's internal rivals had decided to send him packing. In their view, either Späth or Rita Süssmuth should lead the party.

Spath didn't appear fully decided to challenge Kohl. But he thought that he would probably be unable to refuse to serve if strong party circles asked for it. He told me: "If this happens and if I decide to do it, I will need you in Bonn." I declined, telling him that I was the Head of McKinsey Germany, and could not just give up my position.

But Späth replied: "If this happens, you will simply have to do it." At this moment, it became clear that Spath wanted me as a minister if he became chancellor. I called Fred Gluck and explained this difficult situation. He didn't like the thought of having to find a successor for me.

Spath discussed the matter again with a couple of close confidants shortly before the Bremen party congress. He wanted to call the members of the party executive committee and ask the crucial question: "What do you think about Kohl?" Once he had measured current opinion, he wanted to attend a party executive committee meeting immediately prior to the party congress and state: "We cannot continue with the Kohl situation. We have to put it to a vote." But it turned out that while unease about Kohl was great, few wanted to depose him.

The party congress started the next day, and a sick Kohl put himself in the limelight like a world leader, according to CDU politician Helmut Linssen, who was a close personal friend from university. Kohl said that he had spoken to Gorbachev, Mrs Thatcher had assured him of her support, and French president Mitterrand had told him: "You will get through this, all of us have gone through dark times."

Kohl then proceeded to make a frontal attack on his rivals: there were CDU members who carried daggers in their robes, who wanted to depose the party leader as opposed to supporting him in a difficult situation. Kohl talked about a breach of trust, and everyone knew whom he meant.

The old fighter had nipped the coup in the bud. Lothar Späth wasn't even elected to the executive committee. Kohl's supporters ridiculed Späth, saying that he had come to Bremen as an eagle and left as a boiling hen. Then came the East German revolution, a historical event for Helmut Kohl who became the hero of German reunification. Spath in turn quickly lost media goodwill. German magazine *Der Spiegel*, which had supported him as the conservative hopeful, wrote negative columns about him. Only a few months later, he also lost his position as Baden-Wurttemberg's prime minister.

Spath and I did continue our close partnership after these events. We co-authored five books, developed a ten-point program for reconstruction in the new German states and I appeared at several occasions in his n-tv talk-show *Spath am Abend*.

It was gratifying to see him become the most successful CEO of an East German company (Jenoptik), by a substantial margin, notwithstanding financial support of several billion marks provided by Treuhand. Later, he became a successful investment banker with Merrill Lynch (which enabled us to play give-and-go from time to time), and then the great CDU hope as member of Edmund Stoiber's team for the 2002 parliamentary elections. He became the most popular politician within two months. As late as autumn of 2010, when we sat in a restaurant, I witnessed passers-by coming up to him and begging him to run again for office. Späth passed away on March 18th, 2016 and the State of Baden-Württemberg paid tribut to a great leader.

When the liberal democrat Helmut Haussmann became the German economics minister in 1988, he looked for advice outside of political circles. He established a small circle of advisers, the "Spatzle Quartet". Its four members were then the Boss executive Uwe Holy (who is still in the fashion business with Strellson), the then BMW Head of Development Wolfgang Reitzle, Willem van Aghtmael then the CEO of Breuninger Stuttgart's retail and department store, and myself. The quartet met with Haussmann every six weeks to discuss current issues.

One of these evening sessions dealt with coal production, the enormous subsidies provided by the government and how to put an end to those. Haussmann had announced that he would present his views on the future of the Ruhr and Saar coal mines the next day at a press conference. We as his advisers had thoroughly prepared the topic. We presented numbers, arguments and comparisons in order to convince him that severe cuts were warranted. We suggested cutting public subsidies by half as a first step – and the liberal minister agreed.

At eight in the morning, the Ministry of Economics was already surrounded by miners who had painted their faces black. They blocked access and didn't let the minister through, until he agreed to receive a delegation of the protesters. The discussion took place an hour later, and at 10 am Helmut Haussmann stepped forward to meet the press. He declared that he had gained new insights and that the status quo with respect to coal production should best be maintained. Haussmann certainly was a politician with liberal ambitions and a thorough regulatory approach, but apparently the pressure was too high.

A number of advisory proposals with respect to the German reunification as of 1989, developed by myself or jointly with others, suffered the same fate as our coal-production proposal and disappeared into oblivion without further ado. I realized that at that time economic arguments didn't play a role. The reunification process was designed taking into account political considerations. I could only gauge economic aspects, and these were catastrophic. It was already difficult to find a rationale for the "welcome money" received by East Germans in the West, but it was even less understandable to set the exchange ratio of East German marks into Deutsche marks to 1:1, against better judgement.

It was not only politicians who decided to ignore the facts. I presented McKinsey's initial conclusions that the East German economy was trailing the old Federal Republic's not by 20%, as was commonly believed, but rather by 60% or even 80%, to Detlev Karsten Rohwedder, the first head of the Treuhand, and later also to a circle of heavyweight politicians called the "elephant round". My conclusion was as follows: "This will never work, because the East German economy is not competitive."

This dose of realism wasn't enthusiastically received. Jens Odewald, then CEO of Kaufhof and president of the Treuhand's supervisory board, proceeded to give me a roasting. He disputed our analysis and accused me of not having any national sentiment. In those days, warnings were not popular, and I couldn't gather any support. Some clients who had encouraged us to produce a study in order to provide more substance to the critique levied against economic reunification also disappointed me. But now, as our realistic approach was sacrificed on the altar of national sentiment, they patted us on the back and offered consolation, saying that the timing for the realistic analysis just hadn't been right.

CHAPTER 18

EAST GERMANY
AND UNIFICATION

I was in Düsseldorf when the wall fell on November 9th, 1989. I thought that it could have only happened on November 9th, not a day earlier or later. November 9th was a historic date, since Friedrich Ebert had proclaimed the Republic on the ninth of November, the Hitler-Ludendorff coup took place on that day, as did the 1938 "crystal night" pogroms. On this ninth of November 1989, Alfred Herrhausen had accompanied Helmut Kohl to Poland, and I remember how they flew back immediately, how the chancellor appeared in West Berlin and was booed by the masses, and how people applauded when Willy Brandt arrived. There was an incredible feeling of euphoria, it was a great moment in time.

I had developed an interest in the GDR (German Democratic Republic) during my student days. Whoever was interested in politics in the sixties was interested in the GDR. After World War Two, the GDR had been created as a socialist state in the Soviet-occupied zone of Germany. The division of Germany as an expression of the global East-West divide was the pre-eminent political topic of the day.

I had been the political leader of the Student Association of Higher Business Colleges and in that function put the German division on our agenda. I also organized a seminar on the question of German reunification. It was virtually impossible for a West German citizen to explore the GDR, with the possible exception of its capital East Berlin. Because of the special status of Berlin as a whole, the SED (Socialist Unity Party of Germany) could wall in its citizens, but was unable to prevent access from West Berlin with daily visas.

I made frequent use of that opportunity. When in Berlin (most frequently in the company of classmates), we visited the Eastern part and poked around. One day, we met three female East German students. I am still in touch with one of them, Gaby Schwarz. I visited from West Berlin, with a bottle of whisky in my backpack, and we parted company shortly before midnight, as West German citizens had to leave East Berlin by the end of the day. Like thousands of others, I returned via the "Palace of Tears" – Friedrichstrasse Train Station was then the GDR's central border crossing point and a place of forced farewells for many.

Later, when I headed McKinsey's German operations, I tried to establish contacts through official channels with the GDR's Ministry of Foreign Trade. I never received any response. One day, however, I managed to establish contact. I accompanied a Krupp executive when a meeting had been set up in East Berlin's Hotel Metropol with Gerhard Beil, a member of the GDR's government and in charge of Foreign Trade from 1986 to 1990. This was my first meeting with a high-ranking representative of the regime, and I was shocked as to his behaviour. He told us that the Metropol was "his hotel", and that all conversations in the rooms were recorded in order to eliminate public enemies. The meeting with Beil was useless. Quite the contrary, I had a heated discussion with the Krupp executive as to whether it made any sense at all to do business with such characters.

In 1987, Rosemarie and I received an invitation via the politician Kurt Biedenkopf to participate in an exchange of scientific knowledge and views in Leipzig. Virtually all of the GDR's distinguished economics professors participated, including Jurgen Notzold of Leipzig's Karl Marx University. We discussed economic and technological change, but couldn't establish a rapport. We were too far away from a common understanding of business and economics. Notzold and his colleagues called economic and technological adaptation "Adaptations to the Five Year Plan."

These economic experts, most of whom – just like Gerhard Beil – had studied at Berlin's economics university, the "University for Planned Economics", were purist defenders of a "bigger-and-better" approach. They proudly pointed out the success of their exports to Comecon, the Council for Mutual Economic Assistance, which was the Eastern Block's economic union. But calculations were made in tons, as opposed to any realistic measurement. At the same time, the GDR tried to obtain foreign exchange from the West, no matter how. Alexander Schalck-Golodkowski's shadowy realm, aptly named "Commercial Coordination", traded in arms, cultural assets or blood plasma, organized imports of hazardous waste and last but not least made millions from bounties paid by the West German government to free political prisoners.

Representatives of the regime used occasions such as our Leipzig conference to mechanically recite the official success story of the GDR's economy. But one only had to roam the streets of Leipzig in the margins of the conference, and contradictions became obvious. Streets were full of potholes, and entire parts of the city were in a state of dilapidation. And if we westerners tried to eat in "Auerbachs Keller", we received a dose of GDR everyday economics: it was pot luck to be able to sit at an empty table, and service was a disaster.

Nevertheless, McKinsey remained interested in the GDR. In 1988, prior to the fall of the Berlin Wall, McKinsey's German partners held their annual partner meeting in Dresden. The reason for that was that I had remained in contact with Jürgen Nötzold and other economists, and I believed that we could learn from an exchange of views. We completed our agenda in the Hotel Belvedere's conference room. One of my colleagues repeatedly pointed out that our conversations were likely being recorded, but we didn't care and did business as usual: Which clients should we focus on? What was the state of various projects? Who should be promoted to partner?

The social program provided us with interesting impressions of GDR businesses. We visited the energy combine "Black Pump" in Spemberg, Brandenburg, the Meissen porcelain manufacturer and the glass manufacturer in Ilmenau. We didn't gain any real insights from the visits, but we recognized from whatever we saw that McKinsey consultants would have a lot of work here. However, no East German government would have ever hired McKinsey, still less paid in foreign currency.

Our Dresden meeting ended with a gala event at the Hotel Belvedere, to which we invited the GDR officials we had been in contact with during our stay. The atmosphere was relaxed, and I decided to take a stab at making some humorous closing remarks: "We always have difficulties drafting the minutes of our meetings. It would be fantastic if the GDR could provide us with copies of their recordings!"

This banter didn't go down well. Our GDR guests rewarded us with deafening silence. Later, I received a letter from a GDR official stating that I had blatantly broken GDR laws and that they had even considered my arrest. Fortunately, that was not what happened, but authorities took their revenge: when our group left the GDR the next day at the Helmsdorf border crossing point, we were held up for over an hour, without any discernible reason.

After the turnaround had been forced by peaceful citizens, the Treuhand organization was put in charge of shaping the future of the GDR economy. I was among the very first advisers helping to make decisions such as which companies had to be liquidated, which companies could be turned around and which could be immediately sold to private investors. McKinsey was involved in this process with up to 30 consultants and I remember my first visit to a plant in June 1990 during the course of this engagement. It was the VEB machine-tools combine called 7th October in Berlin, and formerly a heavyweight of the GDR economy. Its boss Karl-Heinz Warzecha had achieved cult status as he had achieved a lot within the tight restrictions he was forced to operate under. Other than myself, McKinsey directors from Switzerland, Japan and the US tried to get a first impression. We were shocked with the state of the company and its lack of productivity compared with Western competitors. As of mid-1991, the Chancellery organized several so-called 'elephant rounds' with respect to the 'reconstruction of the east.' Approximately 50 of the Federal Republic's most important business executives and several ministers got together. I was also invited to participate in these rounds probably because McKinsey on its own initiative had produced a fairly critical paper dealing with development of the new states. The paper described an alarming difference of productivity in the former GDR enterprises called combines. Depending on the industry, we estimated that they were trailing West German companies by 60% to 80%. Instead of closing down all the industries, we suggested including a structural component in the productivity calculation for selected combines and regions (for example, the Bitterfeld Chemical Triangle) in order to move away from the rigid application of typical productivity calculations. In addition, I had given a controversial interview in January 1990 in *manager magazin* talking about the most appropriate strategy for making headway in developing the new economy. For example, I recommended a sponsorship model between West German companies and their old GDR locations.

I was very nervous at the first meeting as I wasn't invited every day by Helmut Kohl and his ministers in Bonn and it was exciting to participate in such a group of heavyweights. Three rows formed around the huge conference table: executives of the biggest companies sat in the first row, including Heinrich von Pierer (Siemens), Edzard Reuter (Daimler), Manfred Schneider (Bayer), Hilmar Kopper (Deutsche Bank), Jens Odewald (Kaufhof), Dietmar Kuhnt (RWE), Ulrich Hartmann (E.ON) and naturally Birgit Breuel, then the head of Treuhand; representatives of medium-sized companies were seated in the second row and, for example, people like myself sat in the last row. I let my eye wander in the Chancellor's direction and to a young, plain-looking woman. When I inquired about her, I found out that it was Angela Merkel. She hailed from the east and was referred to as Kohl's 'girl'. She became his Minister for Environmental Affairs in 1994.

Kohl, appearing to virtually direct the participants, led the three-hour meeting confidently. He described how conscripts from the old and new states now entered military service together and how in general swift progress was being made in the new states. He was supported by – of course positive – reports from Treuhand head Birgit Breuel and also by reports of the planned investments of 30 listed companies. Even the French and the British wanted to invest at that time in the former GDR. Thus it stood to reason that Kohl could present himself as the great statesman. For him, there were no insurmountable issues, only opportunities.

But one time something almost threw him. At the occasion of one of these meetings, which took place on a quarterly basis, Schleswig-Holstein businessmen Tyll Necker, head of the German Industry Association (BDI), presented industry's issues with respect to the upcoming introduction of the care insurance scheme on January 1, 1995. Necker said it was "too expensive and it would lead to personnel expenses reaching unknown heights." While Necker was still speaking, Kohl turned red, his hair stood on end and he started to tear into Necker: "What on earth do you think we should do when the population gets increasingly older? And by the way who reconstructed this country after the war?" Kohl said that he was sick of the constant bickering in industry because businessmen were the first to start whining and complaining about everything and then to turn around and make extraordinary efforts and earn lots of money.

The Chancellor ranted and no-one in this elite group tried to contradict him at that moment. The risk of being dismissed from this circle was just too high. I felt sorry for the Schleswig-Holstein businessman because I knew that he had been asked by other participants to be their spokesman and to convey their views to "the fat one" and now he was all on his own.

The meeting continued in an atmosphere of gloom, the attack on Necker, the man from the north, reverberated. I presented a suggestion for sponsorship of the remaining combines. I thought that the West German companies should just take over and build up their former East German assets for example Daimler in Genshagen, close to Berlin, and BASF in Bitterfeld. Those companies unwilling to accept sponsorship would have to pay a duty and I presented an idea about how to provide on-the-ground training for 10,000 managers from the new states. These were creative ideas but they failed – there were just too many advisors around at that time. On that evening, Helmut Kohl was the guest of honor of the German retailers' association and the German hotel and restaurant association. He was enthusiastically welcomed and it was conveyed to him that they had already heard about the day's events but he could be sure that nothing similar would happen that evening. Hearing that, Kohl must have felt vindicated that his occasional distrust of business wasn't misplaced.

But back to the new states which presented a tempting opportunity for McKinsey. Directors Axel Eckhardt and Hartmut Emans were among the up to 30 consultants working for us in the east. They came to me during the summer of 1991 and said that they would like to acquire a company from Treuhand. It was a company with a long history in mechanical and electrical engineering which had originally been part of the AEG Group, then was nationalized in the GDR and subsequently converted into Elpro AG by Treuhand. It also owned a significant real-estate portfolio. My answer was clear: this was not possible because we are advising Treuhand. (If any of us acquired Treuhand assets, it would cast a negative light on McKinsey.) And before going on vacation, I communicated my position to my colleagues in a memo. They were free to bid for the company provided they left McKinsey before so that McKinsey's reputation would not suffer. I also wrote that if their plan didn't work out we could certainly discuss their return to McKinsey. After that, they called me to say that they wanted to stay and would not bid for Elpro.

I couldn't believe it when my old McKinsey colleague and then Treuhand board member Wolf Klinz called me after two weeks and said: "Your two guys showed up today. They made a presentation and it doesn't look bad. I could imagine their bid being successful." I was furious: How could they bid for the company when I had virtually prohibited such action and they had explicitly accepted my view? I tried to call them immediately but they were both away from their offices, one because of an illness and the other because of a training event.

I called New York and discussed the matter. In my view, they had tarnished McKinsey's reputation so severely that they had to be fired. The then managing partner Fred Gluck said: "If you think that's the right thing to do, it's fine. If you find another solution, that's fine too. I will support whichever decision you make."

I managed to reach Alex Eckhardt during the evening and asked: "How did it go in Berlin?" Now he was the one filled with consternation. Then he said: "We can explain everything." I said loud and clear: "You will have to vacate your offices no later than 10 am tomorrow!"

The next morning I instructed our CFO Rainer Roggendorf on how to deal with the two colleagues: "Empty their offices, take away the keys, and get them to leave the office no later than 10 am" The termination virtually happened in front of everyone, which was akin to shooting by firing squad. It was tough, but I wanted to make an example. The firm's reputation had to be protected without compromise.

This case caused quite a stir within McKinsey. I was aware that many partners and colleagues thought I had acted too harshly. But I am still convinced the firings had a deterrent effect. I never ever saw any similar incident at McKinsey.

Today, practically no big company is headquartered in Eastern Germany. The East German economy still has a productivity lag of 25%. A total of about 1.6 million people have left the new states for the west and some areas such as Mecklenburg-Vorpommern are increasingly deserted.

The case of the GDR shows that the consequences of 65 years of misguided development can't be corrected in 20. It will take at least another 20 years to find the way.

CHAPTER 19

BROKEN LEGS, VANITY AND OTHER COMPLICATIONS

B eing a consultant meant that I primarily advised people, and we frequently established close relationships. I will go through thick and thin with people I feel close to. That was the case for Mercedes-Benz CEO Werner Niefer, who passed away in 1993. We had established a close relationship, which went beyond a purely professional level. This relationship stood the test when Niefer found himself in a bind in Italy, in 1990. After a leisurely lunch, Niefer wanted to drive himself to the airport. He took the steering wheel of a bus for which however he had no driving license. He lost control over the bus in a bend and caused an accident, as a result of which a tourist from Stuttgart suffered severe leg injuries. She was immediately tended to by paramedics while everyone waited for the police to arrive. When the police didn't show up, an Italian lawyer recommended that Niefer and his colleagues go to the airport, and that he would take care of things.

Subsequently, the matter caused a big stir, and press reports talked about hit-and-run and a missing bus driver's license. Niefer, CEO of Mercedes, only had a Brazilian bus driver's license! In this crisis situation, he called me. I was in New York at that time, together with Mark Wossner, then CEO of Bertelsmann. I immediately took a flight to Stuttgart to assist Niefer and his wife at this difficult time. He had gotten himself into trouble, but he was a friend and I wanted to help him to the best of my ability, although I couldn't do much more than providing support in this difficult situation. Shortly thereafter, Daimler's annual meeting was held and numerous questions were raised with respect to this issue. Niefer's reputation clearly was tarnished.

I had first met Niefer in 1983, when McKinsey did its first project for Daimler in the Mercedes transporter plant in Dusseldorf. While we worked on the project, Daimler head of sales Hans-Jurgen Hinrichs invited me to their national Sales Conference in Bremen, where I did a presentation. Werner Niefer was also present; he was at that time the Daimler board member responsible for production.

We hit it off right away. It also turned out that his parents owned the restaurant "Stag" in Notzingen, close to my mother's home town.

One of her brothers had even worked in that restaurant and may well have held the little Niefer in his arms. My mother still remembers walking the 14-kilometer return trip from Wendlingen to Notzingen in order to pay a "little visit" to the Stag. Once Werner Niefer discovered that we were from the same region, he reverted to our local dialect whenever we met.

We met rather frequently. McKinsey was hired to analyze the entirety of Daimler's German plants, which was in no small part due to Niefer's influence. He wanted all of his plants to focus on performance and results, and to prevent overheads from getting out of hand. A personal relationship of trust developed, such that we discussed many topics unrelated to McKinsey projects.

One recurring topic was his disappointment about not having been picked for the top job when the then CEO Gerhard Prinz suddenly died in 1983. He never got over it. We discussed the attempt to create an aeronautics company under the Daimler roof, and we also exchanged views on creating a new holding company structure, which got him the CEO job at the automobile subsidiary Mercedes. Other topics from his network found their way on to the agenda, and he usually asked for my advice during weekend phone calls: "Could you perhaps take a look at this?"

Our families had developed such a close friendship that he even visited my mother in Neckarhausen for meals of a regional dumpling specialty called "Maultaschen", or he gave her a ride back on his plane from a sanatorium in Kärnten.

We were shocked when Werner Niefer died shortly after he retired, at the age of 64. His memorial service in Notzingen will remain unforgettable, where he was buried to the sound of Ludwig Uhland's 1809 poem *I had a companion*. I am still in contact with his wife and son.

Not all client contacts lasted for a longer period of time or took a personal character. The following took place in northern Germany. McKinsey had done a project for an automotive supplier, for which we charged 800,000 marks. The company's CEO called me and said that our invoice significantly exceeded his estimate, he had only earmarked the sum of 200,000 marks which was all he could pay us. He suggested to simply not charge anything, in which case we would be mandated for another project in the following year.

I was speechless, but then recovered and told him that we had done what was expected of us and that he should pay our invoice. The CEO then replied asking me to take an entrepreneurial stance: making an investment in this relationship now would certainly pay off later. Our conversation was rather unpleasant, but as McKinsey's office manager, my job was to establish a clear position. We had provided a service for which the client had to pay. I certainly didn't order their products and then say: "Just give them to me for free, and I am sure to come back."

On my return to Dusseldorf, I dictated a letter unequivocally requesting payment. The money finally arrived.

Consulting projects in the financial-services industry remained exceptional. During the early eighties, Commerzbank, for the first time, decided to implement the overhead value analysis, which McKinsey had developed and perfected. We won the mandate, which was my first banking project. I have never experienced a company where management mocked competitors as much as Commerzbank management did. It looked almost as if the company was running all on its own, since top management's attention was clearly devoted to other topics than running the bank. Later, when I conveyed these impressions to Martin Kohlhaussen, my fellow Hochtief board member and former Commerzbank CEO, he readily agreed. He very energetically reoriented Commerzbank's strategy, which had a long-term effect on its corporate culture.

I worked on other projects in the financial-services area, but neither of those turned me into a banking specialist, as I remained an 'industrial man' at heart. We participated in a project to develop options for Dresdner Bank's future and were caught unawares when all of a sudden a merger between Deutsche Bank and Dresdner Bank, – called an 'Uberbank' by *Business Week*, was looming on the horizon. Deutsche Bank's investment bankers ultimately killed the merger and the transaction fell through at the last moment.

We also played a role in Allianz's takeover of Dresdner Bank. Allianz's plan was to turn the bank into a natural distribution channel for their insurance products. It turned out to be Allianz's worst investment, among other things because the concept of a bancassurance group had not been fully internalized by employees. People turn to banks in order to invest their money or to apply for a mortgage, whereas an insurance salesman knocks on people's doors to sell his services. These two worlds don't meet. Allianz sold Dresdner Bank to Commerzbank, after taking hefty write-downs on the value of the participation. My former colleague Martin Blessing, the new CEO of Commerzbank, made good progress in integrating the two banks.

We did a presentation in 1989 for the biggest German commercial bank, Deutsche Bank, where we explained to Herrhausen that it made more sense for them to sell their stakes in industrial companies and to expand their banking activities abroad in order to become a real global player. They executed this strategy by acquiring BAI (the former Bank of America) in Italy, British investment bank Morgan Grenfell as well as Bankers Trust Company in New York.

Alfred Herrhausen called me one night to announce that Deutsche Bank intended to acquire Roland Berger strategy consultants. I was aware that Deutsche Bank was interested in us. Their "chief ideologist" Johannes Wieland had inquired several times whether it appeared possible for them to take a stake in McKinsey. After we responded with an unambiguous "no", it was clear that they were looking to buy another consulting company. I thanked Herrhausen for the information, but told him that I didn't think this step made sense. Conflicts of interest between bank and consulting company were simply far too great, and business clients were unlikely to consider them independent advisers. But I was too late; the decision had already been made.

Berger made a spectacularly weak presentation on the Japanese banking market at the occasion of the first event dedicated to the reorganization, but sending him packing wasn't really an option. After all, he was now part of the family. After a few years, however, consulting ceased to be considered part of Deutsche Bank's core activities and subsequently was sold.

Herrhausen deserves credit for letting us continue with the lead role on the reorganization. He continued to sell Deutsche Bank's industrial stakes and to further develop international banking activities.

By the end of the eighties, Herrhausen was aiming to reorient Deutsche Bank and to implement clearer structures. He wanted to increase the efficiency of their German branches (which operated with a fair degree of independence). Another goal was to upgrade Private Banking (the bank's favorite business area was corporate banking), and to create a "shared services" department where all shared activities such as IT, marketing or corporate real-estate services were centralized. The intention was to not only introduce this new structure to all branches, but also to reflect it at board level. Until that time, each board member performed a number of tasks, which included being in charge of specific branches or geographic areas in addition to their technical area of competence.

These structures were supposed to be streamlined and clearer areas of responsibility were to be established.

Deutsche Bank's board, led by Alfred Herrhausen, met on November 21, 1989 to discuss such reorganization. I wasn't there, but heard from Herrhausen afterwards that he felt like a boxer after 12 rounds at the end of the event. His fellow board members talked and talked, and the more they talked the less they knew what they wanted to discuss. Things remained vague.

Herrhausen wasn't overly amused by his colleagues' behavior. Four days later, he was at my house in Munich together with German minister of economy Helmut Haussmann and publisher Hubert Burda. After Deutsche Bank's CEO described his state of exhaustion, Burda suggested that he take a two-year sabbatical from Deutsche Bank in order to exclusively focus on economic reunification issues.

This was my last encounter with Alfred Herrhausen. Five days later, on November 30, 1989, he was assassinated by terrorists.

At that time, banks were not our main clients. A study for Krupp Industrietechnik in the mid 1980s led to a contact with Berthold Beitz, the grand old man of Krupp AG. I saw him regularly and could even sit at his side and participate in meetings when he interrogated board members and discussed deviations from forecasts. His style was to ask me afterwards what I thought about various people.

This was a critical period for Krupp, which wasn't doing too well. When one day Dieter Spethmann, CEO of Krupp's competitor Thyssen, showed up at Beitz's office to disclose that he wanted to acquire Krupp, Beitz called me and told me about this outrageous offer. I had to travel to New York for McKinsey on that day but promised that I would give him my thoughts once I arrived in New York.

I developed an aggressive defence strategy on two pages which consisted of turning the tables on Thyssen AG by making an offer for it. Spethmann wasn't pleased and in particular because Beitz called Günter Vogelsang, president of Thyssen's supervisory board and a former Krupp executive. Vogelsang did not know anything about Spethmann's plans or at least pretended not to. Thus both groups remained independent because the time wasn't right for such a type of merger. But several years later they started by integrating their steel divisions and subsequently completed a full merger.

During the 1950s, Berthold Beitz, a close confidante of the industrialist Alfred Krupp, had become executive manager of the Krupp group. After Krupp's death, Beitz became the executor of his will and head of the Krupp foundation, which held a majority stake in Krupp. Beitz was without any doubt a great, historic figure of the Ruhr area but he wasn't uncontroversial. Businesses didn't like the fact that he was in favour of workers' participation and when banks annoyed him, he used to say "my divisions are close to the Left." He never denied being close to the workers' side.

On the occasion of one of his frequent tussles with the holding company board members, I wrote him a very critical letter about his mistakes. I explained that at times he was too impatient and withdrew his support for executives too early if the results didn't turn out as planned. Beitz was so unruffled that he showed the letter to his closest associates. He was 78 years old at that time. Beitz once arranged for us to do a study on the future of the International Olympic Committee (IOC) of which he was a member. My colleague Lukas Muehlemann and I analysed the organization and suggested to its Spanish president

Juan Antonio Samaranch to restructure and separate the commercial side from the games. We received a rather harsh reaction with respect to our organizational idea: "This is the dumbest thing I have heard," Samaranch said. "If you don't have money, you don't have power." The IOC's new orientation was finished before it started. Beitz liked our concept because he thought that the IOC President was way too powerful.

My relationship with Beitz continued to his death. He became something akin to an idol for me which probably also had something to do with the fact that he saved the lives of hundreds of Jews during the National Socialist regime. I once told him that I would have liked to be like him had I been an adult under the National Socialist regime. He replied that I would have probably been the type of guy the Nazis would have targeted.

In addition to old industry, we also dealt with software companies. My childhood friend, Ulrich Brixner, former CEO of DZ Bank, put me in touch with Dietmar Hopp, one of SAP's co-founders. After a couple of meetings, Hopp offered me a seat on SAP's supervisory board, which I couldn't accept because such mandates were not compatible with my McKinsey role.

However, our contact resulted in McKinsey receiving a project for the first time from SAP. Our task was to determine how SAP should best position itself in order to do business with the financial-services industry. We presented our results to CEO Hasso Plattner, who was also one of the four founders of SAP.

It was a memorable event, as Plattner knew everything better, specifically with respect to technological issues. A few years of intensive cooperation followed and Dietmar Hopp and I developed a close working relationship. I liked the down-to-earth approach of the former IBM employee who had set up his own business together with three colleagues and unexpectedly became rich. He reacted very harshly when he heard that SAP engineers had acted like Lord Muck at the airport.

Dietmar Hopp and Hasso Plattner were an ideal match. One of them dealt with numbers and the other with technological solutions.

I met Hopp frequently over the last few years when FC Bayern played TSG 1899 Hoffenheim, the tradition-rich football club where he had played in his youth and where he became the lead sponsor and led to the German professional soccer league.

Henning Kagermann succeeded Plattner as SAP's CEO. We also worked well together. We even developed the idea of a Newco, that is a new joint-venture company for SAP and McKinsey in the area of integrated system solutions. My partners at McKinsey however didn't approve this project out of deference to IBM and other clients.

CHAPTER 20

SCANDALS
SURROUNDING
CO-OP & CO

AND COMRADE SCHRODER

I had first studied trade unions during my days at university. Ferdinand Lassalle and August Bebel were the thought leaders of the German labor movement; Karl Marx and Friedrich Engels had first broached the issue of the opposition between labor and capital. These historical figures caught my interest. Otto von Bismarck, the first Chancellor of the German Empire, had prosecuted trade-union representatives with his 'Socialist laws' and had introduced social security in order to take the wind out of their sails. Hitler threw trade unionists into concentration camps. All of that contributed to trade unions occupying a prominent place in my perception of history. In addition, my maternal grandfather Rudolf Brenner was a stalwart social democrat. He worked as a carpenter and farmer, and he and his wife Marie had 11 children.

During my time at McKinsey, I monitored the political path of the trade unionists, particularly as they played an important role in the Bonn political power circles. When Willy Brandt was chancellor, he appointed Walter Arendt, head of the miners' trade union, as Minister for Employment and Social Affairs. Other trade-union leaders such as Eugen Loderer (Industrial Metal), Heinz Kluncker (Public Services and Transport) and Heinz-Oskar Vetter (Confederation of German Trade Unions) were powerful figures in the days when Germany was governed by the socialist-liberal coalition.

I was very keen on establishing a good relationship with these parties. One reason for that was that they were too important to be ignored. Another reason was our image. McKinsey was viewed by trade unions as a bunch of cold-blooded cost cutters, who didn't give a damn about jobs. I wanted to do away with this prejudice, and when I met Vetter's assistant Bernd Otto by accident one day, I asked him to organize a meeting with his boss, the president of the Confederation of German Trade Unions.

My colleague Friedrich Schiefer and I went to see Vetter at the old headquarters of the Confederation of German Trade Unions, at that time still located in Düsseldorf. He impressed us with clear economic analyses, and critical comments with respect to German business leaders: "They should be an available force in addition to labor and capital, but they increasingly constitute an issue." He was convinced that the trade unions were actually better at running businesses. After all, they owned the Bank fur Gemeinwirtschaft headed by Walter Hesselbach, who was called the "red Abs" after Deutsche Bank's first post-war CEO. The trade unions owned Volksfürsorge, a huge insurance company, as well as real estate developer Neue Heimat and retailer co-op, the consumer cooperative. These companies all enjoyed a great reputation. They were a source of revenue and power for the trade unions, and also gave shape to the idea of a social economy. They appeared to resolve the conflict between labor and capital, to everyone's benefit.

I stayed in touch with Bernd Otto, and met him repeatedly with the goal of facilitating contact between union officials and McKinsey. We first made inroads with respect to a trade union owned company when Otto was appointed director of human resources at the co-op in Frankfurt. He helped us get in our first study, an economic diagnosis in the area of the social economy.

We analysed co-op's situation and the results were alarming. The company was deeply in debt. They sourced goods at relatively high prices, sold them cheaper than their competitors and at the same time paid higher salaries. Consequently, its financial situation was bad and they were teetering on the brink of insolvency. McKinsey developed a restructuring program, which was executed in the co-op's regional branches, co-op's business being organized along the lines of a federal organization. The restructuring program produced satisfactory results, such that co-op got out of the danger zone and at least reached the break-even point. The fact that the co-op later turned into one of the greatest economic scandals in German post-war history is an entirely different story. The board had diverted company funds to private channels in Switzerland and Liechtenstein and was indicted on counts of breach of trust, false accounting and personal enrichment. Bernd Otto received a prison sentence of four and a half years.

While working on the co-op project, supervisory board president Alfons Lappas put me in touch with Albert Vietor, CEO of Neue

Heimat. This was a housing company owned by the trade unions, which increasingly made its mark on the real-estate development market. Now and then, Neue Heimat built entire parts of towns. These estates were not exactly pretty sights, but they met expectations and tenants for such subsidized housing were happy. When the government led by Willy Brandt and Walter Scheel enacted their revolutionary urban planning programs, causing a huge boom in urban redevelopment, Neue Heimat played a role.

McKinsey was tasked with developing an economic diagnosis for Neue Heimat. When we presented our initial findings to the supervisory board, Germany's most important trade union leaders were sitting at the table – amongst those Eugen Loderer, the former lathe operator from Heidenheim, his big hands betraying a manual worker, and Heinz Kluncker, whose demand of a 10% salary increase for public employees had shaken the government. We recommended new structures for the rapidly growing construction group, delegating more responsibility to its regional organizations. Subsequently, these measures were adopted.

Prior to our study being finished, an internal report found its way to the news magazine *Der Spiegel*. The report discussed an explosive topic that is private dealings of CEO "King" Albert Vietor and several executives at the expense of Neue Heimat. The report must have been passed on to the *Spiegel* by the secretarial services of the board and led to a front-page story in the June 1982 edition: "Neue Heimat: The shady affairs of Vietor and the comrades". The article caused a huge scandal, and Neue Heimat never recovered. Later, it was sold for one mark to a bakery group and then became insolvent.

McKinsey took on other projects for trade-union owned companies, in order to continuously combat prejudice. For example, we worked with Volksfürsorge, the Bank fur Gemeinwirtschaft and BGAG. The latter functioned as a holding company for the unions' various participations. Its task was to make sure that membership contributions of the then nine million members of the Confederation of German trade unions were invested in a meaningful way, and to grow the unions' assets. Our job was to develop a fitting strategy and controlling system. Unfortunately, it became clear fairly soon that there was an overwhelming need for immediate restructuring, but the long-term liquidity prospects were not great. Lappas was sentenced to a prison term in 1994 during the course of the co-op scandal, and that marked the end of my contact with the trade unions' economic affairs.

Our work for the trade unions and their businesses helped us establish a reputation less tarnished by prejudice. Labor leaders, officials and employee representatives stopped viewing us as cost cutters, responsible for mass firings and business-related redundancies. They saw us more as independent advisers who had nothing against employees, but who could contribute a lot when it came to the strategic positioning of a company.

But the concept of social economy failed. The carefree package for the worker who shopped at Konsum, bought insurance from Volksfürsorge, purchased his house from Neue Heimat, all of that financed by Bank fur Gemeinwirtschaft, remained an illusion. All of the trade unions' businesses were sold or liquidated, as they were unable to compete and because union leaders are not the better managers.

When I heard about these wheelings and dealings, I thought: the higher you climb the further you fall. I knew Otto, Hoffmann, Kaspar and Werner really well, they had been clients for a long time. But I couldn't fathom why all these frauds happened. It had certainly looked somewhat strange how they built up the boards, drove expensive cars and paid themselves high salaries. They were a clique, that helped each other get rich, poked fun at trade union officials and thought that no-one would notice the false accounting. They were light years away from people like Vetter, Loderer or Hesselbach.

Media clients were a different kettle of fish. When Bertelsmann founder Reinhard Mohn decided to relinquish management duties and to join the supervisory board, he looked for an appropriate structure for his group. On the one hand, he wanted to effectively retain control as he remained the majority shareholder, on the other hand he wanted to install a top management team to run the business and make sure that they were given all the opportunities to develop on a professional level. McKinsey organized a trip to the US for Mohn so that he could take a first-hand look at how US media groups were run.

I accompanied him to visit 12 companies. We met with top executives such as Reginald H. Jones of General Electric, the grand old man of US industry, and Arthur O. Sulzberger of the *New York Times*. In addition, we met with top management of Dow Jones, Times Warner Inc. and Twentieth Century Fox. In the end, we concluded that Bertelsmann needed a supervisory board much more involved with company strategy than the classic German supervisory board, which exercised a pure control function.

We conducted one of the last interviews on this matter with Manfred Fischer, whom Reinhard Mohn had installed in the meantime as his major domo. We asked him what he as CEO expected from the supervisory board, and Fischer replied somewhat cheekily: "I expect to be left in peace." Afterwards, Mohn said, somewhat resigned: "I told you so!" I knew that this was the beginning of the end of Fischer's short tenure as CEO.

Six months later, Fischer was replaced by Mark Wössner. Wössner worked with Mohn much better than Fischer could have ever done. Under his leadership, the company became very successful, and revenues and profits increased significantly. McKinsey's work for Wössner, while competing somewhat with the very confident management, focused on identifying areas to further improve this first-rate company.

We had an inauspicious start. Wössner was still Deputy CEO when I met him for the first time in Gütersloh. He told me that I needed to know that no consultant had ever presented an idea that he didn't have or could have had himself.

Wössner's creed was what he called "distancing". He wanted to have at his disposal the best technology in all areas, significantly ahead of the competition – and he generally succeeded. He also thought that the best young people should come to work for Bertelsmann. He was the only German CEO noticed by business schools, and managed to convince young Americans, French or British that Gütersloh was the Mecca of the media industry. One employee representative commented that Wössner alone turned the Mohn family into billionaires and that speaks for itself. Under Wössner, Bertelsmann became a truly excellent company which could hold its own against the best in the world. One can only speculate what would have become of the company if the Wössner-Middelhoff tandem had remained at the helm. I never understood why Wössner didn't get the recognition due to him, which should have catapulted him into the managers' "Hall of Fame". The former client became a close friend.

Mark Wössner was a demanding businessman, and he turned Bertelsmann into a global leader. When his tenure as CEO ended, he joined the Bertelsmann Foundation. While Reinhard Mohn considered the foundation his baby and managed it correspondingly (sometimes he took charge, sometimes he kept it on a long leash, sometimes a project was done in Gütersloh, sometimes elsewhere in the Republic), Wössner wanted to organize things professionally, with a clear strategy and clearly defined responsibilities. After Wössner handed over management of the company to Thomas Middelhoff, the idea was for him to continue for ten years at the top of the company, as president of the supervisory board and Head of the Bertelsmann Foundation. But he left the company after a disagreement with Reinhard Mohn over the hiring strategy for international executives, and moved to Munich.

Bertelsmann remained a client under Thomas Middelhoff. I enjoyed working with him, as he was very active and wanted to move the company to the digital age. When Gerd Schulte-Hillen, the newly appointed head of the supervisory board and former CEO of Bertelsmann print media subsidiary Gruner + Jahr threw in the towel in May 2002, he called me in despair and asked me to become president of the supervisory board. He said that Mohn had already agreed to it. I hesitantly accepted, but Schulte-Hillen changed his mind the next day and went to Mohn to revoke his resignation. A little later, Middelhoff lost his job after a dispute with Mohn and his fellow board members.

There were also extremely difficult cases. It wasn't exactly easy for a consultant to work with Deutsche Bahn. When Reiner Maria Gohlke was at the helm of Deutsche Bahn, from 1981 to 1991, we noticed that our proposals immediately landed at the Finance Ministry in Bonn. That led to an appointment with the later President of the Federal Republic Horst Köhler, then Under Secretary for Finance. While Deutsche Bahn lost market share in freight, it would have to be prepared for the new age.

Turning an agency like Deutsche Bahn into a commercial enterprise presented an immense challenge. However, Deutsche Bahn had dispatched excellent staff to the team we worked with, which made things a bit easier. McKinsey worked on important strategy issues for the subsequent CEOs Heinz Dürr, Johannes Ludewig and Hartmut Mehdorn. When finally my long-time friend Rudiger Grube took over as CEO, I had already retired from McKinsey and worked as an independent adviser. From my perspective, managing Deutsche Bahn is probably the toughest challenge on offer for a German executive.

We also worked with Deutsche Post and Deutsche Telekom and helped turn a government agency and a public sector company into powerful, listed companies. I considered it a personal challenge to work with my old colleague and fellow mountaineer Klaus Zumwinkel. I wasn't personally involved in projects at McKinsey, but I was for Deutsche Post, because Zumwinkel, who had spent 12 years at McKinsey, attached great importance to my keeping an eye on them, which I did, to our mutual benefit. At the same time, I advised him with respect to his future role with Deutsche Post. He was extremely strict when it came to the use of company property and paid for each stamp he took for personal purposes. He had inherited assets in Switzerland and probably hoped that these would be forgotten.

My personal view is that his engagement for a minimum salary, at that time against the Christian Democratic Party's views, was a major factor in him being downright humiliated. The way in which he was taken into custody by police in his house in Cologne had little to do with human dignity. Worse tax evaders have been treated with more dignity.

Zumwinkel understood that he made a big mistake for which he paid dearly with the loss of all of his functions in addition to the fine imposed by a judge. It was out of the question to expel him from our mountaineering club, the Similauner.

Thomas von Mitschke was a great project manager for the Deutsche Post account, so that it wasn't necessary for me to review the results. It would have required an enormous effort for which I simply didn't have the time. I did the same with Zumwinkel as I did later with Werner Seifert, CEO of Deutsche Borse: I regularly got a general overview. Both companies Deutsche Post and Deutsche Borse, metamorphosed from dull agencies into competitive international businesses.

The wonderful turnaround story of adidas AG was particularly inspiring. The company had been without a leader after Adolf Dassler died in 1978. Dr Albert Henkel, a lawyer representing the family, seized the opportunity to create a powerful position for himself in the post-Dassler era. Unfortunately, he knew very little about the branded company's business, which soon led to an existential crisis. I will never forget how Dassler's four daughters, who approached me through Christoph Malms in our Zurich office, asked me to tell him that his time was up. The general view was that Dr Henkel had overplayed his hand; he should be fired and replaced by a "real" CEO. Malms and I discussed the qualifications required of a future CEO of the sporting-goods manufacturer. We agreed that the Swiss manager Rene C. Jäggi should be appointed.

Henkel now had to be informed of the new developments. I told him that the shareholders wanted to pull the plug on the current business relationship. He was visibly dismayed and asked for time when he heard that I had been mandated by the shareholders to deliver the message. He almost threw a fit when he heard that the shareholders were waiting in the next room. He stormed out of the office and was driven back to Herzogenaurach, adidas Group's global headquarters seat. The shareholders were grateful, and Jäggi was enthroned.

I watched the company's future development very closely. After a few turbulent years and several ownership changes, Robert Louis-Dreyfus managed to turn adidas around and it became profitable again. Herbert Hainer, another mountaineering friend and soccer enthusiast, has been leading the company for the last 13 years with great success.

Personally, I wasn't always successful with clients, as demonstrated by the following cases documented by press coverage. Commerzbank's board compared me to an architect who wanted to rebuild the entire house at the occasion of a basement renovation. Then there was the case of Höchst, where I was involved in a heated argument with CEO Wolfgang Hilger in presence of the entire board. The altercation helped my internal standing, but I caught a lot of flak with Höchst. Finally, I would mention the case of Grundig, where Max Grundig initially praised us to the skies based on Berthold Beitz's recommendation, but subsequently tried to shoot the messenger when we presented a highly critical report.

Our relationship with Volkswagen was off to a rocky start. One day, I got a call from Niedersachsen prime minister Gerhard Schröder asking whether McKinsey could do a project about a potential turnaround of Osnarbrück car company Karmann – Karman produced the Karmann Ghia line of cars for VW. The cost would be split between the state government and Volkswagen AG. We produced a project schedule and prepared for a trip to Osnarbrück in order to develop an initial analysis, when we received a call from VW headquarters. They considered the trip pointless and suggested that we should instead simply determine in close cooperation with VW's finance department which Karmann resources were useful for VW, and that was all. Some toing and froing ensued, as we wanted to develop a proper analysis of Karmann's situation, and VW wanted a valuation of the human assets they were going to acquire.

When we came to a standstill, I called Gerhard Schröder and relayed the conflicting positions. The prime minister laughed and said that VW CEO "Ferdinand" (Ferdinand Piech) was a particularly hard-nosed guy, but that these issues could be resolved in a meeting of all relevant parties. Schröder then summoned Piech, VW CFO Bruno Ardelt, Wilhelm Karmann jr., Karmann CEO Rainer Thieme, and myself and Felix Brück of McKinsey. The meeting was scheduled for 9 am in the parliament's restaurant in Hannover, where the chairs were still standing on the tables.

When Ferdinand Piech arrived, he told me and Felix Brück succinctly: "That's something you'll do once and once only." As I tried to explain how this meeting came about, he repeated several times: "That's something you'll do once and once only." Schröder kept us waiting for half an hour. When he arrived, cheerful as always, and said that the meeting had been my idea, I wished that the earth would swallow me up.

We debated the issue for some time, and everyone held opposing views. All of a sudden, Schröder said: "But I don't think you're that far apart. With a bit of goodwill, you should be able to resolve the issue." He then left, citing pressing matters of state, which had to be attended to. Piech and Ardelt left without a backward glance, Thieme thanked us and we looked crestfallen.

I had met Piech a couple of times in Wolfsburg and the meetings had been very professional. He said what he wanted, and we considered whether we could provide any help. Already in those days, I had to give it to him that he knew his cars backwards. Actually, things were not that bad and the fact that he had McKinsey was an expression of esteem. What he didn't like was that we didn't function as he saw fit and that he had been summoned to Hannover by his "majority shareholder". He was visibly furious.

Shortly thereafter, Schröder called me into his office. He sat there, cigar in hand, and told me not to be so sensitive and that we should conduct our study as planned. Shutting down Karmann was not an option for him, in stark contrast to Piech who wanted nothing more than to close Karmann's operations down. Schröder wanted to save Karmann's 6,000 jobs by all means, and that was what happened at that time. However, in April 2009, the small carmaker became insolvent.

CHAPTER 21

CLIMBING MOUNT CHIMBORAZO WITH REINHOLD MESSNER

OR WHO IS THE BETTER MANAGER?

Climbing Mount Everest without oxygen? Experts considered it physiologically impossible, as no human being could survive at an altitude of 8,850 meters without supplementary oxygen. Reinhold Messner thought: I will give it a try and prove that it's possible. Indeed, he climbed the world's highest mountain in 1978 without any supplementary oxygen and lived to tell the tale. He gave an interview, which I watched on TV. I was fascinated by this unstoppable young mountaineer.

My friend Christian Neureuther, winner of several Ski World Cups during the 1970s, knew Messner personally and told me: "If ever you'd like to engage Messner for a presentation, I'll be happy to organize it." An opportunity arose in the summer of 1981 at a McKinsey partner meeting in Munich. I wanted to introduce the McKinsey people to an utterly exceptional person, hoping that the encounter would provide them with a lasting benefit.

I received Reinhold Messner on the third and last day of the event during the afternoon at the hotel Bayerischer Hof. He was 37 years old and appeared almost boyish. His beard wasn't quite as full as it is now. When he began his presentation, the room fell quiet. He talked about the changes in extreme mountaineering since the British mountaineers Andrew Comyn Irvine and George Lee Mallory died on June 8, 1924 during the first ascent of Mount Everest. Or since Austrian mountaineer Hermann Buhl, the first person to ascend Nanga Parbat in 1953, and several years later fell to his death when a cornice dropped on him while climbing Chogolisa in Pakistan (7,654 meters). Messner explained the progress made in mountaineering equipment since that time, and what differentiated the modern mountaineer from his ancestors.

We were addressed by a man who had proved that he was capable of incredible physical and mental performance, and who also got to the bottom of technical, ecological and philosophical questions of mountaineering like virtually no-one else. My 130 McKinsey colleagues sensed that he was part of a very special breed.

After this event, I wanted to know more about Reinhold Messner. Why did he climb mountains and why did he climb them the way he did? I read a lot of his works and materials on him and invited him twice more to give presentations, and we became friends. We started to meet socially, and once with our families on Messner's castle Juval in the South Tyrolean mountains near Meran.

When I turned 50 in 1991, my separation from Rosemarie was quite recent and I didn't feel like celebrating. Nevertheless, I organized a celebration with friends, Reinhold Messner amongst them. He presented me with a climbing rope and said: "Take it as a symbol. What just happened to you is like when a rope team separates. That happens frequently, but not during a mountain tour, that's where people stay together. Why don't you take up mountaineering? I know Robert Schwan, the soccer club executive, and he took it up at the age of 60. You are only 50, give it a try!" He then proceeded to invite me to accompany him on an expedition to Ecuador to trace the trail of Alexander von Humboldt up to Mount Chimborazo, which was going to be filmed by the German TV channel (ZDF) for its *Terra X* series. Messner said: "You will star in this movie!" I replied: "I may possess a few talents, but climbing a 6,000-meter high peak doesn't feature prominently amongst them!" I had been hiking mountains, but that was quite different from actually climbing them. Reinhold Messner was unperturbed and simply said: "You'll do just fine, just tag along." ZDF editor Michael Albus was sceptical. He had provided funding for the operation and thought that I posed a risk for the project. When the three of us met in Messner's Munich apartment prior to the start of the project, Albus asked whether I was sufficiently experienced and what my role was. But Reinhold simply said: "He is my friend, and he'll accompany us." Albus clearly wasn't too happy with the situation. Perhaps a recent efficiency study conducted by McKinsey for the ZDF played a role, as the study hadn't exactly increased our popularity with ZDF staff. Perhaps he was worried that I might throw in the towel. In any event, the ZDF representative continued to pester Messner on the flight to Quito, telling him that "the inexperienced Henzler" constituted a significant risk, while he himself had recently scaled Mount Ortler.

The first practical test came shortly after we arrived in the Ecuadorian capital, during our first training climb on Mount Pichincha, a local mountain close to Quinto. After reaching the summit, we encountered a crevice of a width of about one and a half meters, while descending through a less steep area. There were two ways across: either we had to jump, carrying a backpack weighing 15 kilos, or we had to circumvent it by marching for approximately one and a half hours. Messner jumped across the crevice like a chamois. While Michael Albus was still hesitating, I took a run up and jumped. Then Messner and I lay in the grass for an hour and a half because Albus very reasonably had decided to circumvent the obstacle.

A few weeks later, the ground was sufficiently frozen so that we set out for our climb up Mount Chimborazo. This is a volcano, 6,267 meters high. When Alexander von Humboldt tried to scale it towards the end of the 18th century, it was still considered the world's highest mountain. Humboldt and his friend Aimé Bonpland thought that they had reached heights that were yet unknown, but they didn't make it to the summit. In his novel *Measuring the World*, author Daniel Kehlmann describes the pair debating whether they should claim having reached the summit, when they were forced to abort the ascent. But Humboldt and Bonpland resisted the temptation. We wanted to trace Humboldt's trail as closely as possible in the first place, and subsequently take Whymper's route to the summit. Of course, we had a distinct advantage as our equipment was certainly many times superior to that used by Humboldt, 200 years ago. In addition, mountaineering techniques had improved drastically from Humboldt to Messner.

Marco Cruz, the "Messner of the Andes", and three of his Ecuadorian aides wanted to take us and our camera team to the summit in one go, which presented a significant challenge. Three of us went up on a rope, Reinhold Messner in front, me in the middle and Michael Albus at the rear. It was so dark that I couldn't see the person in front, but only feel his presence via the rope. The tightening of the rope signalled that we could continue. If the rope slackened, it was time to stop. It was freezing cold, and a storm raged in the mountain.

We couldn't see the danger, but we felt its presence. Climbing Mount Chimborazo was an extreme adventure for me, which took me to my limits. The thunderous, frozen darkness caused me to think a few times about how nice it would be to just lie down. The struggle and pain would be over. But then Reinhold Messner pulled on the rope and somehow we continued. Unlike Alexander von Humboldt, I hadn't left a farewell letter, but I had previously thought about what could happen to me. I can't remember the title of the book in which the author describes in great detail how he suffered from appendicitis high up in the mountains, with no help in sight. I discussed this with Reinhold Messner, whose job was to expose himself to borderline situations. It is not possible to just quit or call a doctor or the mountain rescue service. I was aware of that fact, but there's a difference between thinking about these situations at home in front of the fire or actually being in such an extreme situation, where no mistakes are allowed but lots of bad things can happen.

I learned the value of a rope team at Mount Chimborazo. Members entirely depend on each other. You can't step away, whatever happens. I had gone to my physical limits, and Michael Albus wasn't doing much better. The decisive factor was that Reinhold Messner could be relied on. My trust in him gave me strength and confidence. This feeling of trust still exists today, for which I will be eternally grateful to him, as well as for introducing me to real mountaineering. He showed me a new world, which I still enjoy. Messner once told me an anecdote about when he climbed in the mountains with a couple of sherpas (inhabitants of the national park surrounding Mount Everest), when they all of a sudden, without rhyme or reason, stopped climbing and sat down on their packs. When he asked why they had stopped, they replied: "Our souls were not able to move at that pace, and we have to wait for them." In today's globalized world, there is indeed a question as to whether our souls can keep up with the pace of change.

During this expedition to the Andes, the idea of the Similaun Club took shape. Messner and I were sitting in a base camp at the foot of Mount Chimborazo, waiting for the weather to improve. We did some brainstorming, which led to a book entitled *Moving Mountains*. We couldn't start the ascent while it was snowing, so we talked about the entire world and his wife. I asked Messner: "What would you have done if you hadn't become a master of extreme mountaineering?" Messner replied: "I probably would have become an executive or businessman, as these professions provide you with the opportunity to shape things."

We talked about parallels between mountaineering and management, about the creative power required both at the top of a company and at the top of a mountain, the courage to do things out of the ordinary, energy, and knowledge of one's limits, I said: "Maybe we should organize a tour with a couple of top executives. I know quite a few and could bring them together." Messner agreed, and that was the start of it.

Back home after climbing Mount Chimborazo, we started to prepare for the first meeting. Messner was in charge of planning the mountaineering part, and I organized the supporting program and helped put together the group. I approached colleagues, friends and companions. They needed to be physically fit, enjoy adventures, enjoy mountaineering and had to get along well. There was a great deal of interest, and soon we had put together the group, which was to be called "Similauner". Amongst its members were Ulrich Cartellieri, member of the board of Deutsche Bank, E.on CEO Klaus Pilz who unfortunately died shortly thereafter in an avalanche accident, Munich publisher Hubert Burda, my then McKinsey colleague and future Deutsche Post CEO Klaus Zumwinkel, Jürgen Schrempp, who had just been promoted to the top job of Daimler, Wolfgang Reitzle, then Head of Research and Development at BMW and later CEO of Linde, my old friend Axel Munte an exceptionally gifted medical doctor, Cologne Re CEO Jürgen Zech, Peter Hoch, member of the board of HypoVereinsbank, Thorlef Spickschen, head of BASF's pharmaceutical division, Ihno Schneevoigt, Head of HR at Allianz, Reinhold's brother Hubert Messner, a doctor based in Bolzano, and Reinhold and myself. Axel Munte, whom I had met while at university, was our doctor. He had given a demonstration of his medical skills during his residency, when he diagnosed my occasional heart palpitations as Wolff-Parkinson-White syndrome (WPW), a cardiological anomaly having something to do with the impact of electrons on the heart. On a personal level, I had helped him and his wife Heidi to restructure a textile business. Many fellow mountaineers use Axel as the first port of call after mountain tours because of his extensive medical experience.

We met one afternoon in July 1993 in a restaurant in the Schnalstal, a valley at the foot of Mount Similaun, a 3,597-meter mountain in the Ötztal Alps in South Tyrol. We took the cable railway up to a height of 3,000 meters, where we started our tour. In groups of three, we climbed up to Similaun Inn, located at Niederjoch at a height of 3,019 meters. This alpine shelter is more than 100 years old and is simply furnished. The innkeeper is permitted to reserve a few rooms so that we didn't have to sleep on mattresses, which unannounced guests have to do.

The first climb already showed differences in members' strength and skills. Experienced mountaineers such as Ulrich Cartellieri and Peter Hoch did well, but members of the less experienced group had difficulties. The challenge however was similar for all of us. For example, Hubert Burda ("I am the tail-end Charlie!") was so out of shape that Reinhold Messner asked me in the evening: "How could you invite this guy? You have to send him home tomorrow." I tried to calm Reinhold down and Hubert Burda proved to be a tenacious fighter, which came as a big surprise to Messner. We tried to help Burda by distributing some of his load amongst ourselves. After reaching the summit, the brave publisher had to follow Ihno Schneevoigt and his guide Ernst, who took an easier descent from Mount Similaun (whereas we chose a more difficult snowfield). But he fought and persevered. A year later, he joined us in climbing Mount Ortler and proved to be in great shape.

Even back then, we discussed current topics after we got back to the shelter from our mountain tours. If memory serves me right, our first topic was the European Monetary System (EMS), which stirred people's minds at that time. Later, we provided a clearer structure for the discussion part of our annual Similaun meetings by distributing reading assignments to participants, who had to explain the gist of their readings prior to the start of the discussions. Today, it is customary that Similaun members do a presentation which will then be subject of a debate. For example, Ulrich Cartellieri did a presentation on the financial crisis in 2009, and Herbert Hainer, who had recently joined the group, did one on adidas as a "global player". Debates were frequently heated, often until sparks flew. From time to time, we even voted in order to show the diversity of opinion generated by these confrontational discussions.

The first tour after our four-day meeting ended at Reinhold Messner's castle in Juval. We sat together, enjoying each other's company and made plans. Messner pointed out an inscription on his castle: "Vinciturus vincero – those destined to win will win." He recommended this quotation in medieval Latin as a motto for us, a politically organized group which was going to change the world! That didn't happen, even if there were many things we found annoying, such as the sedate and plain politics of then Chancellor Kohl.

We didn't change the world, but our group was in demand. Once word got around as to what we were up to, we were approached – both directly and indirectly- by many who wanted to join. Time and again, I had to make it clear that I wasn't empowered to simply accept new members. Our rules state that every member has to agree to the admission of new members. Indeed, there were cases when a member declared: "If this guy joins, I will leave." Nevertheless, we gradually admitted new members. Over time, other CEOs were carefully selected Jürgen Weber (then Lufthansa), Ulrich Lehner (then Henkel), Georg Kofler (then Premiere), Herbert Hainer (adidas), Jürgen Hambrecht (BASF), René Obermann (then Deutsche Telekom) Klaus Kleinfeld (then Siemens), Kasper Rorsted (then Henkel), Ulrich Wilhelm (Bavarian TV), and Tom Enders (Airbus) were admitted.

Meanwhile, we have in essence become a club of retirees. We still go for mountain climbs in the South Tyrolean Alps each year, together with Reinhold Messner and Hanspeter Eisendle, one of the most experienced mountain guides. We haven't lowered our mountaineering ambitions, but our demands for comfort have increased with age. In 2010, one of our members made the point that he didn't think we should stay in shelters where we had to queue for the only source of water in the morning, toothbrush in hand, exposed to the smell of the person in front. Everyone considered it preferable to stay at a nice inn. We have now rented a room there for our discussions without continuous streams of people asking for Reinhold Messner's autograph.

I have been asked many times why mountaineering attracted managers. I think the reason may be the incredible intensity of such an experience, which is rarely found elsewhere. One gets to know one's body and one's limits. For better or worse, you have to get along with others, eyeball to eyeball. One is exposed to the forces of nature, and one wants to climb higher and higher. Once a peak of 3,000 meters has been climbed, the next step is a 4,000 meter peak. One is also exposed to mountain guides whose mountaineering skills exceed those of the executives by a significant margin.

An executive practicing mountaineering sees new dimensions opening up which are useful in his professional life. He knows that preparation is key, that any tour requires the highest degree of concentration and that things still can go wrong. All kinds of things can happen in the mountains, such as rockfall, or the person in front stumbles or is exhausted and unable to continue. Specifically top executives are in danger of considering themselves infallible after some time in the job. The mountains are a great teacher because one of the conditions of success is to remain aware of danger. There's always something that can go wrong, but absolutely nothing must be allowed to go wrong.

One day prior to our 1994 Ortler tour, a mountaineer fell to his death taking the normal route. When we climbed Mount Cevedale (3,770 meters), we said goodbye to a rope team in the morning at the Casati Alpine hut: a day later, they all perished climbing Mount Königsspitze.

I'd rather not know how many bad investments were made because no-one gave enough thought in the run-up to the fact that the project could also fail, and no-one was willing and courageous enough to say: "We have gone overboard, it is time to cancel the project." Experiencing one's limits as a mountaineer also helps executives: both roles require the ability to give one's all, and it is important to work towards one single point and to drop everything else. One needs the ability to relax, to kick back and to reflect; one needs to relate to others and subordinate oneself, and to correctly assess each situation.

Things only go well in the mountains if one is well anchored, and everyone is able to unconditionally rely upon each other. Otherwise, any ascent would be considered reckless. I like that, and that's perhaps what attracted me to mountaineering late in life.

I am frequently asked whether in our Similaun group strings are pulled, relationships established and deals are made. I think that our group works in the same way as a well-oiled soccer team, provided that not all of our focus and energy is required to make that next step. Whenever we get together or do things together, camaraderie is fostered. I don't know when the term "networking" first appeared in management literature. I never read a book about it. As far as I am concerned, networking is not a means to an end, but rather a fundamental human attitude.

CHAPTER 22

EDMUND STOIBER

THE SLIGHTLY DIFFERENT POLITICIAN

In the early nineties, I started to develop an interest in both mountaineering and Bavarian politics. This led me to meet with the then Prime Minister Edmund Stoiber, whom I met at the FC Bayern Munich soccer club, where he was the president of their advisory board. And when I was a member of the Bavarian-Saxonian development committee ("Miegel-Committee"), I got to appreciate him as an extraordinarily long-term oriented politician. He anticipated early on what it meant for Bavaria if women's participation in business remained at a low level and the number of temporary employment contracts stayed low. During his tenure the role of women increased in politics and business significantly.

During his term as prime minister, he hired McKinsey for a number of projects, for which I was responsible. For example, one project dealt with the issue of how to make best use of subsidies. Would it make sense to pay subsidies to companies in order to attract them to the countryside where they could create jobs? Or was it preferable to focus on strongly developed areas?

Stoiber was fully aware of the fact that it was easier to create a thousand new jobs in Erlangen (a city in Bavaria) rather than in Hof (a town in the same region), but he was aware of the fact that he had to promote more rural areas so as to ensure equal living conditions across the state. I experienced the "art of the possible" in politics, as the fact that the objectively best strategy had to be adapted in such a way that it was considered fair by the population. Edmund Stoiber succeeded brilliantly in this endeavour; he wanted to pave the way for the future for all of Bavaria. From time to time, he and his wife Karin were our guests, and our long-time housekeeper Johanna Schenkl told us that Mr. Stoiber knew the concerns and needs of the "small people" very well. I think this is an appropriate description of Edmund Stoiber.

The project work on economic development done at that time was the basis for consistent promotion of Bavaria's high-tech locations and led to the "laptop and leather pants" strategy. Stoiber wanted to play in the Champion's League of European regions, not unlike his favourite soccer club FC Baycrn.

For an analytically inclined person, it was fascinating to work for him and his highly proficient team consisting of Ulrich Wilhelm, Walter Schön, Karolina Gernbauer, Friedrich Wilhelm Rothenspieler and Martin Neumeyer. Stoiber loved charts and almost devoured their contents. When the McKinsey Shareholder Council met in Munich in 1998, all 21 members around Rajat Gupta lined up in Stoiber's office for a two-hour brainstorming session. This was a unique event in McKinsey history. Stoiber was very sceptical when it came to suggestions, but in the final analysis was a very pleasant client.

Four years later, he became the union parties' candidate for chancellor at the parliamentary elections. For a long time, he led the later social democrat chancellor Gerhard Schröder in the polls. Stoiber was simply viewed as the better chancellor. Six months prior to election day, it looked as if the race was already over. Like many others, I believed that a change of power in Berlin was the will of the voters. As his close adviser, I still don't understand how Stoiber's lead melted away. In the end his advantage was gone as he lacked 6,200 votes. Understandably, this narrow defeat hurt for a long time. I was convinced that he would have become a great chancellor with Lothar Späth as minister of economics and technology for the times. I have always maintained that view and even lost 12 bottles of Zweigelt to Sabine Weber, wife of the former Lufthansa CEO Jurgen Weber, as I had bet on a Stoiber victory. Two outstanding politicians had stood for election, and Stoiber was more than a surrogate.

He achieved more than 60% of the votes in the 2003 state parliamentary elections in his home state of Bavaria, the best result ever. Stagnation or complacency were not part of his vocabulary. He wanted to continue to promote the state, which he had transformed from an agricultural area to a top tech location. Stoiber sold state shareholdings and used the proceeds to develop the requisite infrastructure for high-tech investments. In retrospect, I am pleased that my recommendations resulting from a report on cutting bureaucracy, from my work as a member of the WTB (the scientific and technical advisory committee of the Bavarian government) and the *Bavaria 2020* white paper formed the basis for other changes.

Stoiber reformed the administrative court system and a multitude of guidelines in order to streamline administrative agencies, introducing concepts such as "One-stop agency" or "Sunset" guidelines i.e. if not used they were abolished – Small and medium-sized enterprises received numerous forms of relief, and company formation was simplified. The streamlined administrative structures proved to be a huge benefit for Bavaria as a location for business. Stoiber, following my recommendation, tried to enforce the "Transrapid" train connection because it was the right link to the airport. Unfortunately, the project didn't receive the Christian Democratic Party (CDU) leadership's unconditional support.

Henceforth, Stoiber became a candidate for the positions of President of the EU Commission and the German Presidency. He was an undisputed expert with respect to fiscal and economic policy. For example, he was opposed to Greece entering the European Monetary Union. His star was shining brightly until the 2005 early elections, and strictly speaking also thereafter.

I met Angela Merkel during the World Economic Forum in January 2005 in Davos for a private one-hour meeting. We had a very constructive discussion on a number of topics. Finally, the CDU party's chairwoman said in a very determined manner: "My Dear Mr. Henzler, I know exactly where you're coming from. I know who your master is. You would do everyone a favour if you told him that even if I don't run for chancellor, he will certainly not run a second time. In this case, Koch or Wulff would be chosen." The chancellor later hinted at my role of "Stoiber's adviser" when speaking to a group of businessmen.

Back in Munich, I went to see Stoiber to convey Ms Merkel's views. He listened calmly, but I am certain it wasn't the end of his hopes. In Munich, the failure of Ms Merkel's candidature was factored in if the CDU party were to lose the upcoming Schleswig-Holstein and Nordrhein-Westfalen state parliamentary elections. In that case, all bets were off. Things turned out differently, and the CDU managed to get enough votes in both states to lead the state government. I think it's fair to say that Stoiber, for the last time, saw a small chance on the eve of the 2005 parliamentary elections to make history. In the *Berlin Roundtable*, moderated by then ZDF editor-in-chief Nikolaus Brender, Schröder, who had just lost the elections, kicked up a fuss: "You can't be seriously thinking that my party will enter into any dialogue with Ms Merkel." Would the Social Democrats only enter into a coalition with the Christian Democrats if the latter put someone else in charge?

In the end, Merkel and the Social Democrats formed a coalition government. Stoiber was earmarked for Minister of Economics with additional responsibilities for technological areas in a Merkel-Müntefering government, but decided to retreat to Bavaria at the last minute. I am not sure whether I understand Stoiber's motives for forgoing the position offered in Berlin. However, back in Munich he rigorously carried on with his politics. In retrospect, his mantra rings even more true: "Being top means achieving top performance in all areas." He engaged in intense discussions of his plans with the Christian Social Union (CSU) party and its rank-and-file, but it appeared that a number of party leaders turned away from him (not openly, rather covertly). Despite the undisputed success of his economic policies, a balanced budget and an approval rating of 58%, Stoiber was pushed out.

He announced his resignation with effect as of autumn 2007 during the traditional party congress in Wildbad Kreuth in January of that year. But why did they change the locomotive, why did they get rid of their best man? It probably boils down to a combination of two factors. One, after 14 years as prime minister, there's a certain degree of wear and tear. It happened to Adenauer, Kohl and Spath as well. Secondly, and probably more importantly, Gunter Beckstein and Erwin Huber, who were both roughly in the same age group, saw this as their last chance to succeed Stoiber.

I stayed in touch with Stoiber after his fall from power, as I had completed the *Bavaria 2020* project, which was considered as Stoiber's legacy by many CSU party members.

After a period of understandable disappointment, as certain media organizations continued to portray him negatively, he found a new job in Brussels, dealing with cutting bureaucracy amongst other things. He maintains close links not only with Jean-Claude Juncker, president of the EU Commission, Manuel Barroso, his predecessor, and Gunther Oettinger, Digital Economy Commissioner, and also with his old ally Vladimir Putin.

In addition, he became president of a number of advisory boards where his advice is in demand. I experienced in 2011 how clearly Stoiber analyzed the citizens' weariness as to European topics, how he diagnosed problems of the Euro and how he is respected and heard as an elder statesman.

With the benefit of hindsight, the upshot of Stoiber's leaving office at the age of 66 may have been that it enabled him to focus on other areas of interest and to realize that a busy life doesn't necessarily equate to working 24 hours a day, seven days a week.

CHAPTER 23

CONSULTING FOR THE FUTURE

Committees are a widespread phenomenon when it comes to advising governments. Governments appoint committees in order to deal with specific issues. The first committee to which I was appointed was called "Committee for future issues of the Sovereign States of Bavaria and Saxony". As mentioned earlier, it was headed by sociologist Meinhard Miegel, and had been established during the nineties by Bavarian and Saxonian Prime Ministers Edmund Stoiber and Kurt Biedenkopf. I dealt with not only an excellent committee head, but also experienced excellent clients in the form of these two prime ministers. At that time, we predicted that so-called "flaky" employment contracts would increase dramatically ("flaky" was a creation of Miegel describing non-full-time employment contracts, which today amount to 30%). It was confirmed only a few years later that the production-oriented society was a thing of the past. Our request to increase the labor-market participation specifically of women caused quite a stir as well. Finally, our committee offered strong criticism of horizontal revenue equalization between states and recommended that both states bring a lawsuit in the constitutional court in Karlsruhe.

In addition, after my active McKinsey time, I became a member of the Pohl Committee, which was tasked to deliver a report on the reorganization of the German Central Bank and the closure of the State Central Banks (LZB). The committee was named after its president Karl Otto Pohl, former president of the German Central Bank. We recommended a new organizational structure for the bank, which is still in use today; on the other hand, we didn't succeed in shutting down the state central banks. Thus, the North Rhine Westphalia State Central Bank still exists and tries to make monetary policy at Rhine and Ruhr in the age of the Euro.

I also participated in the Baums Committee, named after corporate law scholar Theodor Baums. In 2001, the committee developed the first German corporate governance codex, establishing standards for corporate management and governance. The goal was to turn Germany into a more attractive location for international and domestic investors. We succeeded in establishing simplified structures for shareholder democracy. But we hadn't been given the important task of developing a modern format for shareholder participation and influence. Furthermore, we asked for greater transparency in German corporate governance and noted a lack of independence of supervisory boards. We failed to implement any of these items, which are still as relevant now as they were ten years ago.

Some committees are established as permanent advisory bodies, such as the innovation committee of the German president, which Roman Herzog established in 1997, and of which I was a member. I experienced an extraordinarily analytical president, who challenged committee members time and again to not only criticize the state of affairs, but to point out concrete opportunities for change.

In 2002, Edmund Stoiber appointed me to preside over the Bavarian Deregulation Commission. The commission was made up of members of the Bavarian administration such as Walter Schön, Head of the Bavarian Chancellery, members of the business community such as former BMW CEO Joachim Milberg, presidents of the local chambers of commerce and many other experts. Its task was to comb through the jungle of regulations: where did regulations go beyond the intended target? How could bureaucratic obstacles be eliminated?

While analysing our society tied up in red tape, we diagnosed a number of "endemic" problems. No-one is interested in bureaucratic regulations – but woe betide us if something goes wrong. Politicians and administrative bodies will be publicly accused of failure to implement sufficiently protective rules. As a result, new regulations will be imple- mented in a hurry. The "mad cow disease" provides a striking example. On the one side, farmers were reluctant to accept specific requirements as to the condition of their cowsheds. However, when the first Bavari- an cow died of mad cow disease, it sparked an outcry throughout the entire region. Afterwards, very detailed rules described how cowsheds had to be whitewashed, how passages for removal of manure had to be structured and how remaining forage had to be dealt with.

We experienced a number of similar situations, for example the first rotten meat scandal, the avian flu or the duck disease when 200,000 ducks had to be culled in 24 hours.

According to our analyses, it was clear that our society takes for granted that the government will stand ready to provide help in all sorts of situations. In Munich alone, more than half of all police operations were due to complaints of people keen to take action against neighbours for a variety of reasons, such as noise or parking offenses.

Of course, the government's constant regulatory activity is not exclusively due to pressure from its citizens. For example, technological change causes entirely new issues where regulation is required. Another reason is that bureaucrats themselves and many parliaments try to justify their existence by looking for new areas of regulation. When the commission combed through the bureaucratic thicket, I was reminded of a quote by Frank Josef Strauss, who apparently once observed: "The Ten Commandments contain 279 words, and the American Declaration of Independence 300 words. The EU regulation on import of caramels contains exactly 25,911 words."

What did my commission – established by Stoiber – achieve? After only six months, we delivered a comprehensive report to the Bavarian government, detailing our suggestions for deregulation. One of the tangible results of our report was that registration of a limited liability company now takes only three to four days in Bavaria, instead of six to seven weeks. Requests for building permits have to receive a binding response within four weeks. We achieved several objectives such as a reduction in companies' reporting obligations and numerous other bureaucratic simplifications for small- and medium-sized companies. Our proposal to make the keeping of books and records mandatory as of a revenue threshold of one million euros wasn't accepted. However, the threshold was lifted from 250,000 euros to 350,000, a clear sign that change comes in small doses in Germany.

Our then manifesto stated that company creation should be made easier, that business growth should be promoted and that business's image should be improved. We used a catchy quote by Winston Churchill to introduce our plea for a new and positive outlook for business: "Some people regard private enterprise as a predatory tiger to be shot. Others look on it as a cow they can milk. Not enough people see it as a healthy horse, pulling a sturdy wagon."

The central theme of the commission's report reads as follows: "Innovation, entrepreneurial spirit and willingness to perform are the reasons for employment and economic growth. They are prerequisites for prosperity and a high standard of living, but also for stable social conditions. The main challenge for a government is to make sure not only that these sources don't dry up, but to increase their strength. Only a dynamic economy ensures a high and growing standard of living for everyone and paves the way for general prosperity."

I still subscribe to these conclusions. Our economy can only be successful if it remains competitive in the global division of labor. Innovation continues, and Germany must maintain a leading position. This requires courage, the willingness to quickly react to global developments and constant modernization. Germany's high degree of regulatory activity slows down economic change and interferes with the creation of new and the adaptation of existing companies. An overregulated economy protects what is existing and places new market participants at a disadvantage. It reduces incentives instead of promoting innovation and new activities.

Specifically, Germany as a high-wage country is dependent upon innovation and technological and organizational progress. High wages and high social and ecological standards will only be affordable if innovation occurs at a fast pace. An excellent educational and training system is crucial, as are attractive conditions to promote and reward talent. Germany must convince creative and dynamic young people to stay in Germany and to realize their ideas.

The social market economy must be geared towards rewarding economic performance, personal responsibility and entrepreneurial initiative. We can only adapt to change caused by globalization if we apply a certain degree of flexibility. Economic change must not be viewed as a threat, but rather as an opportunity, and we must make the best of it.

There's not a lack of work, but rather a lack of entrepreneurs. One of the reasons for that is that entrepreneurs don't benefit from high social standing notwithstanding their important social and economic function. Little effort is made to correct this image. Schoolbooks rarely make mention of entrepreneurs and the self-employed. As a result, it doesn't come as a surprise that young people's career aspirations rarely include these professions.

But it makes sense to promote self-employment and entrepreneurship. Statistics show that one new company creates four jobs in three years. If we manage to ignite the spark of business creation within the young generation, we will create the key prerequisite for a dynamic economy.

In a January 1976 interview, *Spiegel* editors asked the following question: "Mr. Henzler, how do you feel about being Germany's number one job-killer?" This stereotype was and still is used for McKinsey, when a whipping boy is needed if companies react to change, adapt to market conditions and inevitably cut jobs. The tougher the competitive situation, the more pressure to cut costs and increase productivity. For certain existing and particularly mature business areas, the replacement of labor by other means of production is the only method worth mentioning. Firms providing advice in this area help to protect the future of our businesses and thus help in saving jobs. That's why I retaliated by pointing out that we had saved numerous jobs and that it was preferable to have 22,000 secure jobs in the automotive supply industry as opposed to 30,000 jobs, which were not that secure. I also emphasized numerous examples where we had instituted sales growth programs. In addition I was asked how I dealt with the trade unions' attacks against McKinsey. I told them that Franz Steinkuhler, who at that time headed the Industrial Metal trade union and sat on Daimler's supervisory board, once said: "McKinsey would have to be invented if it didn't already exist. The trade unions gain new members each time their consultants do a project for a company." When I replied that the trade unions' businesses were in bad shape, he looked rather embarrassed.

It is inevitable that jobs are lost during the transition process from an industrial to a service and knowledge-based economy. But at the same time, new jobs are created because of new products and new industries. While Germans like to look at the economy as something static, it is in reality a dynamic process. In order to reach an overall positive result, companies must prepare in time for structural change, and politicians must provide the framework promoting such dynamism.

In retrospect, I am fairly happy with the results achieved by the deregulation commission. The commission prepared 105 proposals, of which 60 have been implemented to date. Another 30 are being further evaluated, which takes a long time in Berlin and a very long time in Brussels. The time has probably not come for another 15 proposals. However, I have experienced that the bureaucratic hydra always grows new heads. I feel it is appropriate to do the kind of exercise, which our commission did on behalf of the Bavarian government at least every seven years.

I continued with the fundamental thread of the commission, to promote economic growth, in an expert group comprised of the WTB members, FC Bayern executive Uli Hoeness, economics professor Ann-Kristin Achleitner and movie producer Bernd Eichinger (since deceased). The Bavarian government mandated us to analyse relevant domestic and international developments and to make suggestions on how to set a strategic direction reinforcing the basics with respect to children, education and employment, and thus for prosperity, social protection and security.

We presented our recommendations in 2007, on over 400 printed pages. Amongst other things, we recommended instituting a legal obligation for children's day care as of the age of three, comprehensive all-day schooling and a considerable expansion of the university system. We wanted to drastically increase research and development expenditures. We developed a massive investment program, which would have deployed approximately six to eight million euros. In our view, such expense was justified because Bavaria would have been put on a path to significant growth, yielding positive results in terms of employment and tax revenues.

Our report was controversial, since we recommended extending the term for nuclear power production, and also voted in favour of construction of the Transrapid railway between Munich main station and Munich airport. Criticism notwithstanding, our report

Bavaria 2020 became a standard work for forward-looking politics in Bavaria. It was a shame that some people viewed our work as Edmund Stoiber's sole political legacy. As a result, Günther Beckstein, Stoiber's successor as Bavarian prime minister, didn't fully support our report. At that time it appeared reasonable to extend the term for nuclear power production, but after Fukushima there was no political support for it. At best, the CDU party would have benefited from not pushing through the transition to alternative sources of energy at breakneck speed, two weeks prior to the Baden-Württemberg state parliamentary elections in March 2011. No authoritative calculations with respect to the transition had been provided, and no reliable statements with respect to the cost of renewable energies had been made.

The WTB was dissolved in the summer of 2009, as it was fair to say that the topic of technology had arrived in Bavaria and was well established. Instead, the Bavarian government established a new council for future developments, which covered a wider field. The council is an independent advisory body. Its 22 members hail from various walks of life, and are appointed by Prime Minister Horst Seehofer for a two-year term. Its members include the presidents of the Munich universities, professors Wolfgang A. Herrmann and Bernd Huber, Hubert Burda, executives Norbert Reithofer (BMW) and Rudolf Staudigl (Wacker Chemie), as well as Alois Glück, president of the Central Committee of German Catholics (ZdK), historian Paul Nolte (president of the Berlin Protestant Academy) and Margit Berndl (president of the Joint Welfare Organization). I have been appointed Chair of the Council, and have been working closely with Horst Seehofer ever since. In my personal opinion, he has no problem breaking old habits. While he has a reputation for a volatile temper, I must say that I never experienced this. Certainly, he aims to provoke, for example when he questions retirement at the age of 67. He underpins this view with the fact that only 2.3% of all workers of Siemens, BMW and Audi are aged 60 and above. Seehofer thinks that if people do not even work till 65 – why change the retirement age to 67?

It is exciting to identify and provide advice on decisive issues concerning our future in this group. What would a grccn, sustainably developed Bavaria look like? What has to be done to ensure that all school leavers actually graduate with a diploma? Which broadband infrastructure is required in Bavaria, and what are the benefits? How should the relationship between urban and rural regions be managed, taking into account global competition?

These and many other topics were and still are on our agenda. We formed four working groups, and the Bavarian Chancellery has made a small number of staff available, headed by the highly educated Peter Heinrich, who performed his tasks with verve and devotion.

We presented our first interim findings just before Christmas 2010. A storm in a teapot ensued because our Council held a rather sceptical view as to many rural regions' ability to develop themselves, with the possible exception of the areas of natural conservation and the development of recreational activities. Because we recommended that border towns potentially cater to developing centers in nearby foreign countries, provincial politicians revolted, considering that we were traitors to the nation and causing the destruction of their regions. But we only pointed out an obvious opportunity in the 21st century.

Over the course of the next 20 years, Upper Franconia and Upper Palatinate will lose approximately 10% of their population. In addition, the north of Lower Bavaria will be significantly less populated. The remedy of the past, consisting of the odd infrastructure project, is bound to fail. There are many examples of this, such as Hof airport which is virtually unused by air travel; a swimming pool in a small town in the Fichtel Mountains where nobody swims and a town hall in a border region which has no visitors. Construction of the new subway tunnel in Munich alone would have required expenditures of three billion euros over the next three years – which is about equal to the funds available for the entire Bavarian road network for the next ten years. Currently, its implementation is unclear. No industrialized country is able to provide the same living conditions in remote border regions and metropolitan areas.

Jobs are decisive: if jobs are not available and difficult to create, people will vote with their feet. Specifically young people will leave the area and move to where they can find employment.

Realism is rarely "PC" in Germany – in this country, being politically correct all too often requires smoothly packaging up the truth and disguising hard facts, so that no-one gets upset. On the other hand, the business of politics requires that protagonists constantly present themselves in public and put on a good show. When Lothar Späth was prime minister of Baden-Wurttemberg, his spokesman Matthias Kleinert is rumoured to have set the following standard for their cooperation: "Lothar, every day you don't appear in the press is a day lost." Thus, politicians congratulate the soccer player of the year or participate in TV shows, just to get a minimum of media presence.

Apart from this, it doesn't appear that being a politician is a job to kill for. Even if they move up in the hierarchy, they can at best determine policy guidelines. Being an executive in a company allows the definition of strategy to a much higher degree, and to the assembling of the people required to execute such strategy. In politics, ministers generally have to work with existing resources, even if these have been used to chart a contrary course to date.

I have frequently observed the enormous power of administrations when it comes to politics. "Politics comes and goes, administrations are here to stay", as the saying goes.

After intense discussions with Bernd Eichinger, I once suggested in our council to significantly increase Bavarian subsidies for movie production. The relevant officials immediately rejected the request, and of course politicians didn't pick up on that point, either. It is all too obvious that certain ministers have been given speaker's notes by their experts, to which they strictly adhere in negotiations, meetings or public appearances.

One reason for that is that the world certainly has become increasingly complex. Germany exports goods to 190 countries, and imports from 220. Nowadays, more than 50% of the parts making up a German car are bought abroad. The production chain has become so multifaceted that it is virtually impossible to have everything under control.

As a consequence of increasingly complex issues, transparency must also increase. Nothing remains confidential, not even the forming of an opinion or internal brain-stormings. Consequently, politicians have to act at all times with an almost superhuman degree of concentration and caution.

But the trend towards transparency also can be blessing. I watched with interest how protesting citizens forced politicians and experts to drop buzzwords and to clearly explain and justify the major railway isolation project "Stuttgart 21", while also constructively dealing with criticism.

Time is up for top-down decisions, specifically when it comes to major projects or technologies. Certain politicians take the opposite approach and only look to the political barometer. I believe that the most efficient way to reach decisions and results in a democratic state governed by the rule of law is to engage in constructive debate with all societal strata and reasoning and stop manoeuvring and concealment.

People such as myself can contribute by making their expertise available. The Bavarian Council for future developments, and more commissions such as the Töpfer Commission on ethics in energy issues, which was established after the Fukushima nuclear catastrophe, and various other commissions illuminate the coordinated system of politics. It would not work the other way round. The sum of my experience with politics leads me to believe that I would not have made a good politician. It is a good thing that I never had to prove this fact.

A politician's week usually starts with an analysis of the Sunday night talk show. That was the case for hosts Sabine Christiansen and Anne Will, and that was the same for Günther Jauch. Participants ask: "How did I do last night?" Those who didn't participate check whether their party members followed the party line or whether new signals were issued by their opponents. But the general result was, to quote Shakespeare: "much ado about nothing." Soapbox speeches are made, the contents of which are already known, and no real discussions take place. Such Sunday palava could only become an institution in a "media democracy".

In stark contrast, executives have to act in markets, which have become not only international but global. As a result, markets have grown, but so has international competition. What appeared to be established all of a sudden becomes hotly disputed. Businesses have no choice but to accept the rapid change of technology, and its impact on the supply chain is hard to gauge. Today's investments must be correctly allocated for the long term, at least ten to twenty years, and not for the short term. Politicians like to leave businesses holding the baby when it comes to a lack of ad hoc changes, insufficient growth, lack of innovation and rising unemployment.

There are politicians on one side who need results here and now, and businesses on the other side, which have to engage in long-term planning – time horizons diverge more and more, causing difficulties in communication, up to breaking off all dialogue. Businesses accuse politicians of using empty speech bubbles, and politicians accuse businesses of having a sole desire for profits, being ruthless servants of shareholder value or even being unpatriotic when they move production facilities abroad. I think that politicians may not be completely wrong with respect to shareholder value. In my view, the concept of shareholder value was adopted too quickly from the US, but was not fully appropriate for German companies. I always paid attention to emphasize stakeholder value in my presentations, that is the interests of employees, clients and suppliers, in addition to those of investors.

I think we are dealing with a serious issue. A country with a ratio of government expenditures to gross domestic product of 50%, where half of GDP passes through the hands of politicians and bureaucrats, depends upon politicians and business getting along. It is crucial that the government knows, understands and takes into account the legitimate interests of businesses. Businesses must be certain that politicians don't enact nonsensical laws, that they are not unduly burdened by regulations and that laws are applied reasonably. In June of 2011, Heiner Geissler told me: "You know, businesses just like to bitch and moan. When we introduced the catalytic converter, they said that the auto industry was doomed. In hindsight, it became a huge export success. When we prohibited the dumping of dilute acid, waste-management companies complained that we had driven them out of business. When nuclear power plants are closed down, energy companies complain that the commercial basis for their business goes out of the window. In reality, government provides numerous inspirations for innovation."

In the age of communication, business leaders increasingly imitate politicians when it comes to self-projection. They appear in talk shows, give interviews and behave like political players. This includes of course complaining about politicians' lack of competence and playing the blame game: business leaders frequently try and pass the blame to politicians for their own management mistakes and sins of omission. Memory spans are often so short that regulations are criticized today which had been emphatically requested in the past.

Both business and politics are however worse off if they try to lay blame at each other's doorstep in a populist manner. Politicians must accept that businesses have to measure performance against a few clear benchmarks, notwithstanding the fact that they should have stakeholder interests in mind and not just the interests of shareholders. A company that doesn't generate long-term profits will disappear, and jobs will be lost.

Business representatives and executives must understand that politicians must incorporate many more parameters in their decision-making process, which are hard to measure objectively. They must bear in mind that politicians have to cater to much bigger audiences and are dependent on short-term feedback from the anonymous masses. As always, the better one understands the other's position, the more communication between politicians and businesses will improve. This situation is aggravated by the fact that politicians don't exactly enjoy a great reputation in Germany and politics is regarded as a dirty business. This has a long history dating back 150 years.

Parliamentary democracy is a difficult form of government, specifically for Germans, as we find it difficult to get highly qualified people interested in running for political office. Who on earth is keen on daily abuse at the hands of political opponents, the press and all kinds of lobbying groups? Pakistan's former finance minister Hafeez said when leaving politics, "the time of insults and poverty lies behind."

But a loss of prestige doesn't mean a loss of importance. In my experience, it would be beneficial if both sides practiced a revolving-door policy. I believe that business and government should become more permeable in Germany, similar to the US, where it is common practice for executives to heed Washington's call, and after some time in government return to their executive desks. Such cases are still fairly rare in Germany, an example being Werner Müller, minister of economy under Gerhard Schröder, who later became a member of my Strategic Advisory Council for Credit Suisse and heads the Ruhrkohle foundation. Even more rarely do such moves succeed.

It is even more of an exception to find a politician taking a top job in business, such as the former Hessian Prime Minister Roland Koch, who became CEO of construction company Bilfinger Berger and was fired in 2016 for underperformance.

An exchange of top personnel could contribute significantly to preventing a lack of communication between both hemispheres. And quality would increase if the best people pursued careers in both areas, and not only in business.

CHAPTER 24

THE ALPINE UNIVERSITY

AND TEMPTATIONS TO BECOME AN EXECUTIVE

The first idea for a McKinsey training center came from my Dutch colleague Max Geldens. He frequently sat next to me in Shareholder Council meetings, and being a gifted cartoonist he not only sketched impressions of participants, but also produced numerous sketches of a castle in Wales. His dream was for the castle to become McKinsey's training center. I thought this was a fantastic idea, as our conferences and meetings were usually not held in exciting locations.

As I lectured at many McKinsey seminars, I saw many of these locations and it became clear that they were not the calling card that an excellent consulting firm needed. The seminars were one to two weeks long and frequently featured "soul-searching trips", that is trying to determine our position vis-à-vis McKinsey, and whether we wanted to stay with the firm any longer. This was an important exercise as we continuously lost consultants whom we would have liked to keep. In my view, the ambiance of the firm's training efforts also played a role with respect to this issue.

I picked up Gelden's idea of a McKinsey training center and pushed it through the organization. Together with my colleagues Lukas Mühlemann, Christian Caspar and James Goodrich, I travelled all across Europe in search of the right spot. We found the Chateau du Lac close to Brussels, a beautiful old hotel on the shores of an idyllic lake. It would have made a great location for McKinsey training. However, just before signing, the hotel owner included a couple of clauses in the agreements pursuant to which we would have had to yield to other guests during high season. This was not acceptable, so we regretfully stepped away.

In the meantime, I met and married Fabienne in 1994, my second wife, when she was a project manager at McKinsey. True to the old Marvin Bower-principle that in case of relationships developing within the company, one of the participants had to leave, Fabienne left McKinsey in 1993. In any event, she would not have been at ease being married to the office head. She and I discussed the usefulness of training centers in great depth, and she was always supportive of the project.

I assigned the further search to a team of three associates. They looked at locations in the new German states, and also at the Swiss Bürgenstock, high above the shores of Lake Lucerne.

Meanwhile, Kitzbühel businessman Ernst Freiberger had renovated the old Grand Hotel in the Tyrolian ski resort. He wanted to turn it into a five-star hotel (Ritz Carlton), but local hoteliers were reluctant to accept another hotel of that category. Subsequently, he decided to build a rehabilitation center, but that plan also encountered local resistance. But Freiberger's concept also included a training center of 30 rooms for McKinsey. One day, he asked me whether we wanted to rent the entire building complex.

The building would have been a great fit for McKinsey. But did McKinsey really want it?

I thought it was a joint project for all offices. But New York declined. Fred Gluck had nothing against the German office implementing the project, provided the German partners were on board. He must have heard that my project was somewhat controversial even in Germany.

New York had more or less told me to bring about a decision of the German partners by secret ballot. I put the topic on the agenda of our next partners' meeting in Gravenbruch, close to Frankfurt airport, as the last item for Saturday afternoon. It was midday, and there wasn't much time left until the flights departed. Once more, I promoted the idea and explained the concrete concept. Then it was put to a vote, yes and no on yellow pads. Fifty-five colleagues were present, and more than two-thirds voted against my project.

I was speechless and furious. Why did the German partners take issue with the project, other than for reasons of stinginess or faint-heartedness? Gluck apparently was in possession of information, which I didn't have. The vote also appeared to be an affront against me as I had been closely identified with the project. At a later meeting, with the Brazilian partners also dialling in, I put the project to another vote – and lost again (but this time only 55% of the partners voted against it). After that, I discussed the consequences in a phone call with New York. Rajat Gupta, who had been elected Managing

Director, was a managing partner whom I trusted blindly and with whom I worked closely, recommended a pragmatic approach: "Take yourself out of the line of fire and form a working group!"

Usually, I made fun of the old management rule: "If nothing else works, form a working group!" But this time, I stuck to the rule. Wilhelm Rall, a senior partner in the Stuttgart office, possessed a conciliatory nature and presided the committee. The committee conducted lengthy interviews with all partners, painstakingly collected all pros and cons and finally proposed a concept designed to make the training center project a reality.

The partners met again in Frankfurt, and the plan was once more presented. I said: "All those against the project should stand up and give their reasons." When nothing happened, I declared: "Thank you very much. From my perspective, the project has been unanimously approved." There were some rumblings in the room, but the decision had been made.

I had deliberately overturned the usual voting procedure, because it was clear to me that the vote would likely have been "no", or at best "yes, but…". I was fully behind the concept, and there was no turning back.

The McKinsey training center in Kitzbühel opened its doors in February 1999. Its official name is Alpine University, and it has become a vibrant place of education and encounters, where McKinsey people from all over the world meet to exchange views and develop ideas in beautiful surroundings. I still organize evenings around the fire every six weeks for young associates in training at the facility.

Success has many fathers. Today, everyone is proud of the thriving facility. I frequently hear: "Wasn't it a great decision we made back then?" I did a presentation in 2010 for 200 McKinsey consultants from our Tokyo office. It turned out that 65 of them had been to our Alpine University. It is hard to imagine a better flagship for an excellent international firm. And none that could have been better for me.

"This feels like a boot camp!" said Wolfgang Altenburg, then Chief of Staff of the German Army, when I invited him to give a presentation at one of our winter retreats. Indeed, the average age of our consultants was probably around 30. They were indeed barely past the rookie stage. McKinsey had fairly young staff compared with other companies. One of the reasons for that was that most consultants left the firm sooner or later. Either they were forced out on grounds of performance, or they received attractive job offers from clients.

I also seriously considered becoming an executive when top German companies approached me. When Edzard Reuter was CEO of Daimler-Benz, he asked me whether I was interested in the top job at DASA. I felt honoured by Reuter's approach, but it raised a number of issues: I was hesitant to run a company whose business I didn't really know. I had no clue about the aerospace business. I knew that the defense business made up a significant portion of DASA's production and output, and I certainly knew what that meant: government influence was high. Whether governments could agree to buy a new anti-tank helicopter or not could have a bearing on DASA's future.

I could have acquired the requisite technical skills and learned the defense business. But would that have been a fascinating job? This business dealt with highly regulated government affairs – see the discussions surrounding the potential sale of 200 "Leopard" tanks by Germany to Saudi Arabia during the summer of 2011. At the same time, product development cycles were long, sometimes taking more than ten years, and the additional recurring issue of money ending up in dark channels. Niefer once told me about MTU's involvement in the sale of submarines to Israel and said at the end: "Consider yourself lucky that you don't know all the details." Also, I hadn't served in the military, which was a first in the Henzler family history. I had never held a rifle in my hands. The whole business was just not for me. Edzard Reuter later wrote in his memoirs that he had found a great candidate for the DASA top job, but the candidate didn't accept his offer.

Deutsche Bank CEO Alfred Herrhausen, who also presided the Daimler-Benz supervisory board, offered me two interesting jobs:

CEO of tyre and rubber company Continental, after the then CEO Helmut Werner left to join Daimler, and a newly created board position at Deutsche Bank as Head of Corporate Development. But after careful consideration, I also declined these offers.

Herrhausen then asked me: "But Mr Henzler, you certainly don't want to remain a consultant for the rest of your life?" My response was evasive, but correct: "Right now, I prefer to remain a consultant. But let's see what the future brings."

I received offers time and again, and sometimes I discussed these with my colleagues. As chance would have it, my boss Ron Daniel, Managing Director of McKinsey, and I were in Paris at the same time. We took the opportunity to meet at Orly Airport, back in 1977, to discuss current topics.

I had met Ron Daniel for the first time in 1976 at the occasion of a McKinsey conference on the Bahamas, when he was Head of the New York office. He was of course much more experienced than I, a partner for just one year. We got to talk in the margins of the conference. He wasn't a flashy type of character constantly telling everyone how great he was and about the important deals he was involved in. He took an interest in me, the young German colleague. He asked me about my experience with clients and how I coped with McKinsey's international set-up. I sensed that his interest was real.

Ever since I became Head of McKinsey's German offices, we met once a month at various occasions and had a number of talks, including about personal issues. He was a mentor who helped me wherever he could, and he was also a role model.

He was well-read and possessed a huge amount of knowledge, which was reflected in everything he said and did. The door to his office on the 23rd floor in our Park Avenue offices in New York was always open. One could only admire how he understood the implicit messages conveyed during these conversations, for example if someone needed help, or if certain things were not going right in the teams, or if someone was bored or out of his depth. Ron Daniel always drew the conclusions, but elegantly and without attracting attention.

I thought that Ron's handling of management and leadership tasks as well as his approach to client service could almost be called sage. I was probably not the only McKinsey employee who said to himself: "My goal is to be like Ron Daniel one day." I still haven't reached that goal, I am not wise enough.

As we sat across from each other at Orly Airport, he suddenly said: "You should leave the firm. You are the guy who gets an offer a week. That's not good for you, and that's not good for McKinsey. You should leave." I was shocked. But we first discussed our topics, before Ron Daniel came back to the pressing issue: "But if you decide to leave, you should only leave for a first-class organization, not a shitty company!"

On the flight back to Munich, I thought about what he had just said. He must have heard about an offer to become CEO of a mail-order business. Was this a first-rate company? I was grateful for Ron Daniel's advice. After the flight landed, I called him and told him that I had decided to stay with McKinsey.

The work or rather life at McKinsey was great fun. What would happen if I took the CEO position of a big company? I knew that there was a big difference whether one spent his career within one company or whether one joined laterally. I had seen many examples of laterals that had a hard time, specifically if they joined from McKinsey and if they were successful. Helmut Panke encountered this issue as CEO of BMW, as well as Klaus Zumwinkel as CEO of Deutsche Post, Werner Seifert as CEO of Deutsche Borse or Allianz CFO Friedrich Schiefer. There were few compelling strategies when it came to successfully joining big companies from McKinsey.

Another item contributed to my rather sceptical views. Particularly in large companies, executives don't have enough time for their real job, although a fair amount of time should free up because of advances in information technology and an increasing degree of specialization. When in former times knights unsheathed their swords in order to impress others, nowadays executives pull out their diaries. A new appointment? Certainly, in four months.

This type of behaviour is not only due to executives' self-importance. I was able to watch Werner Niefer from close by: his diary was filled with unavoidable events considered a must, such as lunches, automobile fairs, board meetings, negotiations with suppliers, so much so that there was little room for manoeuver. How could he make time for important clients or rethink corporate strategy? I didn't cherish the thought of having my life mapped out for months ahead. Whenever I had to make a decision on a job offer, I was reminded of the fact that I enjoyed a lot of freedom at McKinsey, relatively speaking.

In addition, I had the opportunity to help shape things. People frequently talked about McKinsey's power in German business. I agreed with Alfred Herrhausen's views on the power of banks. He said: "We don't have power, we exert influence."

McKinsey and myself did exert influence. If we rejected a strategy, board members had to come up with good reasons to convince us, otherwise the supervisory board would have asked unpleasant questions. If we advised against acquiring certain companies, that advice was usually taken to heart. In retrospect, I think that it wasn't problematic for many board members to hire McKinsey for certain types of situations. Our great reputation was certainly one of the reasons.

Just like Herrhausen, I would not lay claim to having been powerful. Our power was limited. Edzard Reuter and Alfred Herrhausen once conducted a vigorous debate on the topic of the "Power of Banks". At this point, I realized that McKinsey had comparatively little power. German boards liked to receive advice, but made all the decisions. Thus, as stated earlier, while I played a role in Daimler's acquisition of Dornier, I didn't participate in the AEG acquisition shortly thereafter. Given my relationship with Siemens, that probably made sense.

When I once read that it wasn't a good idea to be on bad terms with Henzler as he knew the entire world, I felt that I had a position of influence. On the other side, I knew all too well that the role of a consultant was that of a service provider, or rather a servant. In his lecture entitled *Journey to the East*, Robert Greenleaf, founder of the modern "Servant Leadership" movement, depicted the modern service provider as the real leader, notwithstanding his serving function. By serving a company, one could gain significant influence. It was always clear to me that knowledge is power, and even more so for a management consultant, and only a thin line separates knowledge from abuse of knowledge to further one's power.

Because I was certain that things were going well for me at McKinsey, I didn't get too frustrated when for once I wanted to take a job but didn't get it: Siemens CEO Bernhard Plettner had offered me a position as Head of Sales of his group's components division. We discussed the position, but he ended up not making an offer after the last round of interviews. At first, I was dismayed, but quickly realized that it was better the way it was.

CHAPTER 25

RISE WITH LESS INFLUENCE AND A FAREWELL

The 1998 annual meeting took place in Passau. I had convened a meeting of all 700 German McKinsey consultants on the university campus in order to discuss current management topics, together with colleagues from our international offices. My friend from university days and the then president of the University of Passau, Professor Walter Schweizer, hosted the meeting. Traditionally, the last evening was spent discussing our own firm's situation.

I went to the microphone and reported on client, project and staff developments. The news was generally very good, but certain exceptions had to be acknowledged. The Russia crisis was in full swing. We counted 25 young Russians amongst our associates, who were providing for their families with their McKinsey salaries. Because of the crisis, our Russian projects were terminated and they were afraid of being let go. I had discussed assignments earlier in the morning with my partners. I made an emotional speech telling them: "You'll never walk alone. You are part of the big McKinsey family, we will not abandon you." Thunderous applause ensued. All Russian associates received assignments in Germany. I then said: "Let me tell you something on my own account. After 14 years, I will resign from the position as Office Manager. It was a wonderful time, but now the time has come for others to take charge. I just hope that you'll have the same spirit when I come back in 20 years." Silence reigned. I had only informed the 75 partners previously, the vast majority was completely caught by surprise.

Rajat Gupta, then global Managing Director of McKinsey, rose to speak and spontaneously delivered a laudatory address. *Manager magazin* wrote in November 1998: "According to Gupta, ever since the times of McKinsey founder Marvin Bower, no-one has done as much for the firm as Henzler." And the article went on to say: "Even the most hard-nosed among the consultants became misty-eyed." I was of course very touched as the assembled McKinsey participants stood up and gave a standing ovation.

I had slowly come to terms with the decision to relinquish the top role at McKinsey's German offices. I was fifty-seven years old and had three years to go with the firm. When I started at McKinsey, I was consultant number fifty-one in Germany. When I became Office Manager, we had a hundred consultants and now, fourteen years later, that number had grown to seven hundred.

A period of tremendous growth lay behind and inside McKinsey and Germany I got the nickname "growth Herbie". Our expansion required my full commitment with respect to recruitment, organization and staffing. As the German offices grew in importance, the Office Manager's role reflected such growth within the international organization. I wanted to work more with my best clients, and I believe no-one would have disputed that I did a pretty good job in that respect. The Passau meeting thus looked like an appropriate point in time to make a clean cut.

We held a big office management farewell party where Reinhold Messner and Wolfgang Schäuble delivered speeches, and an era came to an end. Messner said he had learned at least as much from me as I had learned from him, and that I was much better at mountaineering than he was at management. Schäuble, with whom I share regional roots, said that he had always listened to me with excitement, and had benefited much from it. He wasn't doing very well at that time, since the CDU took a nose-dive, Schröder appeared to be a good chancellor and he was dealing with a tax scandal with respect to party donations.

At the same time, we were thinking about how to best take some weight off Rajat Gupta's shoulders in his role as Managing Director. By now, McKinsey had more than 70 offices globally. The firm's highest representative had to regularly visit everywhere. Gupta was chronically overworked. The solution consisted of establishing an Office of the Chairman, which dealt with a number of management tasks. An American, Don Waite, was in charge of finance, and Gupta asked me whether I was interested in becoming Chairman for Europe. I was pleased and accepted the position. From then on, I was Head of Europe. This position claimed about half of my time, and the other half was spent advising my long-time German clients such as Siemens, Bertelsmann, SAP, Daimler and others.

I spent three exciting years in that role, even if I had to get accustomed to having less influence. Office Managers had much more power to directly make decisions, compared with a Head of Europe who hovered above it all without his own dedicated staff. From my office in Munich, I frequently traveled to our Eastern European offices, which I had mostly set up myself and which gave both the firm and me a lot of pleasure.

There was a lot for the Head of Europe to do on the Iberian Peninsula. Against the will of the Spanish but to the delight of the Portuguese, I separated the Portuguese office from Spain to gain efficiency. The London office also required my attention, time and again.

Then my sixtieth birthday approached. Sixty is McKinsey's age limit. Rajat Gupta had let me know that he was prepared to enact a "lex Henzler": I could have stayed on for three or five more years. I flirted with the idea for a short time, but then remembered how difficult it had been for many partners to retire from McKinsey. I frequently had to tell them: "You are sixty now, so unfortunately that's it."

Of course, I felt honoured that McKinsey considered making an exception from this rule and didn't want me to leave. But I gave them a polite "No, thanks" so as to avoid availing myself of something which I had denied to others. The firm's principles had to be applied without exception. At the end of 2001, I had my last day at McKinsey, after 31-and-a-half years. There was a partner meeting in Munich, and I had asked our best athlete, Stefan Kupfer, to break a bundle of thin logs. Notwithstanding his best efforts, he didn't succeed. When I showed him how easily it could be done by disassembling the bundle and breaking each single log, my message came across loud and clear: you are strong united as a group, but if you are divided, you may not last for long.

My colleagues threw a farewell party. Jürgen Kluge, then Head of the German practice, organized a party in the Kaisersaal of the Munich Residence. He presented me with a trip to the Kailash Mountain in the Tibetan Gandise mountain range as a farewell gift. In addition, he funded a "Herb Henzler Scholarship" at the Wharton

School of Business in the University of Pennsylvania, endowed with 30,000 US dollars per year, and also announced that an extension of the McKinsey training center in Kitzbühel would be named "Herb Henzler Hall". The press reported: "Mr McKinsey departs". That was it, the end of my McKinsey career.

Manager magazin interviewed me at the occasion of my departure. They asked how things had changed for big German companies during my more than 30 years with McKinsey. In essence, my response was: "The complexity of management tasks has increased manifold."

Thinking back to the seventies when I joined McKinsey, we were dealing with what was called "Germany AG", that is banks and industrial companies forming a closely-knit web, and executive board members mutually joined their respective companies' supervisory boards. Pharmaceutical companies were led by doctors, electrical companies by electrical engineers and chemical companies by chemists. It was an era of steady growth, export activities were hugely successful and management remained largely unchallenged. Press events generally went as follows: "Business is going well, and work is fun. Any questions?" Thirty years later, CEOs had to constantly provide information. A CEO has to explain company strategy to shareholders, staff, analysts and the public, and also has to provide information as to why certain decisions were made and forecasts had not been achieved. Quarterly reports had to be prepared every three months. Increased pressure also meant increased wear and tear. In the old days, it wasn't rare for a CEO of a German company to remain in position for ten to fifteen years. Nowadays, their shelf life decreases more and more – actually it has halved.

A particular feature of German corporate governance contributed to putting additional strain on management. The corporate governance model was one of shareholder democracy, that is shareholders had been granted far-reaching information rights and rights to appeal decisions made by corporate bodies. Shareholder meetings thus required enormous efforts, but results were mixed. Board members painstakingly prepared for weeks in order to avoid falling into potential traps. Costs for the annual shareholder meeting easily reached double-digit million euro amounts. In the end, it isn't even clear whether valid resolutions have been taken. Frequently, some minority shareholder will challenge resolutions, which usually leads to lengthy lawsuits or deals whereby the board pays for the challenge to be revoked. Such shareholder meetings take only a fraction of the time in Switzerland, the UK or the US, and are less costly and more efficient. I told *manager magazin* in the fall of 2001: "We badly need international investors, but they turn their backs with horror on German governance practice."

I think this still holds true. The German attempt to make proceedings for shareholder meetings and legal protection for minority shareholders more than perfect doesn't exactly make for attractive investments in German companies. In addition, there is workers' participation, blurring the dividing lines in corporate management and undermining the role of the supervisory board, because decisions are not reached by means of objective exchange of arguments, but rather behind the scenes, as is normally the case in politics.

Leading a company requires a competent and cooperative board to efficiently manage the company, and a supervisory board to effectively control the board whilst having the company's future development in mind. But, efficiently leading a company also requires the right business environment, provided by the government, and in particular corporate governance. Immediately prior to my retirement, McKinsey had prepared a study proving that corporate governance, that is a codex containing a code of conduct with respect to company management and supervision, had an impact on the valuation of a company and thus on the attractiveness of a business location. According to the study, international investors were prepared to pay 20% more for a top-managed company. Looking at the market value of the Dax 30 companies, applying a 20% price increase would have resulted in an additional 120 billion euros of value in October 2001. Good corporate governance pays, and even more so today. However, according to Uli Lehner, chairman of DT and Thyssenkrupp, nowadays social topics such as the quota of women in corporate functions, the ecological agenda of the company etc. are integrated into corporate governance debates. They have nothing to do with company leadership. Surely, that can't be the aim of the exercise.

Good company leadership must be measured by three benchmarks: shareholder value, that is a company's value, market share in domestic as well as the most important export regions, and the quality of top management. CEO performance must be measured by whether they develop and recruit a sufficient number of top performers, and whether future leaders who could become board members ten years down the line are already within the company's ranks. CEOs must also be able to present their own successor, if possible not chosen because of his resemblance to the current CEO, according to the maxim: I am doing just great, so I should best pick a guy like me!

The 21st century CEO must be a playmaker, who shapes the game. He must know what to expect from everyone, and he must be able to get maximum performance from everyone. He must also focus on critical issues in strategic development, which could be an acquisition today and expansion in Asia tomorrow. But he must be wary of trying to do everything at the same time. It is crucial that enough time is spent thinking about long-term issues, goals and visions.

I had the privilege of advising top German companies for more than 30 years. During that time, financial markets, experts and also the general public have been placing higher and higher demands on corporate management. The economic environment changed radically. The buzzword "globalization" captured the most radical change.

In Germany, people were accustomed to the fact that there was a huge demand all over the world for products "Made in Germany". We were basking in the success of our exports, whereas imports were generally limited to primary products and consumer goods not available in our country. But traditional borders started to disappear, with respect to products, capital and also workers.

Many Germans felt threatened. All of a sudden, Japanese cars and cameras became available in the German market. They were cheap and of good quality. The German consumer liked to purchase imported goods, but the German worker feared for his job. As a matter of fact, many factories were closed because they couldn't remain profitable in a globalized market. Many asked the question whether globalization would cause unemployment in Germany.

Quite to the contrary, Germany is one of the major beneficiaries of globalization. I had predicted that there would always be enough work. But I wouldn't have thought that the labor market would develop that well. One of the reasons is Europe. Europe took the risk of developing the integration model, which has become an economic success. The European Single Market has become beneficial for everyone, but in particular for Germany, which has been able to export many of its goods without bureaucratic obstacles. The euro has been most beneficial for the Germans, as it enabled them to make a significant portion of their exports without incurring the risk of currency fluctuations.

It would be in Germany's interest for all politicians and political parties to make a big effort to draw attention to these effects. For populist reasons, many watch on the sidelines or even participate in demonizing the euro. But the euro, even if it has to be propped up, is not jeopardizing our prosperity, it is rather one of the reasons for that prosperity. Without the euro, dramatic devaluation games would have been played by the European currencies, to everyone's detriment.

Globalization must be shaped, just like the European common market. The financial crisis of 2008 has shown just how much globalization has already advanced. For the first time, a crisis spread around the whole globe and not a single continent was spared. Politicians must learn that deregulation has its limits, and that a global economy needs global regulation. In that case, it will contribute to solving global issues.

CHAPTER 26

———

LIFE AFTER MCKINSEY

MY ONE-MAN COMPANY

"**W**hat next? Feeding ducks in the English Garden?" *Manager magazin* asked that question when I retired from McKinsey. But the devil finds work for idle hands. My Swabian genes probably wouldn't permit any degree of idleness.

Of course, the last three decades had been stressful, but it was almost always a "good" kind of stress, which demands much personal strength, but doesn't use it up, which frays nerves but doesn't ruin them, which fires you up but doesn't burn you out. I was still full of beans after McKinsey.

Lukas Mühlemann had asked earlier whether I would consider taking on new responsibilities. My former McKinsey colleague had moved into business and become CEO of giant Swiss bank Credit Suisse. When his bank made plans to acquire Dresdner Bank, he positioned me for a senior management role. However, the merger never happened.

Mühlemann and I discussed a role with Credit Suisse during the summer of 2001, a couple of months before my retirement. We agreed on the role of "Counsel to the Chairman", which would require three days of work per week, and most importantly that I would work out of a Munich office.

I started my new part-time job on January 1, 2002. My office was located in the Prince Alfons Palais in Bogenhausen, just a few kilometres away from my former McKinsey office. The former residence of a Wittelsbach prince, who supposedly lived there surrounded by 121 cats, had been turned into Credit Suisse's Munich branch, and I received a nice office. What exactly was my new function? I was fairly new to the industry. As stated before, I wasn't a banker and had to find my way into the world of Private and Investment Banking, the two divisions of Credit Suisse at that time. Investment bankers worked on IPOs and mergers and acquisitions globally. Private bankers gathered and managed assets of high net worth individuals. Both divisions were on a roll during those times of internet hype, and a lot of money resulting from the bubble needed to be invested.

Credit Suisse established over 40 branch offices in prime locations in many big German cities and tried to attract clients with assets north of 20,000 euros. Shortly thereafter, the internet bubble burst, and with it this business model. The branch network was thinned out. Credit Suisse didn't place its hopes on customers having realized some capital gains, but rather focused on wealthy customers who are not easily shaken.

I didn't deal with the operative aspects of banking in my new job. I was still a consultant, albeit an internal one. I dealt with new ways of recruiting, coaching of management and numerous other projects. But I was also a sparring partner for Lukas Mühlemann with respect to strategic, business or leadership issues, as my title of "Counsel to the Chairman" indicated.

The world of banking was relatively new to me. However, certain aspects were quite similar to my old world, enabling me to make operative use of my experience as a consultant. Thus, I was involved in a number of acquisitions and financings, for example when the family owners of the *Süddeutsche Zeitung* were looking for investors to save the well-known media company. When Schaeffler tried to acquire Conti during the height of the financial and automobile crisis, Maria Schaeffler was grateful to Credit Suisse and myself when we showed up at a meeting in 2009 with two of our directors and a team and were able to offer support during those difficult times.

The bank and I had entered into a three-year agreement. After that period, a decision was to be made whether or not to renew. The first year was barely over when my friend Lukas Mühlemann lost a power struggle and was removed from his position. Profits were down, and at the same time his past caught up with him when he was blamed for Swissair going bankrupt when he was the Vice Chairman of its board. With Lukas Mühlemann gone, I had lost the partner with whom I had negotiated and concluded my agreement. But his successors Walter Kielholz, Hans-Ulrich Doering and Urs Rohner continued the cooperation. Brady W. Dougan, Credit Suisse's then CEO and I signed ninth extensions of our agreement.

With three days per week spent on Credit Suisse matters, I had at least two days left for other activities. One day is spent sitting on supervisory boards, previously on Hochtief's board, then at FC Bayern Munich as well as on the advisory board of international law firm Freshfields and being a member of the advisory board for Mainstream Renewable Power in London, where I advise the leading offshore wind power company with respect to further expansion. Mainstream Renewable develops offshore wind farms all over the globe and then sells them to power companies. I believe this is an investment for the future, because the farms are built so as to not ruin the landscape and in places where the wind always blows. Unfortunately, the great hopes have dimmed in recent years.

Most of my remaining time was spent on pro bono activities. I am an active member of the board of trustees of the Franz Beckenbauer Foundation and the Messner Mountain Foundation. I had started doing pro bono work while still at McKinsey, and a project particularly close to my heart came through Ion Tiriac.

Tiriac was a gifted Romanian athlete, and the only athlete having achieved top performance in both tennis and ice hockey. We became friends. I met him through contacts at Daimler. Werner Niefer used to call him "the gipsy". "Gipsy, what do you think?" And Tiriac was fine with that. He and I had many discussions in private about Romania's independence. As a consequence of the East-West Conflict, the Romanians boycotted the 1984 Olympic Summer Games in Los Angeles, like the Russians and 18 other socialist countries. We debated Nicolae Ceausescu's horrible dictatorship for hours – in those days, the Iron Curtain was still very much alive. Tiriac said again and again: "These goddamn communists, they really screwed us up!" When Ceausescu was deposed and shot dead by the military in 1989, Tiriac asked for support for his friend Petre Roman, the first democratically elected Romanian prime minister. One day, Tiriac suddenly showed up with Roman in tow at my house in Kitzbühel and introduced me to his friend: "You have to meet him!"

We drank coffee and talked about how things went in his country and whether I could help Roman and Romania in my function as Head of Germany at McKinsey. I finally said: "OK, I'll go to Romania and have a look."

I flew to Bucharest together with two colleagues, where we talked to representatives of the Ministry of Finance and many businesspeople. Romania's capital appeared very European and Mediterranean, but the socialist heritage was still present in both business and government. I thought long and hard about whether McKinsey was in a position to help. In the following year, I helped by preparing the Romanian Central Bank's presentation for the IMF.

Later, we also provided support for a Children's Village in Brasov (Kronstadt), located in the historic region of Siebenbürgen. Tiriac said that orphans had been left behind there in extremely bad conditions after the communist regime was toppled. I immediately pledged McKinsey's support.

The plan was for the children to be relocated to three newly built orphanages, where they would also receive schooling. Tiriac's sister was going to head the program, and McKinsey helped with a pro bono study – each McKinsey office initiates pro bono studies for non-profit organizations, institutions and projects – and many individual donations. In the end, Boris Becker took responsibility for one of the orphanages, Tiriac for another and McKinsey for the third.

The orphanages still exist. Each donor became "godfather" to one child, and they all did very well, either they are at university or they became outstanding athletes. In contrast to "faceless" donations, I always had the impression of having done something really useful for the children. Many McKinsey people paid monthly contributions for the village, similar to club fees, and there were specific donations at Christmas. I collected donations of 20,000 euros on my sixtieth birthday. That is during life after McKinsey.

In addition, I am actively mentoring young management talent. According to *Gablers Wirtschaftslexikon*, mentoring is defined as knowledge and experience of an experienced person being passed on to an inexperienced person. Other definitions are more extensive and also encompass the mentor's motivation. Sometimes such motivation is defined as a personal interest, sometimes as sympathy. In my case,

I simply enjoy interacting with people and have the desire to pass on some of my knowledge and experience.

I had already participated in McKinsey's mentoring program when I was still relatively young. It was common practice for partners to mentor young associates, so I took over mentoring for six young consultants and accompanied them during their first years on the job. I asked for a lot of detail about their current projects and discussed their roles. I often played the ombudsman who provides support in a difficult situation and mediates in case of conflict. But I also often asked my mentees to take a look in the mirror in order to further their self-awareness. Candor and clarity are important in order to develop valued mentees.

Today, together with 80 other top executives, I mentor a couple of students and in addition one participant of the Bavarian Elite Academy each year. This institution is devoted to developing the leadership qualities of promising students, and mentoring is an important part of the elite program.

I am also a honorary professor at Munich's Ludwig-Maximilians University (LMU), where I don't limit myself to teaching as a faculty member. I am also available for students to discuss a variety of items such as: Should I do a PhD? Should I study abroad and if so, where? Does a second degree make sense or is it just a waste of time? I believe that I provided pretty good advice quite a few times when it came to setting the course for a satisfying professional life.

I remained attracted to the institution of the university, the alma mater provider of intellectual nourishment, notwithstanding my choice of a different career path. I kept in touch with LMU from where I had graduated, and presented a lecture at least once a year. I enjoyed lecturing, but there was also a professional motivation as McKinsey was constantly looking for the best university graduates.

In 1989, I was invited by the West German University Presidents' Conference to attend their annual meeting in Hamburg and do a presentation on the topic of German universities' standing in the business world. I didn't hold back and provided criticism using strong words: I accused professors of too much moonlighting and also said that their research assistants were the ones who did the real work.

I complained that they spent too much time attending seminars and congresses instead of looking after their students' needs. In addition, I presented the US system as a model where universities cooperated much more closely with the business world and in some cases were even fully funded by businesses. The *Handelsblatt* reported the next day that my presentation "had caused strong disagreement: university representatives and students were worried about the selling out of academic freedom and the loss of the possibility of comprehensive education – inherent in the university system – in favor of more job-oriented training. Peter Fischer-Appelt, the then president of Hamburg University, told me: "It is easy to criticize, but why don't you do your bit to help universities get better?"

A few months after that event, my old professor Edmund Heinen asked whether I was interested in an adjunct position at his chair at LMU. Time was a scarce commodity – as a McKinsey office manager, I participated in managing an organization set on a course of tremendous growth, both in Germany and abroad. But Hamburg University president Fischer-Appelt's admonition to do something myself was still present. I had also criticized the German universities' isolationism and asked for an increasing amount of practitioners to be invited to lecture, as well as for professors to broaden their horizons in the real world, even if their lifelong tenure didn't exactly provide a lot of incentive in that respect.

Now the time had come for me to stand up to the challenge and to provide my own contribution. I accepted Heinen's invitation and continued to lecture even after my retirement from McKinsey. In 1992, I was named an adjunct professor of business administration department.

In the course of discussions with students over the years, I observed increasingly "green" tendencies. However, these discussions were not always conducted in a rational manner. I have a vivid recollection of a discussion about ecological requirements in the automobile industry. I made a remark that the entire amount of transport-related emissions of greenhouse gases could be compensated if people ate less beef. Student protest against my remark was unanimous, as if I had made a politically incorrect statement.

I also participated in the McKinsey Germany sponsored competition "CEO of the Future" as a jury member and mentor. My goal was the same, to pass on knowledge and experience. Students and young professionals had to write an essay in order to apply for a slot in the competition. The chosen ones received leadership training, had to solve problems using teamwork and then presented their solutions to a real CEO. The three best candidates received a so-called "career budget" of several thousand euros and above all personal mentoring by a jury member.

I founded a discussion roundtable composed of participants in this competition and mentees of the Bavarian Elite Academy. These 15 young people, calling themselves "Herb's Hopefuls", met twice a year with me for a weekend. They received reading assignments, and we then held discussions until the small hours of the morning. In addition, we were in touch by email and I also talked to them personally with respect to career issues.

I hold great hopes for these young people, and I believe they will make things happen. In the meantime, the participants have developed close relationships with each other. One year, they sent me a group photo from a mountain trip, adding a sentence: "You have touched our lives." Such a sentence is a mentor's greatest reward.

My life after official retirement took shape as a one-man company, less stressful than my McKinsey job, but no less varied.

CHAPTER 27

COMPUTER TRAINING FOR THE FOOTBALL TEAM AND FRANZ BECKENBAUER

A PHENOMENON

I still remember the excitement when the German national football team first played a foreign team in 1950, Switzerland, in front of 100,000 spectators in Stuttgart. Germany won 1-0. The World Cup was held the same year in Brazil, but I was told that Germany wasn't allowed to participate because of World War Two, as had been the case for the 1948 Olympic Games in St. Moritz and London.

The national team had been my constant companion as a boy, and the "Bern Wonder" occupied a privileged place in my childish soul. I just had to watch each game broadcast in 1954. We didn't have a TV at that time, so the men in our village went to a pub called "Mountain" in nearby Raidwangen. The pub had a TV, but children were not allowed to sit with the grown-ups. Thus, we had no choice but to watch from outside, looking through the windows. The victories against Austria (6-1) and Hungary (3-2) were simply unbelievable.

I was in seventh heaven when I was invited to celebrate the national team's World Cup victory in 1990 in Rome, this time as a friend of Franz Beckenbauer. I didn't stand outside a pub looking through the window, but was really close to the team – a childhood dream had come true. I remained close to the national team via FC Bayern, which generally provided the core of the players.

I was keen to engage in-depth with Oliver Bierhoff, who I'd met on a flight from Frankfurt to Munich during the summer of 2005. Bierhoff managed the German national team and, in addition to being an athlete, had obtained a degree in economics from the University of Hagen by distance learning. He appeared to be fascinated by McKinsey and even thought about relocating the national team's training center for the 2006 World Cup to McKinsey's Kitzbuhel premises. In the end, his plan didn't work out as it would have been impossible to keep the press at bay. The decision was made in favour of Berlin.

I felt honoured when Bierhoff asked me to do a presentation on team building at McKinsey immediately prior to Germany playing France in Paris in the summer of 2005. He wanted my presentation to be part of a wider education initiative for national team players where they would learn computer skills, read interesting books and think about investing their money – after all, their football career would only last a comparatively short period of time. Bierhoff wanted to increase his players' knowledge base.

I was introduced by Jurgen Klinsmann, a fellow Swabian, and now the 22 selected national team players were sitting in a hotel in Cologne listening to *me*. I have fond recollections of the ensuing discussions, in particular because I noticed that a number of players – and both Klinsmann and Bierhoff themselves – showed a lot of interest. My presentation drew parallels between the performance-oriented organizations McKinsey and the national football Team. More specifically, I said: "You are one of the chosen few, teamwork is everything and you get fired if you don't perform."

I don't think it would be an exaggeration to say that Jens Lehmann would have received top grades had I been required to rank performance at the end of this memorable evening. For example, he asked: "I am now living in London, could you please give me your views on how the German economy could make up ground on the British economy?" There were other bright minds such as Christoph Metzelder, Arne Friedrich and Bastian Schweinsteiger. When Jurgen Klinsmann and Oliver Bierhoff invited me for a last drink after my presentation, Schweinsteiger sat about 20 meters away from us reading an autographed management book of mine. I was quite surprised about his level of interests and signed the book with few personal comments.

But I think we achieved a lot. In the old days, the joke was that players would only leave their rooms when they had finished reading the popular German *Fix and Foxi* comics. Fortunately those days are gone. Nowadays, all players have a computer and can also say something about their prospects.

Shortly prior to the 2006 World Cup , I organized a workshop on crisis management for the team of coaches. The goal was, inter alia, to understand how to manage the competition between goalkeepers Oliver Kahn and Jens Lehmann so as to generate into positive energy.

Or, what if someone suffered from cabin fever, went AWOL? What if that person was Michael Ballack?

During the "summer fairy tale", Jürgen Klinsmann and I exchanged a number of emails discussing the insufficient returns from corner kicks. I wrote: "Dear Jurgen Klinsmann, I think our yield from corners is catastrophic." In the old days, a corner was considered half a goal, but for the German national team corners were almost meaningless, both during the preparation period and actual matches. Klinsmann replied: "Right on, the Italians score 60% of their goals after set-pieces. We still have to work on that." Franz Beckenbauer commented on my presentation to the national team as follows: "I just hope they can still stop the ball after your intellectual upgrade."

During the winter of 2009, Klaus Behrenbeck, Oliver Triebel and I organized another workshop with Oliver Bierhoff and the team of coaches, at McKinsey in Kitzbühel. We counted German National Coach Joachim Low, assistant coach Hansi Flick and goalkeepers' coach Andreas Köpcke amongst the participants. The workshop was entitled: *Effective team building? How to overcome persistent impediments, how to become a 'complete' person.* The atmosphere was fantastic.

But above all, one has to be realistic: the guys' job is to play football. The national team is the apple of the eye of all Germans. Sepp Herberger's response to the question of why so many people liked to watch football was: "Because they don't know how the match will end." This point is of course not comparable with McKinsey, but what's comparable is the unconditional requirement to produce top performance. You are either top or you are fired. McKinsey fires people after two bad reviews, but football is a bit more tame. When Jürgen Klinsmann was let go as Bayern Munich's coach, the club occupied second place in the German National League, and had just lost the Champions League quarter-finals to FC Barcelona. These things happen. But all of a sudden, the supporters were against us and we had about 60,000 people screaming in the stadium: "Fire Klinsmann!" Of course, we had to act faced with this expression of popular sentiment. In addition, Champions League qualification was jeopardized.

Another difference is that McKinsey is far more stable than the national team. In football, players are constantly taken out of service. Players sit on the bench or even on the stand, their contracts are not extended or they read in the newspapers that they are just about to be sold. An enormous amount of uncertainty is thus created, unless players are amongst the few considered so good that they create their own rules. At McKinsey, staff can make almost statistical calculations: one consultant out of every five makes partner, and 40% of the partners become senior partners (directors). This system guarantees a certain degree of stability.

In my view, Franz Beckenbauer is a phenomenon. "Oh, you are from Germany. Isn't that where Beckenbauer is from?" I encountered that reaction wherever I told people that I was a German citizen. Beckenbauer is probably a synonym for Germany.

We had met at a Lufthansa event in 1985. We started talking and soon realized that we were going to be something like neighbours in the near future. He had just moved to Kitzbühel, and I was just getting a house constructed there. As of that date, we continued to meet.

I introduced him to Werner Niefer in a Munich restaurant named "Wörnbrunn". The Daimler executive and the football manager got along well and started a business relationship which has lasted to this day. At that time, Daimler-Benz had just entered the world of sports sponsoring in a big way. Beckenbauer was the German national team's coach and fit the ticket extremely well. Soon, he became a staple of Mercedes advertisements. His popularity increased even more when the German team won the 1990 World Cup under him. The relationship between Mercedes-Benz and the national team which I had engineered continues to this day.

When Beckenbauer was about to become president of FC Bayern Munich, he asked me to become the club's treasurer. I was intrigued by the proposition, but my McKinsey colleagues rightly advised against it. In such a position I would have participated in negotiating the stadium rent with the City of Munich, which was also a McKinsey client. McKinsey also did work for the second German TV channel (ZDF), and I would have been in a position to negotiate broadcasting rights via the DFL, the German Football League. The situation was rife with latent conflicts of interest.

In the mid-nineties, Beckenbauer got me to join the club's advisory board, and when he decided to spin off the football business into a separate corporate entity (AG), I was also elected to the AG's supervisory board. I became one of three members of its general committee and headed the audit committee.

Through Franz Beckenbauer, I got more deeply involved with the world of football. He made sure that I participated in a workshop on organizational issues organized by the German Football Association (DFB). He introduced me to Joseph Blatter, the Swiss president of the Federation of International Football Associations (FIFA), which led to a project for McKinsey. Today, I am still reflecting about the wrongdoings, about corruption in selecting the world cup – yet, when you tried to shape an organization and to establish an information system you had no clue about such allegations at that time.

In November 2009, Beckenbauer resigned from his position as president of FC Bayern Munich. The former team manager Uli Hoeness became his successor and was at the same time elected to the FC Bayern AG supervisory board. He became president of the supervisory board in the spring of 2010.

I was to experience the changing of the guard at the club's top very soon thereafter. Hoeness called and asked me to meet him at 7 am in the morning at his house in Bad Wiessee on the Tegernsee. I drove out to his house and he told me right away: "I have to tell you something you won't like." He then told me that he had sold 10% of the AG's shares to Audi, and that the investor requested a seat on the supervisory board. Of course, I understood Audi's position. He then asked me to resign from my position on the supervisory board, but to continue as a member of the advisory council, as this shouldn't make a big difference.

I was deeply disappointed by Uli Hoeness's proposal, even more so as I had invited him to become a member of my "Bavaria 2020" Team of the Future. But I decided to play ball. I resigned from the supervisory board, but kept my position on the advisory board. I still try to be an active member of the advisory board and feel close to the "Bayern family". There wasn't any impact on my relationship with Franz Beckenbauer. I have been a member of the board of trustees of the Franz Beckenbauer Foundation since its inception. When Uli Hoeness fell upon hard times in 2014 (tax evasion), I stood by him and his wife. Today as his jail sentence comes to an end, I see him regularly on his stints in our FC Bayern offices.

Beckenbauer and I also discuss private matters. He embodies philosophical wisdom combined with a down-to-earth Munich approach. I admire his talent to master difficult situations with almost playful ease. Perhaps for these reasons, he has become something akin to an all-purpose magic bullet in German sports. He was one of the main drivers for bringing the 2006 football World Cup to Germany. After that, he was also tasked in July 2011 with bringing the 2018 Winter Olympics to Munich. The *Münchner Abendzeitung* wrote: "Do it again, Franz". Unfortunately, Munich's candidature wasn't crowned with success, which certainly wasn't his fault.

He calls himself a discontinued model in the advertising industry. But I don't buy it.

CHAPTER 28

MANAGEMENT
BETWEEN LONDON,
RUSSIA AND THE
FINANCIAL CRISIS

I n April 2008, I packed my bags, but not for a single trip. My second wife Fabienne, my three children and I were ready to relocate to a new city, a metropolis where plumbing and wiring in houses supposedly constantly broke. We were undaunted and moved to London.

Credit Suisse asked me to help develop a management program for key clients in the British capital. I had developed and implemented a number of such programs while at McKinsey, so I was happy to accept. Shortly thereafter, we moved into a house in Knightsbridge, a centrally located part of London.

A year earlier, in April 2007, Credit Suisse CEO Brady Dougan had asked his 100 top executives via an Intranet survey: "In your view, how long will the bull market last with share prices clearly going up?" There were very few sceptics; more than 80% thought that the bull market would last for at least three more years, likely longer. But the crisis was already rearing its ugly head. On New York's Wall Street, Bear Stearns, an established investment bank, was making headlines because of subprime mortgage investments turning sour. Bear Stearns was acquired for a knockdown price by its competitor JPMorgan Chase.

This transaction was the writing on the wall and the financial crisis subsequently broke out. At Credit Suisse, we thought that we could get through unharmed as our exposure to the US real-estate market was fairly insignificant. But then Lehman Brothers went under, which caused a huge debacle. Interbank dealings, which are essential for the functioning of financial markets, practically came to a standstill. Combined with the general level of uncertainty, the result was that credit for the real economy was virtually unavailable. Thus, the financial crisis turned into a global recession.

Credit Suisse did not remain unaffected. Conceptual work became difficult, as survival was the main concern. The level of uncertainty became clear when colleagues reported in meetings that they thought Coutts & Co., a private bank for the ultra wealthy, would collapse, or that they had restructured their own assets, divided among as many international banks as possible, and were keeping money in their mattresses. Credit Suisse was also forced to take considerable write-downs on certain assets, as market values were the applicable standard for valuations, and market values were in free fall everywhere. Fortunately, Credit Suisse found a new significant shareholder in the Middle East: the Emirate of Qatar bought 10% of its equity. Consequently, Credit Suisse was spared asking the Swiss government in Bern for help, while a number of German banks had been forced to apply for emergency funding to their government. Brady Dougan steered our ship through the storms with a steady hand.

As to the second crisis during the summer of 2011, I am inclined to quote Ludwig Erhard, the second chancellor of the Federal Republic, and a former Minister of Economy. Erhard once said that 50% of economic activity is based on psychology, and psychological sentiment during the summer of 2011 was rather negative, no matter what governments said. In addition, banks increasingly lacked trust in each other and preferred not to do any business as opposed to taking any risk (most of the business is done among the investment banks).

I was able to observe the real world impact of the financial crisis in London. Banks located in Canary Wharf, an office complex in London's Docklands and the center of investment banking, reduced staff by 25% and more. Those affected had made good money and spent at least a portion of it. Now restaurants were empty, shops lost customers and real-estate brokers were left with nothing to do. It took about a year until the UK slowly started to recover from the crisis. Tables at the "in" restaurants started to fill again, and the real-estate market stabilized, even if at a lower level. The British continued their daily lives and cultivated their quirks, which sometimes gave rise to suspicion that their claim of not being a part of Europe might actually be correct.

My personal life in London turned out to be more difficult than anticipated. I had hoped to nurture interesting contacts outside of the bank, but that wasn't quite the case. While McKinsey London welcomed me with open arms, I never managed to gain entry to English social life.

Sports probably worked out best. I met Peter Kenyon, chief executive of Chelsea through contacts at Bayern Munich, and gained entry to English football circles. In May 2010, during the Champions League Finals in Madrid, I introduced Dean Ashton, Tottenham executive who was in charge of organizing England's candidature for the 2018 World Cup, to Fedor Radmann, who worked on the German 2006 World Cup organization team. I was hoping that Radmann's help would increase the likelihood of success of the English candidature, but to no avail. I would have loved to spare Prime Minister David Cameron and Prince William the humiliation, but England only received two votes in 2010 in Zurich, instead of the thirteen required.

London is a fascinating city, but when I had accomplished my task after three years and went back to Munich, I felt like the angel Aloisius in Luwig Thoma's satire *A Munich guy in Heaven*. God doesn't really have much use for him and sends him back to Munich, as a messenger. Aloisius is overjoyed to feel Munich soil under his feet, and I felt quite the same.

Through Credit Suisse, I got introduced not only to England, but also to Russia. I met a man called German Oskarowitsch Gref on the fringe of a partner meeting of the German McKinsey offices in 1999 in Moscow. At that time, he was Deputy Minister for the administration of government property in the government of the Russian Federation, and rose to become Minister of Economy a few months later, in May of 2000. Gref was looking for influential advisers who could help with an ambitious project: how could a country churning out excellent scientists and engineers also train excellent management talent?

We debated in a small group how to achieve this goal. Rajat Gupta, McKinsey's Managing Director at that time, was also part of that group. He had relevant experience in this matter as he had founded the Indian School of Business in his native country, in Hyderabad. The Armenian industrialist and banker Ruben Vardanian and others also participated in developing and promoting the idea of a Russian Business School.

One word with respect to Gupta: as stated before, I always trusted him but he fell short with respect to the McKinsey values of trust and integrity. When it transpired in April 2011 that he had violated insider trading rules – wiretaps of a phone conversation were being offered as proof –, he was removed from all boards he was sitting on, and all ties to McKinsey were severed. He had caused a great deal of damage to McKinsey by passing on information to an investor friend details of discussions by the Goldman Sachs' board, of which he was a member. The *New York Times*' headlines in April 2011 read as follows: "Can McKinsey still be trusted?" When I attended a McKinsey meeting two months later in New York, I was asked whether I should have known about this, as he and I had been close. I didn't know anything about this side of Gupta. I am still preoccupied with this matter. Last year I visited him in the FMC, Federal Medical Centre in Devens – being one of the few people in McKinsey that stood by him while he served his one year, 10-month jail term.

One day, I received a call from Eberhard von Loehneysen, Office Manager of McKinsey's Moscow office. He asked whether I was interested in becoming President of what was to become the Skolkovo School of Management. I declined the position because of other engagements, but was happy to join the supervisory board in order to help with the project. Ten personalities were sitting on this advisory body, and we held many brainstorming sessions in order to ensure the school's future success. It was a great moment when Russian president Vladimir Putin presided over the ground-breaking ceremony for the school's building in Skolkovo, in the Moscow region. The land had been donated by Roman Abramovitch, the billionaire owner of London football club Chelsea FC.

The Skolkovo School experienced some difficulties during the height of the financial crisis in the summer of 2008. Certain financiers such as Ruben Vardanian had been badly hit. But the Russians showed how to deal with such a crisis: they asked for help in a friendly but direct manner, and none of the sponsors walked away. The new Russian president Dmitri Medvedev was able to inaugurate the management school on its architecturally interesting campus and to hand out enrolment documentation to the first students. A year later, Medvedev came back to attend the first students' graduation ceremony and gave a stirring speech ("Go, Russia"), asking management talent to develop Russia's economic power.

Credit Suisse was one of the main sponsors, and I had participated in the development of the school's concept and curriculum as a member of its supervisory board. We were proud that an idea on the fringe of a partner meeting had turned into an institution graduating MBAs for the real world. Many wanted to set up their own company, work for big international companies abroad or join new and attractive employers in Moscow, McKinsey or investment banks. We had the impression we were witnessing the start of an era. It appeared that Russia was moving towards a more modern future also with respect to management.

There is a tangible lack of managers in Russia, which is why young managers have no real role models, and few mission statements. Oligarchs can't really function as role models, which is why successful companies are needed, showing young talent how management is supposed to work.

CHAPTER 29

IN THE
START-UP WORLD

I have always been fascinated by the start-up world and the dynamism it had in the US. While we managed to create only one (!) large company after World War Two in Germany – thanks to the five founders of the team of Dietmar Hopp and Hasso Plattner, there were 300 companies founded in the same timespan in the US listing of the Dow 500. Seeing Jeff Bezos (amazon) and Bill Gates (Microsoft) interact with the "old economy" representatives at the World Economic Forum (WEF) in Davos was like watching Messi and Ronaldo play against my homeland team of VfB Stuttgart.

At McKinsey, in 1998, the time of the dot.com-bubble, we were intensively debating whether the concept of a "McKinsey Capital" – like other consultancy firms (eg. Bain Capital) – had any merits. Eventually, despite our early ground-breaking intellectual work by our partner John Hagel (Center for Edge Innovation), we decided against it. Our focus was on top management consulting and we could not find enough talents to fill the need of our offices around the world. Why should we diffuse our professional development?

On the other hand, we were losing newly hired associates in droves – West Coast offices experienced attrition rates of over 25%. The start-up ventures seemed just too good as a prospect. As we later found, the dot.com-bubble burst and many associates preferred the comparatively rather safe haven of consulting again.

In Germany, this led to a drastic consolidation of the venture-capital industry, where many, like my dear friends from Earlybird, struggled to survive with internal rate of returns (IRRs) of barely 0.5% for a 10-year fund investment. What stayed was the business plan competitions we had introduced with the help of universities and the chamber of industry and commerce (IHK). These helped to bring entrepreneurial thinking to the younger generation and pro-duced a number of high-class start-ups like voxeljet, a 3D-printer company from Friedberg near Augsburg (now listed in New York with a market cap of over $100 million US).

In 2012 I headed a commission to facilitate the start-up culture in Bavaria. With the help of the Bavarian government's impressive head of the president's office Dr. Karolina Gernbauer, we gathered start-up entrepreneurs, venture financiers, university professors and government officials and developed a solution space for an entrepreneurial push. We concluded that of the three ingredients; ideas, money and entrepreneurs, the problem we were confronted with was a shortage of venture capital and a perennial paucity of entrepreneurs. The Münchner Merkur proclaimed in December 2013 that "the country is losing its entrepreneurial backbone". We managed to put up a fund of 100 million euros for investments in Bavarian start-ups, supported the development of entrepreneurial units in the universities (entrepreneurship centers) and created a "factory" for start-ups in Munich named Werk1. At this initial stage this was 2,500 m², and it is supposed to go up to 20,000 m².

I am acting as a jury member for selecting seven new sites for start-ups in the Bavarian regions.

Currently I am the steering coordinator between the various arms promoting a start-up culture in Bavaria and I am moving between government agencies and start-up entrepreneurs. This involves heavy speaking engagements. Recently I was – together with the CEO of Adidas Herbert Hainer – a keynote speaker at the "bits and pretzels" conference in Munich, with more than 3,000 participants.

After some sobering personal investment experiences in East German real estate in the nineties, I'm now a business angel. I invest up to 200,000 EUR in selected start-ups and I counsel the founders, act as a board member or establish linkages through my international network. It is too early to tell whether Munich will ever match Berlin in terms of start-up culture, but the groundwork is laid.

A day in Berlin where I spend time in the start-up bonanza café Oberhof (Berlin Johannesstraße), where computer nerds of all countries develop their apps, convene ad hoc with investors and display their start-up successes or meet with Jan Beckers (Hitfox – entrepreneur of the year 2014) and his dynamic team at the Rosa-Luxemburg-Straße has become quite normal. With Zeotap (an advertising firm for targeted advertising by telcos), Finreach (a Finntech firm that enables quick shifts from old bank accounts to new bank accounts) and eight more start-ups this serial entrepreneurship house has few peers in Germany. It is great to help these folks. An uplifting experience; sensing the unusual dynamism gives you the feeling that the start-up culture is up and running.

Germany needs a vibrant start-up culture badly and the fact that large companies like Adidas and others study the start-up scene intensively and invest big time (for example the runtastic deal for 200 million euros by adidas) gives me hope for new dynamism.

CHAPTER 30

GRAPPLING WITH
THE DIGITAL
REVOLUTION

In my consulting life, I have experienced the fact that long-held convictions can be overturned and proven wrong by technical disruptions. The proud telephone communication technology where Germany was leading the global industry with competent suppliers like Siemens and solid distributors like Deutsche Telekom, had a belief that voice and data networks would always remain separate, that mobile communication had no future, that voice recognition and imaging telephony was technically not possible. All these castles tumbled with the early digital revolution.

In recent years, the pace of change has speeded up considerably. Andy McAfee and Erik Brynjolfsson wrote *The Second Machine Age* with plain but telling points like these: is an observation made by Intel in the 70s. Every 18 – 24 months computing powers doubled (Moore`s law) and this law still holds, in fact we are now on the second half of the chessboard.

- The authors make allegations to the Indian king who had to pay off a counselor. The counselor wanted that in a chessboard each box would get double the amount of rice as the preceding one. (quadratic sequence). The king thought it was a joke – only to find out that the continuous doubling was resulting in more rice than existed in all of India. Well again now on the second half of the chessboard means every development will speed up much more than ever before.
- Whole industries will be unraveled along the lines of Kodak (a company I visited in Rochester, NY in 1963 when they were the icon of photography with about 80,000 employees), which was replaced by Instagram (then 15 people).
- The digital world will overcome perennial shortages, instead of scarcity there will be plenty, instead of expensive things will be cheap, instead of dangerous things will be safe, etc. We will be able to eradicate diseases, battle hunger and avoid accidents.
- Yet "the winner takes it all" is the rule that will govern this world. Examples like Google or Facebook show that the first mover will enjoy a near monopoly. This is hard to swallow for Europeans who traditionally prefer a benign competitive environment.

Andy McAfee asks: "Who is the third-best cello player? Who is the fifth-best pianist?" etc. and indeed when we see that even today soccer star Ronaldo has close to 110 million clicks and cashes in on that, while the whole German national team has only 25 million clicks, it shows the tendencies.

I debated the contents intensely. If we consider that airbnb, founded in 2006 by Brian Chesky, Joe Gebbia and Nathan Blecharczyk, today controls 750,000 beds, Hilton Group owns 715,000 hotel beds, Hilton's market capitalization is approximately $23.6 billion US while airbnb is valued at $25.2 billion by private investors. Likewise we can see how Pinterest (private investors are willing to put up $13 billion US for this online blackboard) and Uber, now valued at close to $50 billion, and it is not hard to see many disruptive changes coming.

Since my days in Berkeley (1968–1969) and my close contacts with the San Francisco McKinsey Office (especially with Tom Peters and Bob Waterman, while they were writing *In Search of Excellence*), I have followed developments on the West Coast very closely. Numerous visits have kept me upto date.

Most recently, I have spent full weeks in situ and visit Stanford and Berkeley, have interviews with luminaries like Sebastian Thrun, founder of udacity, the company that sells online-teaching or Andy Bechtolsheim, founder of Sun Microsystems and many former McKinsey people that now work at Apple, Facebook, Google or Oracle and hence I have been getting an educated impression on what's happening and how German business is positioned in the innovation lab of the world. Back home, I have given numerous talks and written papers on these visits, so that I became a voice on Germany's competitive standing. In a recent issue of *Der Spiegel*, I wrote about the elder statesman of German industry and warned that the Germans are falling behind. In an interview with the leading business journal *manager magazin* in February 2014 I reported on the "severe shortage of German industry in the digital world".

At present I am teaching a course on strategic leadership at the Ludwig-Maximilians University, and giving many speeches on trends in the value chains of whole industries.

I do see some real challenges in our environment:

- Our schools still favor the humanistic education and do not pay enough attention to mathematics, informatics, natural sciences and technology, the MINT subjects. Overcoming the shortages in qualified teachers will take years while other countries like the UK teach coding in elementary school.

- In our universities, where Germany now educates close to 50% of each year's cohort. we are experiencing average ratings in the MINT subjects, leading to a paucity of software-engineers in industry (often filled by sw-engineers from Russia, the Ukraine and Romania). Our Max-Planck Institute has an excellent reputation on an international level, but turns out only highly specialized MINT scientists. But we need to supply many more thousands of computer scientists (at least double the 50,000 computer science graduates per annum).

- Our leading industrial companies, a stalwart of our economy, where 23% of the German GDP is created, are often world champions in exports to the global market place. These are probably world class when it comes to "embedded" software, but when it comes to making business perspectives out of the data we produce in billions of bytes from turbines, automatic gear, trucks, x-ray machines, locomotives etc., it seems this is still a US phenomenon. The Ciscos, IBMs, Microsofts and Oracles of this world have concepts for maintenance management systems (MMS) or products life cycle systems (CPLS), while in Germany heavy intellectual battles on "who owns the data" and data protection laws are being fought.

An impressive example to illustrate this phenomenon:

An average jet engine has about 5,000 sensors and generates about 10TB of operational data per 30 minutes. So New York to London typically generates about 160TB of data. Four engine jumbo jets generates 640TB of data per flight. Now GE may not capture and store all of this data, they store about 1TB of data per flight on average and this gets stored in an Amazon-like data lake environment built by GE through its investment in Pivotal Software.

I enjoy visits to Walldorf where my old friend Dietmar Hopp oversees the development at SAP, a company that has taken on these challenges. I do get the feeling that SAP has come home in this world and has even come to be seen in the valley as an insider.

I get the same feeling when I visit my dear old friends at Festo, a leading global pneumatic company near Stuttgart. Here the combination of hardware and software solutions for automation works and helps industry in 70 countries to become more efficient.

In recent years I have observed how the digital world is changing our knowledge base (i.e. what theoretical underpinning do we have when we do not know the production functions anymore? What positioning should telecommunication incumbents have in the future (more infrastructure or value added services) and how large companies – the arena in which I spend my professional life – are grappling with Diesel software fraud at Volkswagen), legal proceedings (Deutsche Bank) and corruption issues (Siemens). This raises questions on the controllability of global enterprises that employ more than 100,000 people.

A meeting with Michael Patsalos-Fox in New York made me stop and think. Michael is a former McKinsey director and now heads a growing cyber-security firm. Two comments from our New York discussion should be cited:

- A significant amount of our work is proactive security assessments which can include sophisticated penetration testing and ethical hacking aimed at identifying vulnerabilities in networks, software, physical environments and as important, the business processes used by enterprises that compromise security.
- We also have developed insider threat software to identify potential threat actors working inside companies through psycholinguistic analysis of company email. This type of threat identifies people who may be at risk of compromising the safety of a people and assets, eg. could be used in financial institutions, and where public safety is at issue.

However, we do not have enough manpower to fill global needs. This is a spooky feeling in a world that is changing so rapidly and where today's knowledge base is becoming obsolete as we read these lines. The information that is mass produced in 2015 is more than all the information produced in history. A sign of fears – yes and no. Yes – because my mind does not comprehend all the bad things that can happen, no – because mankind can be the great beneficiary of these developments if we manage to control them.

CHAPTER 31

———

SUMMARY OF
A SUMMITEER

The older I get, the more I am conscious about the loss of two friends from university, both lost to traffic accidents. In 1966, while doing an internship in Latin America during the summer break, I met Klaus von der Heyde on a passage to Montevideo. He was studying law in Munich, and I was studying economics. We frequently got together after that first encounter. One day, while attending a seminar of the Konrad Adenauer Foundation in Eichholz, I received a letter from his parents, informing me that Klaus had been in a fatal traffic accident with a Citroen 2CV (nicknamed "The Duck"). I was deeply shocked by the news, as I had seen him only a few weeks before. I was for the first time confronted with the finite nature of life, and a very abrupt type of finiteness to boot. During these first moments, I was unable to get more information about the circumstances of Klaus' death, as it took some time to reach his parents. He hadn't been driving himself, he was just sitting next to the driver who caused the accident. Over the next few weeks, I felt finite, vulnerable and particularly vulnerable in traffic. The metal box of a "duck" doesn't provide a lot of protection.

Sometime after that event, the next accident took place. Eberhard Schmidt was driving home, from Stuttgart to Nürtingen. He had just passed his final exam in veterinary medicine. He was very happy, sitting behind the wheel when he overshot a bend. The car somersaulted several times, and, he was killed right away. Another close friend was gone, and I felt very sad. I lost two more friends during the last few years, Ulrich Brixner and Ernst Hösl. Both had given speeches at my sixtieth birthday party.

Looking back on my life and specifically my professional life, I know that I had been able to remain active much longer than Klaus or Eberhard. Notwithstanding all wistfulness, I feel cautiously proud. When I imagine how far I have come from the small farming village, how much different my current life and the life I have led over the last 40 years is from life in the village, I believe that the bridge I had to cross was wide. It certainly took some time to adjust to the new life and to become successful. However, I believe that I have kept my feet firmly on the ground. When I organized a political beer brunch on the Swabian Alb some time ago, I felt that I could still speak the locals' language and understand their issues. I can understand part of the criticism levelled at "Stuttgart 21". If a Swabian gets told that the project cuts the travel time from Paris to Bratislava, people from Feuerbach don't really see the relevance for their daily lives.

My mood becomes reflective when asking myself the question: did I do enough? I never went into politics and never ran a big company. Had I joined Daimler, Siemens or Deutsche Bank, I would have had a greater centrifugal mass to move around. Today, I regret it less than during the times when I underwent a soul-searching process and tried to determine whether a more exciting world than the world of McKinsey existed. I thought about it a lot. Because I knew many CEOs, a number of situations cropped up where I felt like taking the plunge.

But I never jumped ship. I thought it most important to continue focusing on my chosen area.

Had I gone to work for Daimler, I would likely have gone in an entirely different direction and would have had to lead and manage half a million people. But it doesn't make sense to dwell on these scenarios, as I took a different route.

Today, I am more interested in other topics, the unresolved issues of our times. I hail from farming stock, and my grandmother had eleven children, and my mother had two. I have five children, which is exceptional. Our society has become hedonistic, which includes having less children. We consume here and now, without thinking about what to pass on to the next generation. My brother and I grew up with a sentence our parents repeated over and over again: "We want you to have a better life than ours." It is hard to pass on this sentence nowadays. I am noticing some big gaps between generations, and I also realize that there is an increasing gap between rich and poor – no matter what the Gini coefficient for the German society says. My father died at the age of 71, having been sick for several years; actually after WW II he was often sick for weeks. My mother just celebrated her 99th birthday and she is still the center of our family, of our relatives and even for the village. Her seven grandchildren and six great grandchildren visit her often and keep her on her toes. My brother who became a high school teacher at the Balingen Gymnasium and his wife Ursel (an artist) live near my mother and visit her weekly.

Real wages have not increased over the last ten years until 2012, and one third of the new jobs in Germany are temporary jobs. Workers with short temporary employment contracts will be unable to make sufficient pension contributions to guarantee a reasonable pension. These things are simply not right. Also, the European spirit – prevalent for so long – doesn't appear to be present any more. We just accept that we can travel anywhere, are not threatened by anyone and that the Cold War is over. I feel and have always felt as a European. The big issue will be to manage the balancing act between the European idea and a local identity. If we succeed in this endeavour, Europe's prospects will be good.

Europe is a union of peace, but peace has become a matter of course for many people. Young people don't understand why they should consider this a great achievement, as they have never experienced anything different. They grew up with these great achievements, experienced great economic freedom, and saw how many former communist countries were admitted to the union, which helped by reducing the prosperity gap in the new member countries. But a leadership problem developed, which in turn caused a counter movement. The latter is particularly prevalent in countries such as Denmark and Sweden, where the movement argues along these lines: "Europe just costs a lot of money. It is run by a sclerotic organization in Brussels, and it is unclear whether Jose Manuel Barroso, the president of the European Commission, has anything to say. It doesn't appear to be the case." Reinhold Messner, who was a member of the European Parliament for the Green Party, once said: "There are 27 member countries with a total of 27 foreign ministers, each of whom determines his own foreign policy. It is difficult to squeeze a uniform political will out of the unified Europe."

In general, we should be satisfied. But I realize that our society is anything but satisfied. I recognize a lot of disenchantment with politics, and I see issues with prerogatives of interpretation. Churches have lost it, the same holds true for big organizations such as trade unions, and also political parties, which have trouble finding members. By the same token, people don't vote any more. I feel very pensive about it all. It makes me think that I should have voiced my views more clearly, including on our world's ecological prospects . It is understandable that people want to be able to fly to Mallorca for 29 euros. But I know that the cost to our economy is equal to at least ten times that amount.

For the future, we need to guarantee more information and apply a more scientific approach, which must be communicated in a clear and reasonable manner. We must also make sure that our society doesn't have school dropouts. This well-to-do society must be able to ensure that every child, no matter his or her background, receives minimum qualifications. We must also ascertain that those trained up to an elite level really function as an elite and become prime movers, pulling others along. We must insist on that, and there must be equal opportunities for everyone. I do take issue with the fact that many of my contemporaries lead a life of leisure, consisting of pleasure cruises and playing golf. I think everyone deserves leisure time and relaxation, which however shouldn't turn into the meaning of life, as global issues are just too difficult. Debating for an entire evening whether a birdie should have been played at hole seventeen … No.

Many executives are currently being heavily criticized. There is a lack of comprehension that an executive can earn up to ten million euros in our republic. Someone earning 1,400 euros per month cannot understand this, and rightly so. Of course, board members or directors of a company should earn more, but I believe the vast gap in salaries is not healthy. I don't think it is right if a Munich hairdresser earns a gross salary of 1,400 euros, but has a one-hour commute because she can't afford an apartment in the city.

I reflect more and more as to how to communicate these facts. How could prices be expressed as economic costs? How could it be said more clearly that the real cost of a flight priced at 29 euros is actually equal to 300 or 400 euros? If this were possible, wouldn't this contribute to a new awareness?

When I lead meetings of the Future Council, I try to make it clear to the participants that we have to communicate more clearly where we are headed. The issues we will have to deal with are too significant to just wait and see.

People lack orientation. They don't want to follow anyone, but at the same time don't know what to do, either. A hundred and twenty thousand people attended the final service at the annual Protestant church gathering in June 2011 in Dresden. They were singing and praying under the clear skies, on both sides of the river Elbe. It was a great community event, and few police officers were required because there were no issues, notwithstanding the huge amount of participants. Perhaps these types of events may help to develop a perspective in this incredibly complex world, whose immense degree of uncertainty puts fear in the hearts of people. Who do we sell tanks to, and who don't we? It is not that easy any more to answer these questions, as we don't know whether something meaningful is accomplished or whether a new dictator is being empowered. If I advocate that freshly cut flowers shouldn't be available for purchase all year round and that such flowers shouldn't be brought by cargo flights to Germany, I also know that this will cost 100,000 jobs in West Africa. If we don't want that, we also have to forgo prawns, yoghurt or cheap flights, for the sake of fairness. And petrol will cost a minimum of three euros.

I may not be affected too much, as I could still afford petrol or long-distance travel, but many people couldn't. Is it possible to simply take away the material blessings of the last 70 years?

I believe that I have to be a good role model myself. The Swiss priest and author Jeremias Gotthelf once said: "What shines in the fatherland should and must start in one's home." That means not to get on other people's nerves and to ask others to do things for you, but to rather get things done. As a general matter, a better result for the whole world will be achieved.

We, the older generation, as we have more time to reflect, should say loud and clear: "Future generations, we have to leave you a world that's different from its current appearance. We have to make sure that society is more interconnected." I try to make suggestions at conferences or political roundtables: "We abolished mandatory military service, but why don't we establish a mandatory social year for men and women between the ages of 16 and 21?" I always listen to the same, massive counter-arguments: "Oh my god, we will never be able to get this through. First, we take away a year of a young person's training, and second we can't expect social engagement from everyone. Also, special training is required for social services ...". If we want to bring society more together, we must know that the glue holding things together is not watching a football game in Munich's Allianz Arena, or the common experience of a traffic jam.

I know that 16 million Germans are volunteers – no other European society comes close. We also have very varied clubs and associations. According to CSU politician Alois Glück, president of the Bavarian Mountain Rescue Association, they receive five applications for each available position. The numbers are similar for Water Rescue Services. But the media doesn't report these facts; the information conveyed to the public is pure nerve gas.

In general, there's a lack of convincing role models. My mentee Johannes Elsner held a farewell speech at the Bavarian Elite Academy mentioning a "generation without heroes". The role models I grew up with were certainly exaggerated; the Fuhrer madness during the Third Reich was a perversion. But I don't think that having no role models is a good thing, either. When I ask during my university classes: "Who do you want to emulate, who is your hero?", I generally get silence as an answer. Sometimes, students will say "Michael Schumacher" or "Oliver Kahn". But that's about it. Things are quite different in the US, where names like Bill Gates, Steve Jobs or Mark Zuckerberg come up. Whenever I mention this, the response is invariably: "Why should I become like Steve Jobs or Mark Zuckerberg? I want to make my own way." This has been so to a shocking extent, more than ever, and in my view is an expression of the general sense of isolation.

My role models were Ron Daniel and – in many ways – Alfred Herrhausen. Becoming like them was worthwhile, they were great personalities.

Taking a look at politicians, it appears quite difficult to identify a role model. I met German minister of employment and social affairs Ursula von der Leyen at the World Economic Forum in Davos in 2011, and was fascinated by her. I had the impression that she was real, not plastic. I know minister of Education and research Annette Schavan back from her days in Stuttgart. She is a politician who I can accept. I adore Wolfgang Schäuble; I have to take my hat off to someone who has gone and is still going through life's trials as he has. Angela Merkel is cocky, embodying the will to power. Her reputation is better abroad than at home. While I frequently moan about her tactics, mention has to be made that she has to deal with a weak coalition partner. I still don't understand why Horst Köhler quit the German presidency.

I would tell a young graduate that he is lucky, as he is part of an age group which will decrease by 15% over the next ten years. It is a fantastic economic situation when the supply of highly qualified graduates decreases, but demand increases. The war for talent has already started, and the possibilities are limitless. Thus, young graduates can relax as they will be presented with many choices. The second item I would tell a young graduate is: "Try to understand Asia. Go to Asia, as I went to the US in 1968." For me, there was no other option; in 1968 it was all about the American Way of Life. There simply was no other option. Today, people need to go to Asia.

The digital revolution is another challenge. We don't know how it will end. When the IT revolution started, a specialist was hired who switched on the server and produced stacks of printouts. Today, young people are the children of the revolution and they are expected to know everything, which includes contacting clients via Facebook. Knowledge has become ubiquitous, even if my own brain doesn't constantly want Twitter or Facebook. But the young generation will find new ways to deal with digital media while preserving their privacy. It will also have to deal with more frequent job changes. Employability is more important than the employer, and people will be less of an employee and more of a problem solver. Because the knowledge half-life has been drastically reduced and constantly atrophies, life will become such that knowledge has to be updated every four to five years. In my generation, accepted wisdom was that an economics graduate who knew accounting could live off such knowledge for 40 years. Things will never be the same.

I studied in an ivory tower. Today, schools and universities must deal much more with social development. In parallel, every single person must get involved. There is one saying which for me comes close to a motto: "If the creator has given you more talent and skill, society has a claim on such talent and skill." A university graduate still makes twice the money of a non-graduate. It would be appropriate to give back this additional value one way or another.

I constantly went through phases in my life when I went beyond the limit. I was convinced by growth, by my own organization, McKinsey, that I hired talent wherever I found it. My creed was that good people would create their markets. And all of them made a big effort – we experienced almost linear growth. We were on a steep upward trajectory, for more than 14 years. During that stretch of time, a number of economic crises occurred and it wasn't always easy to convince our business partners that growth was good. Our business partners frequently said: "Let's go back to the roots, we want to be small and manageable. Huge amounts of effort and energy had to be expended to try and convince them of the contrary. I had to work closely with clients, while realizing that I didn't always know the details to the extent I wanted. More and more, I had to rely on my teams, and I thought: "Is that a good thing? Does my counterpart realize that I am not that deeply immersed in the details?" I was afraid of being found out, that a client would say: "You are completely clueless." I was at the limit.

That was also the case with respect to my role at McKinsey. I never wanted to become the New York-based Global Managing Director of this consulting firm, but wanted to ascertain a sufficient degree of autonomy for myself, no matter who ran McKinsey at any given time.

Today, I think that the notion of growth must be redefined with respect to national accounts. A number of new components must be added, such as competitiveness and sustainability. Growing older has also enabled me to see my own personal growth in a new light. I experience personal growth, my knowledge base grows and my ability to help others also grows. What used to take a week is now completed in two days. This is also a form of growth: growth in productivity. Such personal growth is important, and people's enthusiasm will be infectious because they are able to say: "That can't be all, we must improve, become faster, jump even higher." I can identify with improving, but today a big question mark has to be put over the faster, higher, further.

But I would go to the limit again, no doubt about that.

Family portrait with his parents and his younger brother Siegfried, Christmas 1943

Herbert Henzler fell ill as a child with tuberculosis. Here he is in a sanatorium in Schwäbisch Gmünd

As a ski instructor in Austria (Westendorf in Tirol), Herbert made some money for his studies

Herbert Henzler in his element. Skiing has been part of his childhood, to his great passion

Best-selling author and management consultant Kenichi between Fred Gluck and Herbert Henzler

Herbert Henzler talking to Alfred Herrhausen and Hans-Olaf Henkel. Shortly afterwards, the head of Deutsche Bank was murdered by RAF terrorists

A concentrated
listener

With Marvin Bower
who of today
characterized the
corporate image

Herbert Henzler in
conversation with
Vera Niefer and
Wolfgang Reitzle

Disputing with
Ezard Reuter

On the occasion of
the the founding
of the Similaun
group the publisher
Hubert Burda
handed over a gift
to Herbert Henzler

The Germany boss
of McKinsey –
Herbert Henzler
– with his successor
Jürgen Kluge

An unusual
McKinsey
advertisement
for young people
recruitment

Wolfgang Schäuble
and Herbert Henzler

From the left:
Herbert Henzler,
Jürgen Rüttgers,
John McDonald,
Frank Mattern,
Jürgen Kluge,
Jürgen Schröder,
Axel Born

Mark Wössner
former CEO of
Bertelsmann and
former client of
Herbert Henzler.
Still today the
two have been
close friends

Herbert Henzler
– in intensive
exchange with
Henry Kissinger,
former US
Secretary of State

Together with Reinhold Messner on the 3599 high meter mountain Similaun. After this mountain the climbers group consisting of leading managers of the German economy – founded by Herbert Henzler and Reinhold Messner was named

Michael Albus, Reinhold Messner and Herbert Henzler on on Humboldt's Footsteps to the Chimborazo

The Alpine
University – the
McKinsey Training
Center – launched
by Herbert Henzler
– where today
there is a "Herbert
Henzler Hall"

Franz Beckenbauer,
guest in the Alpine
University

As part of the
training program for
national team Mr
Henzler shared his
knowledge with the
German national
football team

As member of the board of the FC Bayern München AG together with Uli Hoeneß, Karl Heinz Rummenigge, Karl Hopfner and Franz Beckenbauer

Martin Walser and Herbert Henzler in a joint interview with the manager magazine on trhe subject: culture enters commerce

Together with Lothar Späth at the book presentation of their joint work "Jenseits von Brüssel"

Herbert Henzler receives the first class Merit of the Federal Republic of Germany from Prime Minister Horst Seehofer for special merits

Already during his time as Prime Minister of the state Bayern Edmund Stoiber appreciated the analysis of Herbert Henzler. They still have excellent relationships, especially regarding the the reduction of bureaucracy offensive of the EU

The Similaun tour – here together with Jürgen Weber

AN INTRODUCTION TO
HERBERT HENZLER

Herbert Henzler is the former German office head and European Chairman of McKinsey & Company. From 2002 till 2012 he was senior advisor to the Chairman of Credit Suisse Group. In 2012 he joined Moelis & Company in the role as Senior Advisor.

Today he is an advisor to the Bavarian Government and board member of several leading companies like FC Bayern Munich and New Silk Route. At Munich university he teaches courses on strategy and organization and acts as a visiting professor at Skolkovo business school in Moscow.